A PLUME BOOK

TOP SECRET RESTAURANT RECIPES 3

TODD WILBUR is the bestselling QVC cookbook author. He's appeared on *The Oprah Winfrey Show*, *Today*, and *Good Morning America*, among others. He lives in Las Vegas.

"The recipes are easy to follow and . . . by preparing your own versions of restaurant meals you will almost always save money."
—*Arizona Daily Star*

"[Wilbur's] recipes use everyday supermarket ingredients to bring brand-name foods to the home kitchen. Perhaps not surprisingly, his recipes are not complex. If anything, they reflect how easy home cooking can be."   —*Star Tribune* (Minneapolis–St. Paul)

"Having this dude on her show must have really tested Oprah's dietary mettle."   —*Entertainment Weekly*

TopSecret Recipes ®

PRESENTS

TOP SECRET RESTAURANT RECIPES 3

The Secret Formulas for Duplicating Your
Favorite Restaurant Dishes at Home

BY
TODD WILBUR

Illustrated by the author

A PLUME BOOK

PLUME
Published by Penguin Group
Penguin Group (USA) Inc., 375 Hudson Street, New York, New York 10014, U.S.A. • Penguin Group (Canada), 90 Eglinton Avenue East, Suite 700, Toronto, Ontario, Canada M4P 2Y3 (a division of Pearson Penguin Canada Inc.) • Penguin Books Ltd., 80 Strand, London WC2R 0RL, England • Penguin Ireland, 25 St. Stephen's Green, Dublin 2, Ireland (a division of Penguin Books Ltd.) • Penguin Group (Australia), 250 Camberwell Road, Camberwell, Victoria 3124, Australia (a division of Pearson Australia Group Pty. Ltd.) • Penguin Books India Pvt. Ltd., 11 Community Centre, Panchsheel Park, New Delhi – 110 017, India • Penguin Books (NZ), 67 Apollo Drive, Rosedale, North Shore 0632, New Zealand (a division of Pearson New Zealand Ltd.) • Penguin Books (South Africa) (Pty.) Ltd., 24 Sturdee Avenue, Rosebank, Johannesburg 2196, South Africa

Penguin Books Ltd., Registered Offices: 80 Strand, London WC2R 0RL, England

First published by Plume, a member of Penguin Group (USA) Inc.

First Printing, October 2010
10 9 8 7 6 5 4 3 2 1

For information about the trademarks appearing in this book, see pages 411–412.

Ⓟ REGISTERED TRADEMARK—MARCA REGISTRADA

LIBRARY OF CONGRESS CATALOGING-IN-PUBLICATION DATA

Wilbur, Todd.
  Top secret restaurant recipes 3: the secret formulas for duplicating your favorite restaurant dishes at home / by Todd Wilbur; illustrated by the author.
      p.   cm.
  At head of title: Top secret recipes presents.
  Includes index.
  ISBN 978-0-452-29645-9
  ISBN 978-0-452-29700-5 (Target edition)
  1. Cooking, American.   2. Chain restaurants—United States.   I. Title.   II. Title: Top secret restaurant recipes three.
  TX715 .W65874   2010
  641.50973—dc22   2010027757

Printed in the United States of America
Set in Gill Sans

For MoMo

CONTENTS

Words cannot express how grateful I am to all the people who help serve up each new batch of *Top Secret Recipes* books:

Thank you to everyone at Penguin Group including Clare Ferraro, Cherise Fisher, Kate Napolitano, Barbara O'Shea, Sandra Dear, Liz Keenan, Laurie Connors, and Anne Banfich.

A big shout-out to Robert Reynolds, Perry Rogers, Colin Smeeton, Shannon Doucett, Ken Langdon, Robert John Kley, Darren Emmens, Melinda Baca, Daniella Paz, and Anthony Corrado.

Thanks to the Stern Show and everyone at Howard 101 for entertaining me during the long hours in the kitchen, and "getting the poison out" so I can keep laughing through the frustrating and tedious process of creating each of these Top Secret Recipes from scratch.

Huge hugs and big kisses to my amazing family for putting up with the craziest deadline of my career. It's really great to be back!

And a superbig helping of gratitude to all of you who read my books; thanks for your support and your kind words over the years. As long as there are people like you who keep cooking with these books and enjoying the recipes, I'll keep whipping up extra batches of these formulas to make sure they are the best original clone recipes available anywhere.

CANDY BARS AND
MAGIC TRICKS

At the age of twelve I was consumed with secrets and sweets.

It was then that I saw the price of candy bars increasing from 15 cents to 20 cents each. As a true candy lover—I was your typical kid, after all—this 25 percent price increase was devastating. Each day I rode my bike for miles around Orange County, California, searching out every liquor store, convenience store, and supermarket where I could spend my lawn-mowing money on any remaining inventory of candy bars that still had "15 cents" printed on their wrappers. To me these wrappers were precious collector's items—symbols of my vanishing preteen candy-loving years.

After spending several months finding as many of the 15-cent wrappers as I could, I continued to build my collection by saving every wrapper for each size of every candy bar on the market. Because I always ate what was inside each of those wrappers I tasted practically every candy bar sold in the United States from 1976 to 1978. I noticed how each candy bar was made, and I studied the list of ingredients on the packaging. After carefully removing and consuming the contents from the packaging, I stored the wrappers in scrapbooks and shoeboxes until I had several hundred in my collection. I stopped collecting the

wrappers a couple years later when the price of candy bars increased again, this time to 25 cents each.

While writing my first cookbook, *Top Secret Recipes*, twelve years after I started my candy bar wrapper project, I found myself in a kitchen creating clone recipes for some of the same candy bars I had collected and inspected as a kid, including Reese's Peanut Butter Cups, Snickers, Almond Roca, Mounds, and Almond Joy. I eventually cloned several others for later books, including Baby Ruth, Milky Way, 3 Musketeers, Twix, Payday, Nestle Crunch, York Peppermint Pattie, Mars Bar, 100 Grand, and many more. As it turns out, my hobby as a kid studying candy bars and their ingredients had planted a seed in me that would later sprout into a facet of my career.

The money I didn't squander on candy I spent at magic shops. In addition to obsessing over candy bars at age twelve, I had become fascinated with illusionists—back then these guys were cool. I bought dozens of magic props and piles of books about magic because I absolutely had to know how all the magicians did their amazing tricks. For me, watching a magician perform on TV was more about figuring out how the tricks were done than about sitting back and being amazed. You might think that knowing all the secrets would demystify the performance and ruin the experience, but I found that understanding the details behind the scenes gave me a larger appreciation of all the work that went into the craft. I actually enjoyed the show even more when I knew how all the tricks worked.

People who create good food have something in common with magicians. They, too, are artists in a specialized craft often reluctant to reveal their secrets. And just as earlier in life when I was compelled to uncover the secrets of the magicians who demonstrate their skills on stage, I now spend my time figuring out how the "magicians" of the kitchen perform their tricks. But what makes my current obsession more challenging than my hobby as a younger man is that there are no shops selling the secrets I now seek to uncover. I must figure out these culinary tricks all on my own.

It was only recently that I realized that these two seemingly unrelated hobbies from the same moment in my childhood were the first signs of character traits that would guide me toward my career destiny.

The First Clone Recipe I Tried

My first encounter with a clone recipe was in college. I was a freshman, and as is the case with most first-year college students, I had very little money. This was an unfortunate situation for many reasons, but especially because living right down the hall of my dormitory was a group of girls who really loved drinking Kahlua, and they really loved boys who gave them bottles of it. To show their devotion to the expensive coffee liqueur, they would peel the fabric seal off the neck of each bottle they finished and proudly tape it to the outside of their dorm room door. By Christmas, their door was about half-covered with the little booze trophies, and the throw rug in their room smelled like Black Russians.

One day my buddy turned me onto a fifth-generation photocopy of a recipe someone had given him. It listed five ingredients—

vodka, sugar, water, instant coffee, and vanilla—that when cooked together under the right conditions would produce a liqueur that tasted exactly like Kahlua. This was too good to be true! We immediately got to a kitchen and converted the cheapest vodka we could find into the party girls' beverage of choice, loaded it into empty Kahlua bottles, and anxiously awaited the weekend. When we presented our female friends with a couple bottles of "special Kahlua," the party was on. And they loved it! The liqueur tasted exactly like Kahlua, but what we didn't realize was that the proof was close to double what's in the real stuff! You can imagine the shenanigans that ensued when everyone downed the usual number of drinks with twice the alcohol content they were used to. It's no wonder nobody noticed when we took the empty bottles home with us at the end of the night to refill again for the following weekend.

The Second Clone Recipe I Tried

Several years went by before I saw my next clone recipe. In 1987, the second clone recipe I tried showed up in my mailbox in the form of a chain letter. At the time, these snail mail chain letters were similar to the chain letter spam that we get in our e-mail inboxes today: Someone tells an inspirational/sad/angry story and asks you to make a copy of the letter and send it to five of your friends. If you break the chain, the letter warns, bad things will happen. Ooh, scary.

The chain letter I got told the story of a woman who visited a Mrs. Fields cookie store and asked for the chocolate chip cookie recipe. They told her that she could buy the recipe for two-fifty, and that she could put the charge on her credit card. She certainly could afford the bargain price of $2.50 for the recipe, so she immediately handed over her card. But several weeks later when the woman received her credit card statement, she was shocked to see a charge for $250! When she went back to the cookie store, they refused to refund her money since she had already received the rec-ipe. So she decided to get even by sending the recipe along with her "story" out in a chain letter, which then proceeded to quickly spread across the country.

To this day no one knows

who created that chain letter, but the story is obviously made up—Mrs. Fields would never sell her trade secret. And the recipe produced a cookie that tasted nowhere near as yummy as one made by Mrs. Fields. When I tried the recipe I knew it couldn't possibly be real since the cookie was downright gross. Just to compare I drove to the Mrs. Fields store at a nearby mall to get the real thing, and that's when I saw the sign. On the countertop was a placard that completely discredited the chain letter recipe and its story—the same chain letter that I had received. "Wow," I thought, "this recipe must have become very popular." I eventually found out that the company had posted similar signs in each of its 450 cookie stores! Indeed, this one little "secret" recipe had become quite a phenomenon. That's the exact moment I realized that people love copycat recipes, especially if the recipes produce copies of well-known products.

My next step was to find out if I was able to improve the recipe so that it tasted more like the original chocolate chip cookie. It was just a cookie after all, and I knew how to make cookies. I got to work in the kitchen and over several days, after making a huge mess and a dozen or so batches, I finally had done it: I had baked my very own Mrs. Fields chocolate chip cookie clone from scratch in my own kitchen. I had just created my first clone recipe of a famous brand-name food!

I shared the cookies with friends, with family, with coworkers, and asked them all what they thought the cookies tasted like. When everyone said, "A Mrs. Fields cookie," I had the confirmation I needed. I decided to create a bunch more clone recipes that would hopefully develop into a cookbook unlike any that had been published before. I got right to work. I found my Kahlua recipe from college, and improved it. Now I had two recipes!

I had no way of knowing it at the time, but this was the very beginning of an adventure that would continue through the next two decades.

From Zero to Ten in 23 Years

It took six years from the day I started writing that first book, *Top Secret Recipes*, for it to land on bookstores shelves.

Not having a formal culinary education made the process of writing the book especially tedious since I had to learn the science of cooking and figure out how to adapt what I had learned to re-creating well-known products. I see now that this worked to my advantage since the recipes were written in such a way that the book was easy to use for folks who, like me, didn't necessarily have a lot of kitchen experience. My recipes required no fancy techniques, commercial equipment, or hard-to-find ingredients.

As I was putting the book together I was working as a TV news reporter in Arizona and Pennsylvania, so I tapped into my experience gathering information to help create the recipes. I interviewed fast food restaurant employees. I educated myself by reading a variety of cookbooks and watching cooking shows on TV. I went to the library to gather information on food production, all the while wishing that someone would hurry up and invent the Internet. I sought out exactly what I needed to know for each recipe on my list, and after several years I had produced the cookbook that previously existed only in my mind.

My art background came in handy when I decided that schematic-style blueprints would be the perfect way to illustrate the "top secret" recipes. I created each of the blueprints by hand, using drafting tools and black ink pens that I bought at a nearby art supply store. When the art was done I made copies of the entire manuscript, sent them out to thirty publishers, and waited impatiently for a response, which I was hoping would come soon because, in an unexplainable leap of faith, I had just quit my job. Thankfully, I didn't have to wait long. Within a few weeks I had offers from five different houses that wanted to publish *Top Secret Recipes*. Of the five, I chose the biggest one, Penguin, only because at the time they were publishing books by a guy named Stephen King, and I figured if they were good enough for him, they probably knew what they were doing.

When the book finally came out it in 1993, it was so different from any other cookbooks on the market that it got incredible media attention. I wound up on several national TV shows and in newspapers, and book sales were off the hook.

The success of *Top Secret Recipes* led to the next book, *More Top Secret Recipes*, which was more of the same type of convenience food clone recipes, and it also sold very well. For the third book, though, I thought I'd try something a little different. For *Top Secret Restaurant Recipes*, instead of creating clone recipes for fast food, snack cakes, and candy bars, I decided to clone recipes for the signature dishes from the country's most popular casual restaurant chains such as Chili's, Cheesecake Factory, and T.G.I. Friday's. This book was nearly triple the size of the first two books and it was my most ambitious project yet, but I had much more cooking experience under my belt and the book turned out really great. I even wound up appearing on *The Oprah Winfrey Show* with that book, which, for any author, is the absolute best show to be on. Today, more than thirteen years later, that book still sells like crazy and is the all-time top seller in the series.

After that I wrote two low-fat clone recipe books (*Low-Fat Top Secret Recipes* and *Top Secret Recipes—Lite!*), a book of drink clones (*Sodas, Smoothies, Spirits & Shakes*), a couple more convenience food books (*Even More Top Secret Recipes* and *Top Secret Recipes Unlocked*), and another book of casual restaurant chain clones (*Top Secret Restaurant Recipes 2*). This book you're holding right now is the tenth book I've written, and a personal milestone. More than 1,000 recipes, 450 blueprints, and 10 books, all inspired by a simple chain letter that triggered a career of cloning recipes that has now lasted for over half of my life.

Happy to Be Here

I truly believe that this book is some of the best work I've ever done.

In this third installment of *Top Secret Restaurant Recipes*, I bring you another batch of original secret formulas with step-by-step instructions for making your own home versions of a variety of signature dishes from America's largest casual full-service chains. All of the big chains are represented here, including Applebee's, T.G.I. Friday's, Chili's, Olive Garden, Red Lobster, Outback Steakhouse, P. F. Chang's, IHOP, and Cheesecake Factory. But this time around I'm mixing things up a bit by including some great recipes from well-known fine dining restaurant chains.

From Spago, I've cloned the chain's famous butternut squash soup that is usually only available in the fall. If you enjoy dishes like this one, but don't care for the fine dining prices, check out that soup recipe on page 365, as well as the clone recipe for Spago's incredible pumpkin cheesecake on page 367. There are also great clone recipes for dishes from other fine dining chains such as Fleming's Prime Steakhouse (pages 153–160), Joe's Stone Crab (pages 207–215) and Mastro's Steakhouse (pages 229–236).

I'm also really happy to finally bring you some clones for dishes from Roy's, the high-end Hawaiian-fusion chain out of Honolulu. There are now thirty-two Roy's restaurants around the country and the number one dish on the menu, Roy's Classic Macadamia Nut Crusted Mahi Mahi, is cloned here in this book (on page 343), along with the way-too-good Hawaiian Martini (page 341), and the ridiculously simple yet delicious Melting Hot Chocolate Soufflé (page 347). You must give at least one of these recipes a try.

And I am pleased to announce that after nearly thirteen years of working the recipe over and over again, I have finally perfected the clone recipe for Pizza Hut's Pan Pizza. I've still got copies of e-mail requests that I received way back in 1997 for this long sought-after clone recipe with a great technique for making a deep-dish crust. One of my goals for this book was that I would do whatever it took to nail this recipe once and for all, even if it meant repeated trips to Pizza Hut to interview employees (which I did). The secrets are—at long last—all here for you to try on page 316.

If you're a fan of lettuce wraps, I've included a few really good recipes for you. After I published my recipe for the Chicken in Soothing Lettuce Wraps from P. F. Chang's in *Top Secret Restaurant Recipes 2*, I had tons of requests for the vegetarian version of that dish. I went to the restaurant and tasted the veggie lettuce wraps and I thought they were even better than the chicken version! They're made using baked tofu with a little mint and lime tossed in there—really good stuff. If you're a vegetarian, or just love these wraps, check out my clone recipe of that dish on page 300.

As I was working on those vegetarian lettuce wraps I discovered a better stir-fry sauce that would help improve my old recipe for the chicken version of the wraps, so I'm including a totally re-worked "improved" clone for the Chicken in Soothing Lettuce Wraps from P. F. Chang's (page 296). And if you like the Thai Lettuce Wraps at Cheesecake Factory, that one's here too, including all three of the incredible sauces. The recipe is on page 86, and just look at that sweet photo of the dish on the front cover of the book!

You've now got a collection of recipes here for a wide range of dishes from cocktails to appetizers to entrées and desserts, so you should be able to find something that will fit perfectly into just about any occasion. Many of these clones re-create the most requested dishes from the chain, such as the Buca Di Beppo Chicken Limone (page 56) and Carrabba's Chicken Bryan (page 70). And many are the signature dishes that have helped put the restaurant chain on the map, such as the Volcano Nachos from Margaritaville (page 225), and one of Oprah's favorite desserts, Serendipity 3 Frrrozen Hot Chocolate (page 358).

Regardless of which dishes you decide to make, I'm hoping you have a great time preparing each one of them and that your diners are blown away by how close your creations are to the real thing. Not only are you going to have a great time amazing your crew with these taste-alike dishes, but you'll also save some serious bucks by cooking your meals at home.

After dusting off my calculator I worked up this comparison of several random dishes from the book and how they stack up with the cost per serving of the same dishes from the chains:

	Original	Clone
Ruby Tuesday Queso Dip	6.99	3.52
Red Lobster Peach-Bourbon BBQ Scallops	9.25	4.44
P. F. Chang's Kung Pao Chicken	13.50	8.65
Roy's Melting Hot Chocolate Soufflé	9.50	2.48
Outback Steakhouse Victoria "Crowned" Filet	21.95	5.31
Olive Garden Chicken & Gnocchi Soup	5.35	1.81
Applebee's Tomato Basil Soup	3.99	1.62
Bonefish Grill Bang Bang Shrimp	9.90	4.05
Buca di Beppo Chicken Limone	19.95	9.99
IHOP Banana Macadamia Nut Pancakes	7.99	3.30
Fleming's Prime Steakhouse Fleming's Potatoes	8.50	2.22
T.G.I. Friday's Parmesan-Crusted Sicilian Quesadillas	9.49	3.62
Joe's Stone Crab Garlic Creamed Spinach	5.25	2.29
Average Cost (per serving)	10.12	4.10
Savings (per serving)		approx. 60%

If my math is right, most of the dishes in this book will end up costing you under ten dollars per serving with the average somewhere around four bucks per serving. That's an average savings of approximately 60 percent versus eating out!

Plus, when you cook from this book you'll be able to re-create the tastes of the food you love with total control over the types of ingredients that are used. If you prefer organic ingredients in your dishes or food that has been grown and raised differently from the food used by chefs at the restaurant chains (who must keep costs down), these formulas give you that ability. And the total cost of your meal, even if you choose to use more expensive organic ingredients, will still be less than what you'd pay when eating out.

You can now plan meals with an appetizer from one chain, an

entrée from another chain, and a dessert from yet another. You can create unique meals that cannot be enjoyed by visiting any one restaurant chain location.

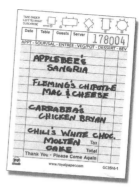

This book gives you the ability to create the type of food that has made the restaurants so successful. But now the food will be coming out of your own kitchen! You will be able to experiment, add your own creative touches, and make these recipes uniquely yours. I hope many of these recipes become a part of your life.

Many years ago, in *Top Secret Recipes*, I wrote, "What was once a world of home-cooked meals is now a world of prescribed and proven secret formulas. This book is an occasion to combine the best of those two worlds." By writing these books I'm encouraging everyone to spend more time in home kitchens, where the process of preparing meals together can be an extremely rewarding event in which all can participate.

Our lives are always changing, that's for sure. Since my first book of clone recipes, many things have changed in my own life. I now have a wonderful wife, a beautiful daughter, and a perfect house. Life is definitely more complicated with all the things that come along when you have a family to think about. But it can also be more enjoyable. I'm still the same person who wants to share his passion for clone cooking with the world. I'm still the guy who will work as hard as I possibly can to make each of my recipes from scratch, over and over and over again, until they are as good as I can possibly make them. And I'm still the guy who vowed from the very beginning to make my work original, to be truthful, and to never cut corners.

I hope this dedication comes through in every recipe you try. Please enjoy this book and all the recipes inside. If you get as much joy out of this book as I put into it, my true destiny has been fulfilled.

Until next time, happy cloning!

APPLEBEE'S RED APPLE SANGRIA

MENU DESCRIPTION: *"Drink in the passions of Spain! A delightful mix of Sutter Home cabernet sauvignon, Shakka Apple liqueur, Dole pineapple juice, Ocean Spray cranberry juice, and grenadine. Garnished with maraschino cherry, orange, lime, and fresh apple."*

The menu description for this quenching cocktail specifies brand names that the restaurant uses to create this drink. For the best clone, I suggest you use the same brands. However, if you must substitute with other brands, I don't suspect anyone will care. I certainly won't, and I promise not to tell anyone your secret. If you can't find Shakka brand apple liqueur, use any sour apple flavored liqueur. If you don't have Sierra Mist lemon-lime soda, you can use Sprite or 7UP. This is just between you and me.

⅓ cup Sutter Home cabernet
    sauvignon
1 ¼ ounces Shakka Apple liqueur
½ ounce grenadine

1 ½ ounces Ocean Spray
    cranberry juice cocktail
1 ½ ounces Dole pineapple juice
Sierra Mist soda (or other lemon-
    lime soda)

GARNISH
red apple
orange wedge

lime wedge
maraschino cherry

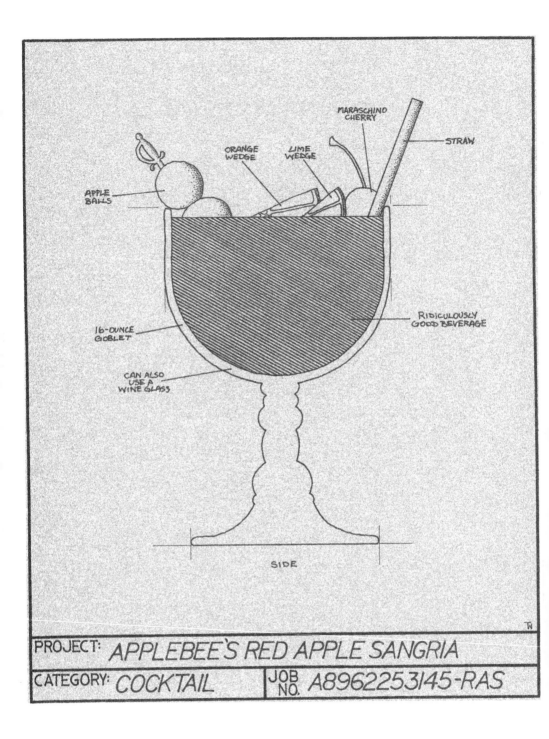

APPLE BALLS

ORANGE WEDGE

LIME WEDGE

MARASCHINO CHERRY

STRAW

16-OUNCE GOBLET

CAN ALSO USE A WINE GLASS

RIDICULOUSLY GOOD BEVERAGE

SIDE

PROJECT: *APPLEBEE'S RED APPLE SANGRIA*

CATEGORY: *COCKTAIL*   JOB NO. *A8962253145-RAS*

1. Fill a 16-ounce glass with ice.
2. Pour cabernet into glass (should fill it about ⅓ up).
3. Add apple liqueur, grenadine, cranberry juice, and pineapple juice, and top off the drink with the soda.
4. Use the small end of a melon baller to scoop 2 balls out of a red apple. Pierce the apple balls on a toothpick.
5. Drop all of the garnishes into the drink and serve with a straw.

• MAKES 1 DRINK.

•   •   •   •

APPLEBEE'S
WHITE PEACH SANGRIA

MENU DESCRIPTION: *"Sutter Home white zinfandel with DeKuyper Luscious Peachtree schnapps, pineapple juice, and lemon-lime soda. Served Mucho size over ice with fresh fruit."*

No need to waste expensive wine duplicating this incredibly re-freshing new cocktail from Applebee's. Sutter Home White Zin-fandel, which runs around 5 bucks a bottle, is the brand of choice at the chain, but feel free to use any white zinfandel on the shelf, even if it's in a box. The wine will be diluted with peach schnapps and other ingredients, so no matter which wine you pick, you'll always get a delicious, thirst-quenching cocktail that's perfect for warm weather hang time.

½ cup Sutter Home white
    zinfandel
1 ½ ounces DeKuyper Peachtree
    schnapps

2 ounces pineapple juice
½ cup Sierra Mist, 7UP, or Sprite

GARNISH
red or green apple
orange wedge

lime wedge
maraschino cherry

1. Fill a 16-ounce glass or goblet with ice.
2. Add zinfandel, schnapps, and pineapple juice to the glass. Fill to the top with the soda.
3. Use a melon baller to scoop 2 balls out of an apple. Pierce the balls on a toothpick, then add to the top of the drink along with wedges of orange and lime, and a maraschino cherry. Serve with a straw.

*   MAKES 1 DRINK.

TIDBITS

Use sugar-free lemon-lime soda for a lower-calorie version.

•   •   •   •

APPLEBEE'S
TOMATO BASIL SOUP

MENU DESCRIPTION: *"A tasty twist on a family favorite. Red, ripe to-matoes slowly simmered in a rich cream sauce and seasoned with basil and select herbs."*

This easy recipe requires two large cans of crushed tomatoes, and your soup will still have the impressive taste and texture of gourmet tomato bisque requiring fresh tomatoes and more work. You may notice that the large amount of basil used here contributes an overwhelming flavor and aroma when first added, but as the soup simmers, the herb mellows to create the perfect clone of the original. And there's no need to make croutons from scratch for the garnish when you can buy lightly seasoned packaged croutons in just about any market.

1 teaspoon extra virgin olive oil	⅓ cup granulated sugar
½ cup minced white onion	2 teaspoons minced fresh parsley
1 teaspoon minced garlic	¼ teaspoon dried oregano
two 28-ounce cans crushed tomatoes	¼ teaspoon salt
3 cups chicken broth	¼ teaspoon ground black pepper
¾ cup heavy cream	
⅓ cup minced fresh basil	

GARNISH

seasoned croutons
shredded Parmesan cheese

1.   Heat I teaspoon of olive oil in a large saucepan over medium heat and then add onion and garlic. Sauté for about I minute. Add crushed tomatoes and chicken broth and bring mixture to a boil, then reduce heat and simmer for 20 minutes. Turn off the heat and let mixture cool, uncovered, for 30 minutes or so. You can let it sit for as long as an hour, if you like.
2.   Pour approximately half of the tomato mixture into a blender. Put the lid on the blender and hold it down with a dish towel. (Mixture may still be hot and you don't want the lid of the blender to pop off.) Blend on high speed for about a minute, pour the mixture into a large bowl or pitcher, then add the rest of the mixture to the blender and blend on high speed for a minute.
3.   Pour all of the pureed tomato mixture back into the saucepan, and then add the remaining ingredients. Bring the soup back up to a bubble, then reduce heat and simmer for 20 minutes. Serve approximately I cup of soup with a garnish of 3 or 4 croutons on top and a sprinkling of shredded Parmesan cheese.

• MAKES 6 SERVINGS.

•   •   •   •

APPLEBEE'S APPLE WALNUT CHICKEN SALAD

MENU DESCRIPTION: *"A masterwork of flavors. Grilled, marinated chicken breast crowns this fresh mix of delectable greens, crisp Granny Smith apples, rich crumbled blue cheese, and sweet candied walnuts. Tossed in our tangy balsamic vinaigrette."*

Sometimes I feel like a C.S.I. To re-create this baby I ordered several of these salads to go, and then sat down with a magnifying glass and carefully picked out each of the bits and pieces and separated them into smaller bowls. Sure, this was tedious work, but it made it easy to measure out each ingredient for the most accurate clone recipe. Next, I cooked a ton of chicken, each with different versions of the marinade, until I found the one that worked. The smoky marinade for the chicken here is basically a brine that adds just the right amount of saltiness and flavor through osmosis, so be sure not to let the chicken soak longer than specified. Of course, the lead performer in any salad is the dressing, since it is responsible for much of what you taste. The tangy balsamic vinaigrette is delicious with honey, Dijon mustard, garlic, and tarragon in there. You can make an easy emulsion out of it with a hand mixer. The best part is that you'll end up with leftover vinaigrette that you can use to make a couple more meal-size salads, and then some. Case closed.

CHICKEN MARINADE

3 cups water
1 tablespoon salt
½ teaspoon garlic powder
¼ teaspoon hickory-flavored
    liquid smoke

2 chicken breast fillets, pounded
    flat (½-inch thick)
oil
ground black pepper

BALSAMIC VINAIGRETTE

¼ cup red wine vinegar
3 tablespoons granulated sugar
3 tablespoons honey
1 tablespoon balsamic vinegar
1 tablespoon Dijon mustard
½ teaspoon salt
½ teaspoon minced garlic

½ teaspoon lemon juice
¼ teaspoon dried Italian herb
    blend
¼ teaspoon dried tarragon
pinch ground black pepper
1 cup extra virgin olive oil

CANDIED WALNUTS

1 teaspoon peanut oil
1 teaspoon honey
2 tablespoons granulated sugar
¼ teaspoon vanilla extract
⅛ teaspoon salt
¾ cup chopped walnuts

SALAD

4 cups chopped romaine lettuce
2 cups chopped red leaf lettuce
2 cups chopped iceberg lettuce
1 apple, chopped into bite-size
    pieces
¼ cup crumbled blue cheese

1. Prepare chicken marinade by combining water, salt, garlic powder, and liquid smoke in a medium bowl. Mix until salt dissolves. Flatten two chicken breasts with a kitchen mallet to ½-inch thick. Drop chicken in marinade, cover, and chill for 3 hours.
2. When chicken is done marinating, blot each breast dry, rub with oil, and grill for 3 to 4 minutes per side on high, until done. Lightly pepper each breast while grilling.
3. Make the balsamic vinaigrette by combining all ingredients except olive oil in a medium bowl with an electric mixer on medium speed until sugar is dissolved. Pour the oil in a thin

stream into the bowl while mixing. Continue mixing for several seconds until the dressing thickens. Cover and chill.

4. Make the candied walnuts by combining in the order listed, peanut oil, honey, sugar, vanilla, and salt in a medium skillet over medium heat. When mixture begins to bubble, add chopped walnuts and stir constantly until sugar begins to smoke and/or caramelize. Immediately turn off heat and keep stirring the nuts so that they do not burn. After a minute of stirring, turn off the heat, and pour nuts out onto a plate. When nuts cool, break them apart if they have stuck together.

5. Build each salad by tossing 2 cups romaine lettuce, 1 cup red leaf lettuce, and 1 cup iceberg lettuce with half of the chopped apple and 3 to 4 tablespoons of balsamic vinaigrette. Arrange greens on a plate and sprinkle on 2 tablespoons of crumbled blue cheese followed by about 3 tablespoons of candied walnuts. Slice each chicken breast into thin strips and lay the chicken on top of the salad and serve.

• MAKES 2 SALADS.

TIDBITS

You can save time by using precooked grilled chicken breast strips that are available in the deli section of your supermarket. Foster Farms is one leading brand.

•   •   •   •

APPLEBEE'S GRILLED SHRIMP 'N SPINACH SALAD

MENU DESCRIPTION: *"Tender spinach, crisp bacon, roasted red peppers, red onions, toasted almonds, and hot bacon vinaigrette—all topped with succulent shrimp."*

Here's another great vinaigrette from Applebee's—a perfectly sweet-and-sour concoction packed with bits of real bacon. Medium shrimp are sprinkled with a secret seasoning blend, then grilled and arranged on top of the 2 large dinner-size salads this recipe yields. You can also split these up to serve 4 smaller side salads. There will be extra vinaigrette, so by adding a bit more spinach, you can even stretch this recipe to serve 6 when that couple who never calls ahead shows up unexpectedly on your stoop at chow time.

BACON VINAIGRETTE

½ cup light olive oil
¼ cup finely minced cooked
    bacon (3 or 4 slices)
½ teaspoon cornstarch
¼ cup red wine vinegar
¼ cup granulated sugar

1 ½ teaspoons Grey Poupon Dijon
    mustard
¼ teaspoon salt
¼ teaspoon coarse grind black
    pepper
¼ teaspoon hickory-flavored
    liquid smoke

SHRIMP SEASONING

1 teaspoon coarse grind black
    pepper
½ teaspoon salt
½ teaspoon garlic powder
¼ teaspoon onion powder
¼ teaspoon paprika
¼ teaspoon rubbed (ground)
    sage
¼ teaspoon granulated sugar

SALAD

20 to 24 medium shrimp, peeled
    and deveined
2 tablespoons butter, melted
¼ cup sliced almonds
16 cups fresh spinach
½ cup diced tomato
    (1 large tomato)
½ cup sliced red onion
¼ cup sliced roasted red bell
    pepper (see Tidbits)

1. Make bacon vinaigrette by combining bacon with ¼ cup of oil—that's half of the oil—in a small saucepan. Place the pan over medium heat and when it begins to bubble, set your timer for 1 minute. After a minute, remove the pan from the heat and let it cool for 3 to 4 minutes. Dissolve cornstarch in the vinegar and whisk the mixture into the oil and bacon, along with the sugar, mustard, salt, pepper, and liquid smoke. Drizzle the remaining ¼ cup of oil into the saucepan while whisking. Cover and chill dressing (it will thicken as it chills).

2. Preheat barbecue grill to high. Combine shrimp seasoning ingredients in a small bowl. Mix this blend with your fingers to break up any clumps of sage.

3. Pierce 5 or 6 shrimp on each skewer. Brush the shrimp with melted butter and sprinkle a little of the seasoning blend on both sides. Grill skewered shrimp for a couple minutes on each side, or until they are done.

4. Toast the sliced almonds in a medium sauté pan over medium heat until golden brown. Toss the almonds often so that they don't burn.

5. Build each salad by tossing 8 cups of spinach with ¼ cup diced tomato, ¼ cup red onion, 2 tablespoons roasted bell pepper, 2 tablespoons toasted almonds, and 3 to 4 tablespoons vinaigrette. Toss gently so that you don't bruise the

spinach. Arrange the tossed salad on a serving plate, then remove the grilled shrimp from the skewers and place 10 to 12 shrimp on top.

• MAKES 2 LARGE SALADS.

TIDBITS

Roast a red bell pepper by placing it directly on the stove over a high flame. Rotate the pepper as it chars until all of the skin is blackened and then plunge the pepper into an ice water bath or seal it in a zip-top plastic bag. After a few minutes you can easily remove all of the blackened skin, and then slice the pepper. You can also roast the pepper in preheated 425 degrees F oven. When the skin blisters, use the bag or ice water bath to remove the skin. Alternatively, you can buy bottled roasted peppers, but I think fresh is a much better way to go.

•   •   •   •

APPLEBEE'S
CHOCOLATE MOUSSE
DESSERT SHOOTER

MENU DESCRIPTION: *"Decadent Oreo chunks, chocolate mousse, and whipped cream make this a rich and creamy treat."*

After searching for an awesome chocolate mousse to clone, I've finally found inspiration in this new dessert shooter from Applebee's. This is a single serving of thick and rich chocolate mousse that is easy to replicate using half a bag of semisweet chocolate chips melted slowly in a double boiler or in a bowl set over a pan of hot water. To make an authentic re-creation we don't want a mousse that's too fluffy, so we'll stir the egg whites into the melted chocolate rather than folding them in. We'll save the folding for the whipped cream. With a little Godiva chocolate liqueur and some chopped up bits of chocolate that go in there, you'll have a great mousse that is made even better when served in a 6-ounce rocks glass along with Oreo cookie crumbs, chocolate fudge topping, and whipped cream.

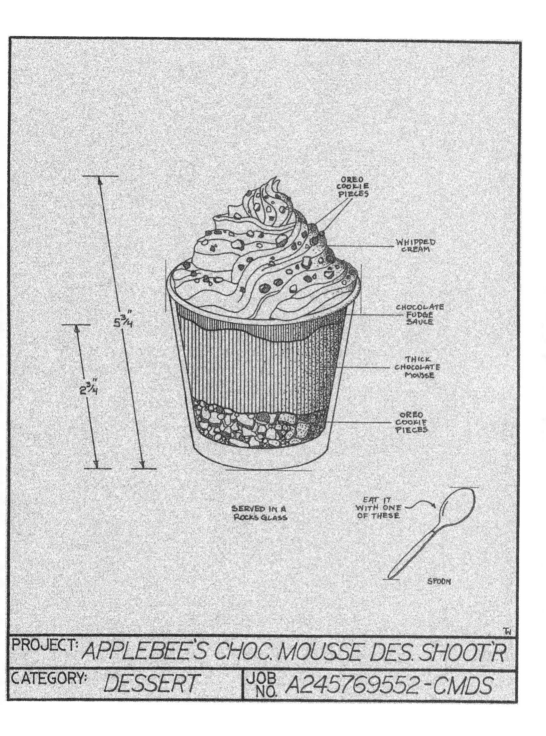

OREO
COOKIE
PIECES

WHIPPED
CREAM

CHOCOLATE
FUDGE
SAUCE

THICK
CHOCOLATE
MOUSSE

OREO
COOKIE
PIECES

5 3/4"

2 3/4"

SERVED IN A
ROCKS GLASS

EAT IT
WITH ONE
OF THESE

SPOON

PROJECT:	*APPLEBEE'S CHOC. MOUSSE DES. SHOOT'R*	
CATEGORY:	*DESSERT*	JOB NO. *A245769552-CMDS*

CHOCOLATE MOUSSE

2 tablespoons salted butter
6 ounces semisweet chocolate
    chips (1 cup)
1 tablespoon Godiva chocolate
    liqueur

1 teaspoon vanilla extract
2 eggs, separated
2 tablespoons sugar
½ cup heavy cream

8 Oreo cookies
½ cup chocolate fudge sauce
canned whipped cream

1. Make a double boiler by setting a metal bowl on top of a medium saucepan filled with a couple inches of water. Add the butter to the bowl, and then set the heat to low. When the butter has melted, add the chocolate chips, except for 1 tablespoon that you set aside. When the chips are melted, add the chocolate liqueur and vanilla. Remove the bowl from the heat and whisk in the egg yolks.
2. In a separate bowl, beat the egg whites until they form soft peaks. Stir egg whites into the chocolate mixture.
3. In another medium bowl, combine sugar with the cream, and then whip the cream until stiff. Fold the whipped cream into the chocolate.
4. Chop remaining 1 tablespoon of chocolate chips into small bits the size of rice. Stir this chocolate into the mousse, then cover and chill the mousse for 3 to 4 hours.
5. Open the Oreos and scrape out the filling (use a knife, not your teeth). Pop the chocolate wafers into a plastic bag and pound on it with a kitchen mallet until you've got a bag full o' crumbs.
6. Make each serving by spooning 2 tablespoons of Oreo cookie crumbs into the bottom of a 6-ounce rocks glass. Spoon ⅓ cup of chilled mousse into the glass, and top it with 2 tablespoons of chocolate fudge topping. Warm up

the fudge a bit in the jar in your microwave (remove the top first!) so that it's easy to spoon into the glass. Spray a pile of whipped cream on top and sprinkle it with some of the leftover Oreo crumbs.

• MAKES 4 SERVINGS.

•   •   •   •

APPLEBEE'S KEY LIME PIE DESSERT SHOOTER

MENU DESCRIPTION: *"This tart and tangy layer of graham cracker crumbs, key lime filling, and whipped cream is a little taste of heaven."*

While working on this clone, I couldn't help thinking of Steve Martin and Bernadette Peters in *The Jerk* enjoying "the best pizza in a cup ever." Applebee's has taken a slice of key lime pie out of the pie pan and put it into a 6-ounce rocks glass. The key lime filling for this clone is thickened on your stovetop, and the topping is made by combining key lime juice and sweetened sour cream. Try to find key limes for this recipe, but any lime juice will work in a pinch if key limes or bottled key lime juice is hard to track down. Chill the filling for a few hours in your fridge before building these 4 servings with graham cracker crumbs on the bottom and whipped cream on top. It's really good stuff. Probably the best key lime pie in a cup ever.

KEY LIME FILLING
4 egg yolks
one 14-ounce can sweetened
    condensed milk
½ cup key lime juice

KEY LIME TOPPING
½ cup sour cream
2 teaspoons key lime juice
3 tablespoons powdered sugar

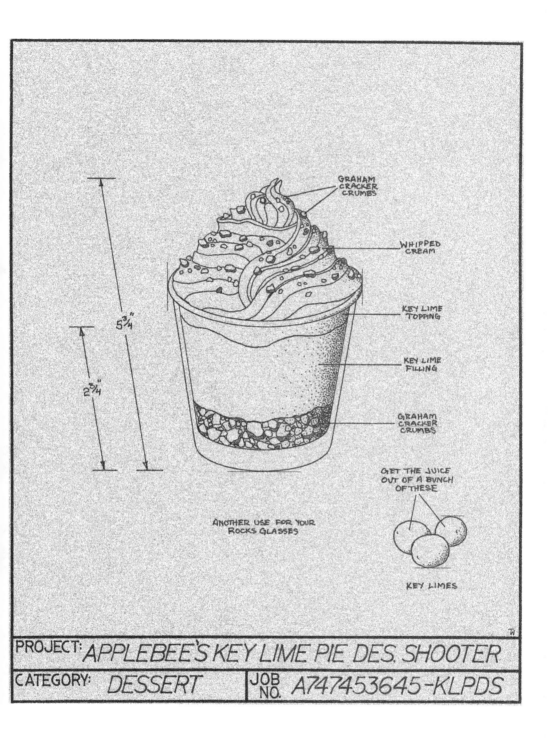

GRAHAM CRACKER CRUMBS

WHIPPED CREAM

KEY LIME TOPPING

KEY LIME FILLING

GRAHAM CRACKER CRUMBS

5¾"

2¾"

GET THE JUICE OUT OF A BUNCH OF THESE

ANOTHER USE FOR YOUR ROCKS GLASSES

KEY LIMES

PROJECT:	APPLEBEE'S KEY LIME PIE DES. SHOOTER	
CATEGORY:	DESSERT	JOB NO. A747453645-KLPDS

*½ cup plus 2 teaspoons graham
    cracker crumbs*
canned whipped cream

1. Beat the egg yolks on high speed in a medium bowl for 2 to
    3 minutes or until light yellow. Add the sweetened condensed
    milk and beat again for another 30 seconds. Transfer this mix-
    ture into a medium saucepan over medium/low heat and stir
    in ½ cup key lime juice. Continue heating for 8 to 10 minutes,
    stirring often, until mixture begins to bubble. Remove the key
    lime filling from the heat and cool, then cover and chill for 3
    to 4 hours.
2. Make the key lime topping by combining sour cream, key lime
    juice, and powdered sugar. Cover and chill.
3. To build each serving, spoon 2 tablespoons of graham cracker
    crumbs into a 6-ounce rocks glass. Spoon in ⅓ cup key lime
    filling, and top it off with 2 tablespoons of the topping. Add a
    pile of whipped cream, sprinkle about ½ teaspoon of graham
    cracker crumbs on the whipped cream and serve.

• MAKES 4 SERVINGS.

•   •   •   •

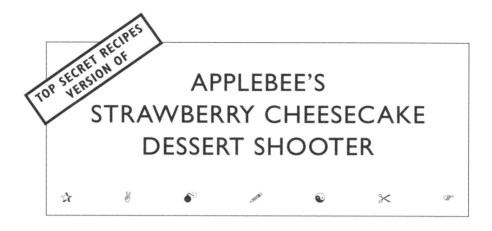

APPLEBEE'S
STRAWBERRY CHEESECAKE
DESSERT SHOOTER

MENU DESCRIPTION: *"Classic cheesecake, graham cracker crumbs, strawberry sauce, and whipped cream make this one to savor."*

Making cheesecake like this means you don't need to crank up your oven and run it for the hour or more that traditional cheesecake recipes require. Since the cheesecake filling is layered into a small glass, you make it ahead of time on your stovetop, which substantially shortens cooking and cooling times. When the filling is chilled, it's spooned into 6-ounce glasses on top of graham cracker crumbs, then thawed sliced strawberries in syrup are spooned on top. After finishing off each dessert shooter with a pile of whipped cream, you get to pass out some spoons, sit back, and enjoy a roomful of "mmmm."

CHEESECAKE FILLING
12 ounces cream cheese
   (1 ½ 8-ounce packages)
2 eggs, beaten
⅓ cup granulated sugar
2 tablespoons sour cream
½ teaspoon vanilla extract

FINISHING
½ cup graham cracker crumbs
½ cup frozen sliced strawberries
   in syrup, thawed
canned whipped cream

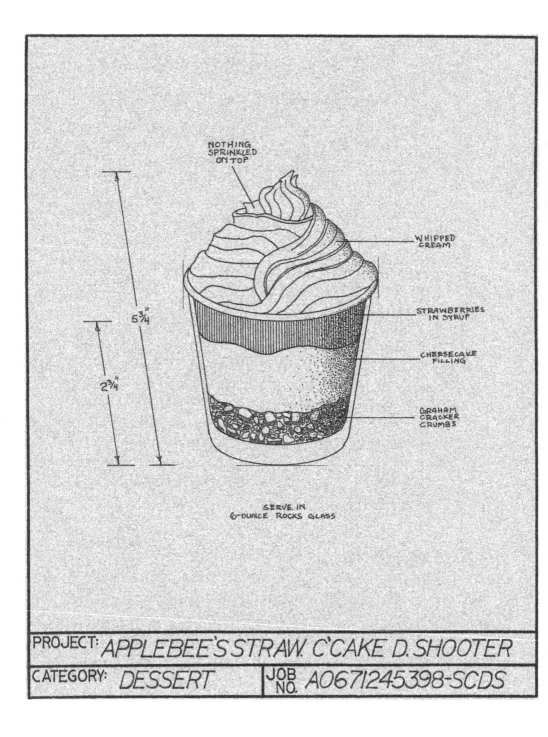

NOTHING
SPRINKLED
ON TOP

WHIPPED
CREAM

STRAWBERRIES
IN SYRUP

CHEESECAKE
FILLING

GRAHAM
CRACKER
CRUMBS

$5\frac{3}{4}"$

$2\frac{3}{4}"$

SERVE IN
6-OUNCE ROCKS GLASS

PROJECT:	*APPLEBEE'S STRAW. C'CAKE D. SHOOTER*	
CATEGORY: *DESSERT*	JOB NO.	*A0671245398-SCDS*

1. Make the cheesecake filling by blending cream cheese, eggs, sugar, sour cream, and vanilla in a large bowl with a mixer on high speed until smooth. Pour the mixture into a large saucepan and cook over medium/high heat, stirring often, for 8 to 10 minutes, until the mixture begins to thicken. Mixture should stick to the spoon when it's inverted. Pour cheesecake filling into a covered container and chill for several hours until cold.

2. To prepare each serving, spoon 2 tablespoons of graham cracker crumbs into a 6-ounce rocks glass, and top with ⅓ cup of cheesecake filling. Spoon 2 tablespoons of strawberries and syrup on top of the cheesecake filling, and top off the dessert with whipped cream.

- MAKES 4 SERVINGS.

• • • •

BAHAMA BREEZE
ISLAND ONION RINGS

MENU DESCRIPTION: *"Thick-cut and coconut breaded, with chili-horseradish and citrus mustard dipping sauces."*

Track down a couple large sweet onions and some shredded coconut for this Island-style twist on golden onion rings. Make 1-inch slices in each onion so that when the slices are separated, you end up with at least 16 wide rings. The breading here will be enough for that many rings, although you might be able to squeeze out a few more. I've also got clones here for the diptastic sauces (check out the secret ingredient that gives the citrus-mustard clone its strong orange flavor without thinning out the sauce). When you're done, you'll have an impressive tower of rings that makes a kickin' appetizer or party dish for at least a half dozen of your crazy friends and family folks.

CHILI-HORSERADISH DIPPING SAUCE

⅓ cup mayonnaise
⅓ cup Heinz chili sauce
2 teaspoons prepared horseradish
2 teaspoons finely minced parsley
pinch salt

CITRUS MUSTARD DIPPING SAUCE

¼ cup orange juice concentrate, thawed
¼ cup Grey Poupon Dijon mustard
2 tablespoons honey

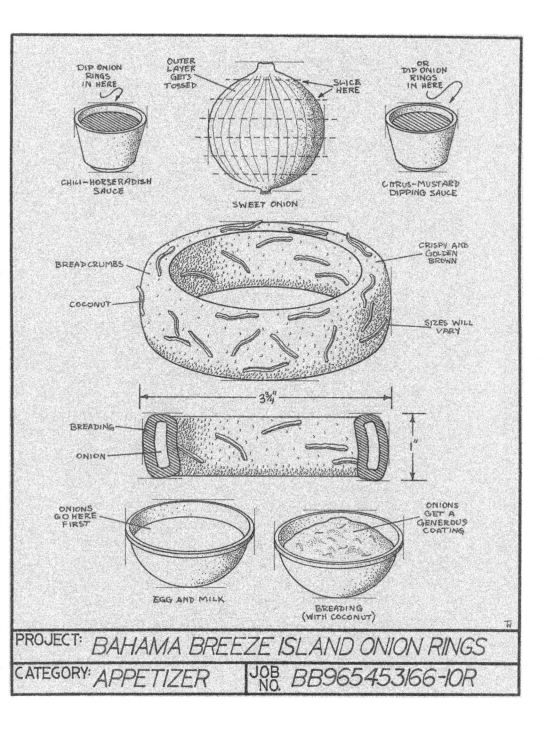

DIP ONION RINGS IN HERE

CHILI-HORSERADISH SAUCE

OUTER LAYER GETS TOSSED

SLICE HERE

SWEET ONION

OR DIP ONION RINGS IN HERE

CITRUS-MUSTARD DIPPING SAUCE

BREADCRUMBS

COCONUT

CRISPY AND GOLDEN BROWN

SIZES WILL VARY

3¾"

BREADING

ONION

1"

ONIONS GO HERE FIRST

EGG AND MILK

ONIONS GET A GENEROUS COATING

BREADING (WITH COCONUT)

PROJECT: BAHAMA BREEZE ISLAND ONION RINGS

CATEGORY: APPETIZER

JOB NO. BB965453166-IOR

1 tablespoon granulated sugar
½ teaspoon finely minced garlic
¼ teaspoon crushed red pepper
    flakes

¼ teaspoon coarse grind black
    pepper
pinch of salt

2 cups all-purpose flour
2 teaspoons salt
1 teaspoon paprika
1 teaspoon ground black pepper
½ teaspoon onion powder
½ teaspoon garlic powder
2 cups plain bread crumbs

1 cup shredded coconut
3 eggs, beaten
3 cups milk
2 large sweet onions, sliced into
    rings, 1-inch wide

6 to 10 cups vegetable oil or
    shortening (as required by
    your deep fryer)

1. Make chili-horseradish sauce by combining all ingredients in a small bowl. Cover and chill.
2. Make citrus mustard dipping sauce by combining all ingredients in a small bowl. Cover and chill this sauce, too.
3. Combine flour, 2 teaspoons salt, 1 teaspoon paprika, 1 teaspoon black pepper, ½ teaspoon onion powder, and ½ teaspoon garlic powder in a large bowl. In another large bowl, combine bread crumbs and coconut. In a third, smaller bowl, combine beaten eggs and milk. When your onions are sliced into wide rings and separated, bread each ring by first dipping it in the egg and milk mixture, then into the flour blend. Go through this first step with 3 or 4 onion rings at a time, allowing them to sit in the flour blend for a bit so that the flour has time to set up and stick to the onions. Dip those same onion rings back into the milk and egg a second time, and then back into the flour blend. Now we switch it up. Dunk the rings back into the wet stuff, and this time give them a coating of bread crumbs. Do that one more time: wet stuff then bread crumbs, and set the rings on a plate. When

all of the rings have been breaded, allow them to rest for 30 minutes so the breading will surely stick when the rings are fried.

4. Heat 6 to 10 cups of oil or shortening to 350 degrees F in your deep fryer. Fry 2 to 4 onion rings at a time for 1 to 2 minutes, until light brown. Drain the fried rings for a minute or so after they come out of the fryer, and then arrange them in 3 towers of 5 onion rings each, with the 16th onion ring stacked on the middle at the top of the 3 stacks. Serve the dipping sauces on the side in small bowls.

• MAKES 6 OR MORE APPETIZER SERVINGS.

•   •   •   •

BAHAMA BREEZE
WEST INDIES PATTIES

MENU DESCRIPTION: *"Crispy pastry with savory beef filling served with seasoned sour cream and apple-mango salsa."*

This is a great finger food appetizer for your next small party since you'll end up with 14 to 16 empanada-like beef-filled "patties" that will be enough for 6 or more people. My server called them "Island-style Hot Pockets." What's cool is that you can make these days ahead of time and freeze them until the party's on. When the time comes, it takes just 5 minutes to fry the patties to a crispy golden brown. Serve them up alongside cool seasoned sour cream and this fantastic apple-mango salsa, and get on with the festivities.

DOUGH

¾ teaspoon salt
2 cups all-purpose flour
¼ cup vegetable shortening
¼ cup cold salted butter
1 egg, beaten
¼ cup whole milk

FILLING

½ pound ground beef (not lean)
¼ cup diced russet potato
¼ cup julienned carrot
2 tablespoons chopped white
    onion
1 teaspoon minced parsley
¾ teaspoon curry powder
½ teaspoon paprika
¼ teaspoon salt
⅛ teaspoon ground cayenne
    pepper
2 tablespoons chicken broth
½ teaspoon lemon juice

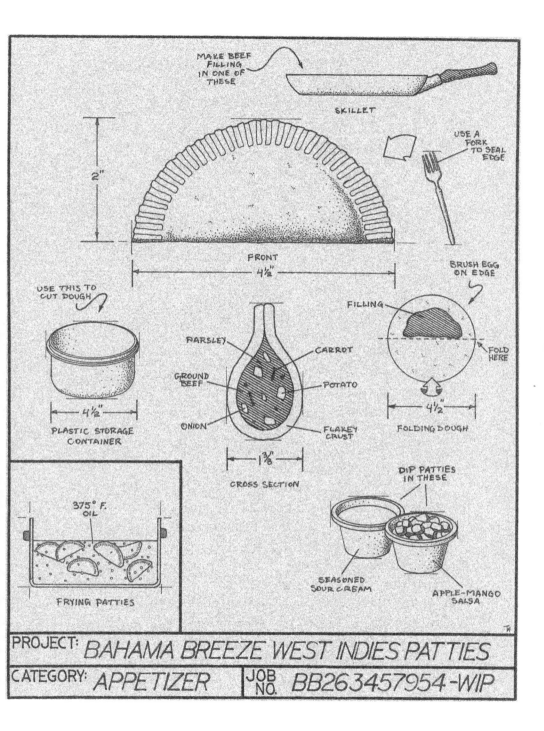

MAKE BEEF FILLING IN ONE OF THESE

SKILLET

2"

FRONT

4½"

USE A FORK TO SEAL EDGE

BRUSH EGG ON EDGE

USE THIS TO CUT DOUGH

4½"

PLASTIC STORAGE CONTAINER

PARSLEY

CARROT

GROUND BEEF

POTATO

ONION

FLAKEY CRUST

1⅜"

CROSS SECTION

FILLING

FOLD HERE

4½"

FOLDING DOUGH

375° F. OIL

FRYING PATTIES

DIP PATTIES IN THESE

SEASONED SOUR CREAM

APPLE-MANGO SALSA

PROJECT: *BAHAMA BREEZE WEST INDIES PATTIES*

CATEGORY: *APPETIZER*　JOB NO. *BB263457954-WIP*

SEASONED SOUR CREAM

1 cup sour cream
¼ cup diced tomato (half of a
    medium tomato)
1 tablespoon chopped red onion
1 tablespoon minced green bell
    pepper

1 teaspoon chopped cilantro
¼ teaspoon salt
¼ teaspoon ground cayenne
    pepper
pinch ground cumin

APPLE-MANGO SALSA

1 cup finely diced Granny Smith
    apple (half of a large apple)
4 teaspoons lime juice
1 cup finely diced mango
    (1 small mango)

1 tablespoon minced jalapeño
1 tablespoon minced red bell
    pepper
1 tablespoon minced cilantro
pinch salt

1 egg, beaten
6 to 10 cups vegetable oil or shortening
(as required by your deep fryer)

1. Make the dough by combining salt with flour in a large mixing bowl. Add shortening and cold butter and use a pastry knife or large fork to cut shortening and butter into dry ingredients until the fat is completely combined. Add beaten egg and milk and stir to bring ingredients together, and then use your hands to form the dough into a ball. Wrap the dough in plastic and pop it in the fridge until the filling is done.
2. Brown the ground beef in a medium sauté pan over medium heat. Break the meat up into small bits as it cooks (a potato masher works nicely for this). When the meat is done, pour it out of the pan, strain off the fat, then return the fat back to the sauté pan.
3. Drop diced potato pieces into a small saucepan of water over medium heat. When the water comes to a boil, drain potato and drop the pieces into the fat in the sauté pan along

with the carrot and onion. Sauté for 3 to 4 minutes over medium heat, and then add the ground beef back into the pan along with the curry powder, paprika, salt, and cayenne pepper. Stir in chicken broth and lemon juice and bring the mixture to a simmer for 3 to 4 minutes. Turn off the heat and cover filling while you make the seasoned sour cream and apple-mango salsa.

4. Make seasoned sour cream by combining all ingredients in a small bowl. Cover and chill.

5. Make apple-mango salsa by combining all ingredients in a medium bowl in the order listed. Cover and chill.

6. When the meat is cool, it's time to fill the dough. Roll out a portion of the dough on a floured surface until it is very flat. Use an upside down round plastic storage container with a diameter of approximately 4½ inches to cut out rounds of the dough. Use a brush to paint beaten egg along the edge of half of the dough. This will help to seal the dough. Measure a heaping tablespoon of filling into the center of the dough, and then fold the dough over and press down along the edge. Force out any extra air when you close the dough. Press down along the edge of the dough with the tines of a fork to seal the dough. When all of the patties have been assembled, cover them and let them freeze for a couple hours to ensure that the seams will hold.

7. Heat 6 to 10 cups of oil or shortening in your deep fryer to 375 degrees F. Fry 4 or 5 patties at a time for 5 to 6 minutes, until golden brown. Flip the patties over as they fry to get both sides evenly browned. Serve patties with a pile of apple-mango salsa and seasoned sour cream on the side in a small bowl.

• MAKES 6 TO 8 APPETIZER SERVINGS.

•   •   •   •

BJ'S RESTAURANT & BREWHOUSE AVOCADO EGG ROLLS

MENU DESCRIPTION: *"Crispy golden wontons wrap a tantalizing blend of avocados, cream cheese, sun-dried tomatoes, red onions, cilantro, pine nuts, chipotle peppers, and spices. Served with a sweet tamarind sauce."*

Avocado egg rolls or spring rolls have been increasing in popularity as an appetizer at casual chains, but they are a bit more of a high-maintenance menu item than, say, southwestern egg rolls or other spring roll variations. Since avocados are quick to oxidize and turn brown, these rolls must be made and served within a 2- to 12-hour time frame. Also, cooks must be careful not to overfry the egg rolls or the avocado inside will become too hot, turn brown, and taste pretty gross. So, if you're planning to serve these later in the day, make them in the morning and let them chill out in your fridge until it's time to fry them up. You can also make the tamarind sauce early in the day and park it in the fridge. You'll need a little tamarind paste for this sauce, which can be found at Whole Foods or specialty stores. If you don't want to clone the sauce as served in the restaurant, you can always use your favorite sweet and/or spicy bottled dipping sauces. And creamy southwestern-style sauces are also awesome on these babies.

1 tablespoon pine nuts

2 ounces cream cheese, softened
   (¼ cup)

1 ½ teaspoons minced sun-dried
   tomato

1 ½ teaspoons minced canned
   chipotle chile

1 ½ teaspoons minced red onion

1 ½ teaspoons lemon juice

1 teaspoon minced fresh cilantro

⅛ teaspoon garlic powder

⅛ teaspoon salt

pinch ground black pepper

3 cups diced Hass avocado
   (3 medium avocados)

6 large wonton wrappers

1 egg, beaten

6 to 10 cups vegetable oil

SWEET TAMARIND SAUCE

1 teaspoon tamarind paste

½ cup dark brown sugar

¾ cup water

½ teaspoon minced fresh ginger

¼ teaspoon minced garlic

1 ¾ teaspoons soy sauce

pinch dried oregano

dash ground black pepper

GARNISH

julienned carrot

julienned red cabbage

chopped fresh cilantro

1.   Toast the pine nuts in a small skillet over medium/low heat for 5 to 10 minutes, or until the nuts begin to brown. Stir or toss the nuts often, and watch them closely so they don't burn.

2.   Combine the pine nuts with cream cheese, sun-dried tomato, chipotle chile, red onion, lemon juice, cilantro, garlic powder, salt, and pepper in a medium bowl. Stir well. Add the diced avocado and stir gently to combine with the other ingredients. Be careful not to mash up the avocado—you don't want guacamole.

3.   Position a wonton wrapper on a plate, floured-side down, with one corner pointing toward you. Brush the edges with beaten egg. Measure ½ cup of the avocado filling into the

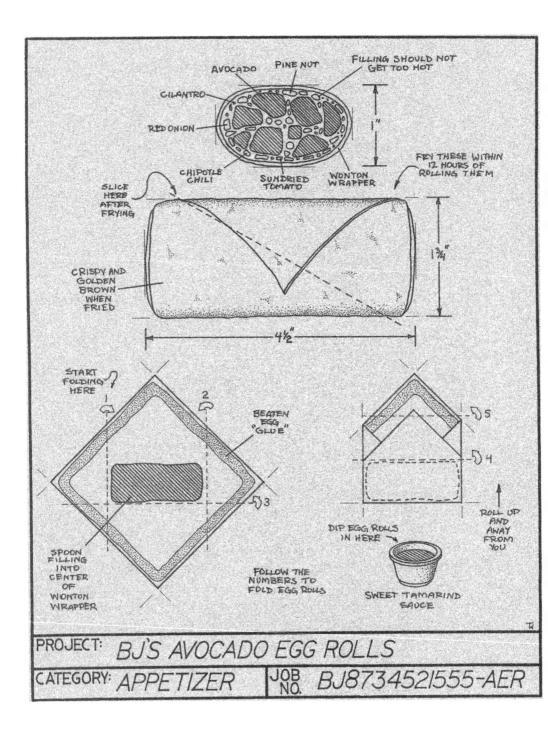

AVOCADO   PINE NUT   FILLING SHOULD NOT
                              GET TOO HOT

CILANTRO

RED ONION

1"

CHIPOTLE   SUNDRIED   WONTON
CHILI   TOMATO   WRAPPER

FRY THESE WITHIN
12 HOURS OF
ROLLING THEM

SLICE
HERE
AFTER
FRYING

CRISPY AND
GOLDEN
BROWN
WHEN
FRIED

1¾"

4½"

START
FOLDING
HERE

2

BEATEN
EGG
"GLUE"

3

SPOON
FILLING
INTO
CENTER
OF
WONTON
WRAPPER

FOLLOW THE
NUMBERS TO
FOLD EGG ROLLS

5

4

ROLL UP
AND
AWAY
FROM
YOU

DIP EGG ROLLS
IN HERE

SWEET TAMARIND
SAUCE

PROJECT: *BJ'S AVOCADO EGG ROLLS*

CATEGORY: *APPETIZER*   **JOB NO.** *BJ8734521555-AER*

center of the wrapper. Form the filling into a horizontal pile that is about 4 inches long by 1½ inches wide. Fold over the left and right corners, and then fold the corner closest to you over the filling and on top of the corner farthest away. Roll the egg roll away from you over the top corners. Be sure to use a little pressure as you roll so that the contents of the egg roll are nice and snug in there. Chill for 2 to 12 hours, but don't go longer than that or the avocado may begin to brown.

4. Prepare the tamarind sauce by combining all the ingredients in a small saucepan. Set the pan over medium heat, and when the mixture begins to boil, set your timer for 5 minutes. After 5 minutes, the mixture should have thickened and reduced to about ½ cup. Pour the sauce into a small serving bowl and set aside until you're ready to plate the dish.

5. To fry the egg rolls, heat the oil to 375 degrees F in a large saucepan or deep fryer. Fry the egg rolls two or three at a time for 4 minutes, or until lightly browned. Drain them briefly when they come out of the oil, but don't let the egg rolls sit too long, as you want them to be just slightly warm, even a little cool, in the middle when served. Slice each egg roll diagonally through the middle and arrange around the small bowl of dipping sauce on a plate that is sprinkled with a garnish of julienned carrot and julienned red cabbage. Just before serving, sprinkle a little chopped cilantro over the entire plate.

• SERVES 6 AS AN APPETIZER.

•   •   •   •

BJ'S RESTAURANT & BREWHOUSE CHILI

MENU DESCRIPTION: *"Chili made with select cuts of tender pork and beef, pinto beans, Piranha Pale Ale, and topped with melted jack and cheddar cheeses, sour cream, and green onions."*

There's nothing that warms the soul like a hot bowl of spicy chili. And since BJ's is a brewery, the 80-unit chain adds an ingredient that makes a steamy bowl of red even better: beer! The Piranha Pale Ale that's poured into the chili pot is very similar to Bass Pale Ale, so that's what we'll use here for our clone (Sierra Nevada Pale Ale also works well). Toss everything into the pot over the heat, and in about 90 minutes you'll have enough chili for 8 hungry mouths. Serve up the chili in bowls, or more impressively, in the center of hollowed-out sourdough loaves. Nice.

1 pound ground beef
1 pound ground pork
2 cups diced onion (1 medium onion)
2 tablespoons chili powder
1 tablespoon salt
1 teaspoon garlic powder
1 teaspoon dried thyme
1 teaspoon ground black pepper

½ teaspoon ground cayenne pepper
½ cup all-purpose flour
2 cups water
two 15-ounce cans pinto beans, with liquid
one 15-ounce can crushed tomatoes
one 12-ounce bottle Bass Pale Ale

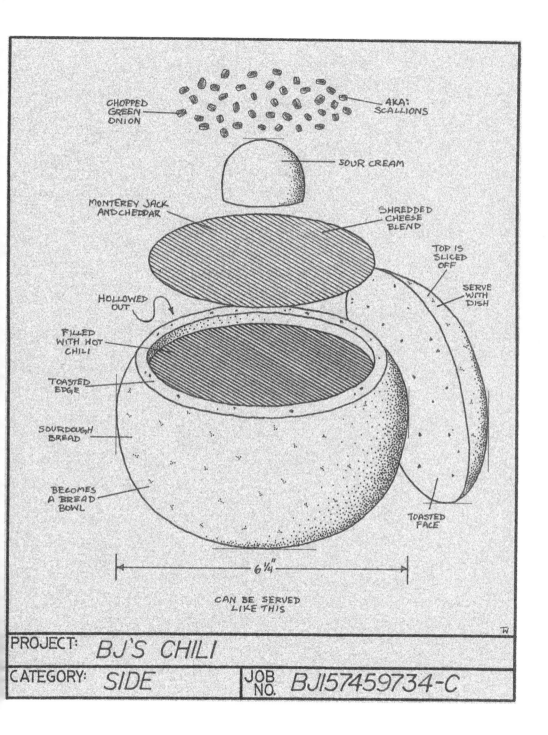

CHOPPED GREEN ONION

AKA: SCALLIONS

SOUR CREAM

MONTEREY JACK AND CHEDDAR

SHREDDED CHEESE BLEND

TOP IS SLICED OFF

SERVE WITH DISH

HOLLOWED OUT

FILLED WITH HOT CHILI

TOASTED EDGE

SOURDOUGH BREAD

BECOMES A BREAD BOWL

TOASTED FACE

6 ¼"

CAN BE SERVED LIKE THIS

PROJECT:	BJ'S CHILI		
CATEGORY:	SIDE	JOB NO.	BJI57459734-C

1 cup shredded cheddar cheese
1 cup shredded Monterey Jack
*   cheese*
½ cup sour cream
½ cup chopped green onion

Rounds of sourdough bread with
*   centers hollowed out (and*
*   keep the tops—see Tidbits).*

1. Brown ground meats in a large saucepan over medium heat. Drain off excess fat.
2. Add onion, chili powder, salt, garlic powder, thyme, black pepper, cayenne, and sauté for an additional 5 minutes.
3. Combine flour with water and add mixture to pan.
4. Add remaining ingredients, bring chili to a simmer, and then let it simmer uncovered for 1½ hours, stirring occasionally.
5. Serve 1¼ cups of chili in a bowl or in a carved-out round of sourdough bread. Mix shredded cheeses and then top chili with ¼ cup of the cheese blend, a tablespoon of sour cream, and a tablespoon of chopped green onions on top.

• MAKES 8 SERVINGS.

TIDBITS

When serving chili in a sourdough bread bowl, combine ¼ cup melted butter with ½ teaspoon garlic salt and ½ teaspoon dried parsley flakes. Brush this over the face of top of the bread you cut off to make the bowls. Also brush a little garlic butter on the top edge of the bread bowl. Flip the tops and the "bowls" over onto the buttered surface on a griddle or skillet that has been preheated to medium heat. Cook for a minute or two, until browned. Serve chili in the bread bowl with the grilled top leaning against it.

• • • •

BJ'S RESTAURANT & BREWHOUSE PARMESAN CRUSTED CHICKEN BREAST

☆　　　　✄　　　　💣　　　　✎　　　　☯　　　　✂　　　　☞

MENU DESCRIPTION: *"Our marinated chicken breast coated with par-mesan cheese and crunchy panko breadcrumbs, lightly pounded and pan fried to a golden brown. Served with white cheddar mashed po-tatoes and steamed broccoli and topped with a lemon chardonnay butter sauce, sun-dried tomatoes, fresh basil, and Parmesan cheese."*

This re-creation lays out a great way to prepare that 4-pack of chicken breasts you dropped into your shopping cart. While you're at the market, head down the aisle where the Asian foods are parked and pick up some Japanese bread crumbs, also called panko. Combining these coarse bread crumbs with shredded Parmesan cheese makes a crispy breading for the chicken that doesn't even need a sauce to taste good. Still, the lemony chardonnay butter sauce used at the restaurant is cloned here, too, so you'll have the complete flavor experience. You'll want to plan ahead a bit for this dish since the chicken fillets will need to marinate in the brine solution for 2 or 3 hours. This dish goes great with another clone recipe, BJ's White Cheddar Mashed Potatoes (page 42).

2 cups chicken broth
1 teaspoon salt

4 large skinless chicken breast
fillets

4 eggs
½ cup all-purpose flour
1 cup panko (Japanese bread
    crumbs)

1 cup shredded Parmesan cheese
½ teaspoon salt
½ teaspoon ground black pepper

LEMON CHARDONNAY BUTTER SAUCE

¼ cup salted butter
¼ cup chardonnay wine
2 tablespoons lemon juice

¾ teaspoon granulated sugar
pinch salt
1⅓ cups heavy cream

light olive oil

GARNISH

2 tablespoons shredded
    Parmesan cheese
4 teaspoons minced sun-dried
    tomatoes

4 tablespoons thinly sliced fresh
    basil

1. Make the brine for the chicken by dissolving the salt in the chicken broth in a medium bowl. Cover the chicken breasts with plastic wrap and pound each one to about ½-inch thick with a kitchen mallet. If breasts are large, you can cut them in half. Add flattened chicken to the brine. Cover and chill for 2 to 3 hours.

2. When the chicken has marinated, remove the fillets from the brine and dab with paper towels to remove excess liquid. Beat eggs in a medium bowl, and pour flour onto a plate. Combine panko, Parmesan cheese, salt, and pepper in another medium bowl. To bread the chicken, first coat each fillet with flour, then egg, and then the Parmesan mixture. Let the breaded fillets rest for a bit on plate in your fridge while you prepare the chardonnay butter sauce.

3. Make the chardonnay butter sauce by melting the butter in a small saucepan over medium heat. Add wine and simmer for I minute. Stir in lemon juice, sugar, and salt, and then add cream. Simmer over low heat for 10 to 12 minutes, until thicker.

4. Add enough oil to cover the bottom of a large sauté pan, and heat over medium/low until hot. You can check the heat of the oil by dropping a bread crumb into it. If it starts to sizzle, your oil is ready. Sauté each breaded chicken fillet in the oil for 4 to 5 minutes per side, until brown. Remove fillets to a paper towel–covered plate until ready to serve. Serve each fillet with a couple tablespoons of butter sauce spooned over the top. Pile a tablespoon of Parmesan cheese on top of each fillet, followed by I heaping teaspoon of minced sun-dried tomatoes and a tablespoon of basil.

• MAKES 4 SERVINGS.

•   •   •   •

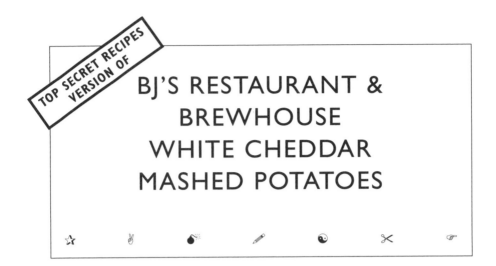

BJ'S RESTAURANT & BREWHOUSE WHITE CHEDDAR MASHED POTATOES

You'll find these easy-to-clone mashers served alongside BJ's new Parmesan Crusted Chicken Breast (page 39), but this is a versatile side that can be served up with tons of home-cooked entrees. You won't need gravy for these rich, flavorful mashed potatoes—just a fork.

2 large russet potatoes
1 cup shredded white cheddar
   cheese
¾ cup heavy cream

¼ cup salted butter
½ teaspoon salt
⅛ teaspoon cracked black pepper

1. Peel and quarter potatoes. Boil potatoes in 6 to 8 cups of water in a pot or large saucepan for 30 to 40 minutes, until soft. Drain potatoes, then add them back to the pan and mash thoroughly.
2. Add cheese, cream, butter, salt, and pepper and heat over medium/low heat, stirring often, until thick.

• MAKES 4 SIDE SERVINGS.

• • • •

BJ'S RESTAURANT &
BREWHOUSE
BJ'S FAMOUS PIZOOKIE

MENU DESCRIPTION: *"A freshly baked, hot out-of-the oven, rich and delicious cookie topped with two scoops of vanilla bean ice cream and served in its own deep dish. Your choice of Chocolate Chunk, White Chocolate Macadamia Nut, Peanut Butter or Oatmeal Raisin Walnut."*

Visit one of more than 90 BJ's restaurants located in the West and Southwest and you'll likely find many giddy diners digging down into one of these deep-dish cookie desserts. Even though the restaurant is known for great Chicago-style deep-dish pizzas and a fantastic selection of custom-brewed beers, it's the Pizookie at the end of the rainbow that gets the most drools. There are currently four varieties to choose from on the menu, so I'm giving you clones for all four below. Each formula makes enough dough for one giant cookie, and the recipes are so easy that you could make more than one with just a little extra effort. You might think that the cooking temperature of 475 degrees F is extreme for a cookie, but since BJ's is a pizza joint, these puppies get cooked in cranked-up pizza ovens, and it works great. Not only will you have your cookie done in only 5 to 7 minutes, but it'll also be nice and brown on top and slightly gooey in the center—all good things for a cookie, right? The restaurants use 6-inch deep-dish pizza pans, but you can bake your clones in any cake pan or pie pan with a bottom that is 6 to 7 inches across.

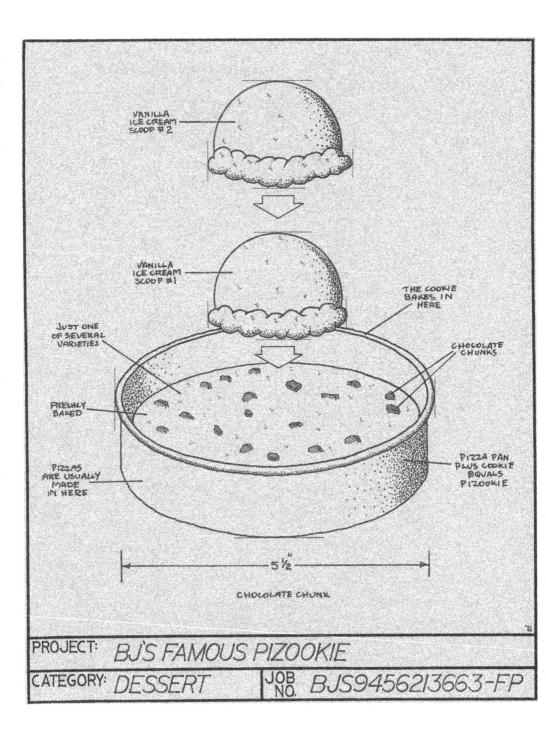

VANILLA
ICE CREAM
SCOOP #2

VANILLA
ICE CREAM
SCOOP #1

THE COOKIE
BAKES IN
HERE

JUST ONE
OF SEVERAL
VARIETIES

CHOCOLATE
CHUNKS

FRESHLY
BAKED

PIZZAS
ARE USUALLY
MADE
IN HERE

PIZZA PAN
PLUS COOKIE
EQUALS
PIZOOKIE

5 1/2"

CHOCOLATE CHUNK

PROJECT:	*BJ'S FAMOUS PIZOOKIE*	
CATEGORY: *DESSERT*	JOB NO.	*BJS9456213663-FP*

CHOCOLATE CHUNK

2½ tablespoons salted butter, softened
¼ cup light brown sugar, packed
1 tablespoon beaten egg
¼ teaspoon vanilla extract

6 tablespoons all-purpose flour
¼ teaspoon baking soda
⅓ cup semisweet chocolate chunks

WHITE CHOCOLATE MACADAMIA NUT

2½ tablespoons salted butter, softened
¼ cup light brown sugar, packed
1 tablespoon beaten egg
¼ teaspoon vanilla extract
6 tablespoons all-purpose flour

¼ teaspoon baking soda
3 tablespoons white chocolate chunks or chips
3 tablespoons chopped macadamia nuts

PEANUT BUTTER

1½ tablespoons salted butter, softened
3 tablespoons creamy peanut butter
¼ cup light brown sugar, packed

1 tablespoon beaten egg
¼ teaspoon vanilla extract
6 tablespoons all-purpose flour
¼ teaspoon baking soda
2 tablespoons unsalted peanuts

OATMEAL RAISIN WALNUT

2½ tablespoons salted butter, softened
¼ cup light brown sugar, packed
1 tablespoon beaten egg
¼ teaspoon vanilla extract
5 tablespoons all-purpose flour

¼ cup rolled oats (not instant)
¼ teaspoon baking soda
⅛ teaspoon ground cinnamon
3 tablespoons raisins
1 tablespoon chopped walnuts

2 scoops of vanilla ice cream

1. Preheat oven to 475 degrees F.
2. Combine all ingredients for cookie of your choice up to but

not including the flour in a small bowl and beat with an electric mixer on high speed until smooth. Add flour and baking soda (plus oats and cinnamon if making the oatmeal raisin walnut cookie) and stir well by hand. Stir in remaining ingredients then press the dough into a small buttered pie pan, cake pan, or 6-inch deep-dish pizza pan.

3. Bake for 5 to 7 minutes or until cookie begins to brown. Cool for a minute or so, add 2 scoops of vanilla ice cream, and go for it.

• MAKES 2 SERVINGS.

•   •   •   •

BONEFISH GRILL
BANG BANG SHRIMP

MENU DESCRIPTION: *"Tender, crispy shrimp tossed in a creamy, spicy sauce."*

Bonefish Grill proudly refers to this appetizer as the "house specialty." And why not? It's an attractive dish with bang-up flavor, especially if you like your food on the spicy side. The heat comes from the secret sauce blend that's flavored with chili garlic sauce, also known as sambal. You can find this bright red sauce near the Asian foods in your market—and while you're there, pick up some rice vinegar. Once the sauce is made, you coat the shrimp in a simple seasoned breading, fry them to a nice golden brown, toss them gently in the sauce, and then serve them up on a bed of mixed greens to hungry folks who, hopefully, have a cool drink nearby to mellow the sting.

SPICY SAUCE

½ cup mayonnaise

4 teaspoons chili garlic sauce (sambal)

1 teaspoon granulated sugar

½ teaspoon rice vinegar

1 egg, beaten

1 cup milk

¾ cup all-purpose flour

½ cup panko bread crumbs

1 teaspoon salt

½ teaspoon ground black pepper

½ teaspoon rubbed (ground) sage

¼ teaspoon onion powder

¼ teaspoon garlic powder

¼ teaspoon dried basil

6 to 10 cups vegetable shortening
    or oil

16 to 18 medium shrimp, peeled
    and deveined

GARNISH

1 handful of mixed greens

1 green onion, chopped (green
    part only)

1. Combine all ingredients for the spicy sauce in a small bowl.
    Cover the sauce and set it aside for now.
2. Combine the beaten egg with the milk in a shallow bowl. Mix
    flour, panko, salt, black pepper, sage, onion powder, garlic
    powder, and basil in another shallow bowl.
3. Bread the shrimp by first coating each with the breading. Dip
    breaded shrimp into the egg and milk mixture, and then back
    into the breading. Arrange the coated shrimp on a plate and
    pop them into the fridge for at least 20 minutes. This step will
    help the breading to stick on the shrimp when they are frying.
4. Heat shortening or oil to 350 degrees F. Use the amount of
    oil required by your fryer or enough to fill a large saucepan
    about halfway.
5. When your oil is hot, fry the shrimp for 3 to 4 minutes, until
    golden brown. Drain on a rack or paper towels. When all of
    the shrimp have been fried, drop the shrimp into a large
    bowl. Spoon about ¼ cup of the sauce over the shrimp and
    stir gently to coat. Stack the shrimp on a bed of mixed greens,
    then sprinkle chopped green onion over the top.

• MAKES 2 TO 4 APPETIZER SERVINGS.

TIDBITS

You can also make this dish several days ahead by following the directions up to the frying stage. But instead of frying for 3 to 4 minutes, flash fry the shrimp for just 45 seconds, and then let them cool. Pop the shrimp into a zip-top bag and into the freezer. When you want to make the dish, simply fry the shrimp for 3 minutes or until brown, and then coat with the sauce and garnish as instructed in step #5.

• • • •

BONEFISH GRILL
SAUCY SHRIMP

MENU DESCRIPTION: *"Shrimp sautéed in a lime tomato garlic sauce with kalamata olives and feta cheese."*

Restaurateurs Tim Curci and Chris Parker opened the first Bonefish Grill in St. Petersburg, Florida in 2000, and, with at least 8 species of fresh oak-grilled fish to choose from on any given day, the chain has since exploded to over 100 units in 29 states. Yes, the fish is very good, and the oak grill is a nice touch, but you should also know that this is a restaurant that likes to have fun with sauces. This appetizer clone is a good example of that. The tartness of the lime works beautifully with the sweetness of the sun-dried tomato to create a scampi sauce unlike any you may have tasted before. Lay this simple dish on the troops before your main course and you will be tonight's kitchen hero.

¼ cup salted butter
2 tablespoons light olive oil
1 teaspoon minced garlic
2½ teaspoons granulated sugar
1 tablespoon lime juice
¼ cup sliced sun-dried tomatoes

⅛ teaspoon Italian herb
    seasoning blend
16 to 18 medium shrimp, peeled
    and deveined
¼ cup heavy cream
¼ cup crumbled feta cheese
4 pitted kalamata olives

1. Combine butter and olive oil in a medium skillet and heat over medium/low heat until the butter is melted. Stir in garlic and let it cook for a minute or so. Add sugar, lime juice, tomatoes, and Italian seasoning and cook until sugar is dissolved.
2. Add shrimp to the pan and turn heat up to medium/high heat. Sauté shrimp for 2½ to 3 minutes, until cooked through, then turn off the heat.
3. Stir in the cream, then pour entire contents of the skillet onto a serving plate. Sprinkle with crumbled feta and kalamata olives.

• MAKES 2 TO 4 APPETIZER SERVINGS.

• • • •

BONEFISH GRILL
CITRUS HERB
VINAIGRETTE

There are a few decent bottled salad dressings out there, but there's nothing on the shelf that compares in taste to this home-made version of the house dressing from Bonefish Grill. Not only that, it's a heck of a lot cheaper to make your own vinaigrette from scratch. And check out the easy steps: Mix everything together in a bowl, microwave for 1 minute, whisk to emulsify, then chill. If you're a salad lover, this is the clone for you.

⅔ cup extra virgin olive oil
¼ cup granulated sugar
3 tablespoons water
2 tablespoons white wine vinegar
4 teaspoons minced garlic
1 tablespoon Grey Poupon Dijon
    mustard
2 teaspoons lime juice

2 teaspoons lemon juice
2 teaspoons minced fresh parsley
½ teaspoon dried basil
¼ teaspoon dried oregano
¼ teaspoon salt
⅛ teaspoon ground black
    pepper

1. Whisk all ingredients in a medium bowl. Microwave on high for 1 minute or until mixture bubbles rapidly around the edge of the bowl.
2. Remove bowl from microwave and whisk for 1 minute until mixture thickens. Cover and chill for 1 hour before serving.

• MAKES 1¼ CUPS.

BUCA DI BEPPO GARLIC BREAD & MOZZARELLA GARLIC BREAD

Get the breath mints ready. The secret to re-creating Buca di Beppo's garlic bread starts with using the right kind of bread and lots of fresh garlic. Bakers at each restaurant start baking bread early each day, so you'll want to find a freshly baked Italian loaf in your market's bakery, and cut it in half through the middle using a large serrated knife. The restaurant used to make the garlic bread with focaccia-style bread, but recently changed the recipe. Either way you go, the fresher your bread, the better your garlic bread will turn out. The garlic cloves are sliced very thin using a sharp knife and a steady hand. Arrange these slices over the top of the generously buttered bread. Then just make sure you each consume at least 1 slice when the lightly brown garlic bread comes out of the oven so that everyone's breath is equally stinky.

1 loaf of Italian bread (can also use focaccia or ciabatta)
½ cup (1 stick) salted butter, softened
6 cloves garlic, sliced thin

3 tablespoons grated Parmesan cheese
2 cups shredded mozzarella (if making the mozzarella version)

1   Preheat oven to 425 degrees F.
2.   Slice bread in half through the middle and spread approxi-

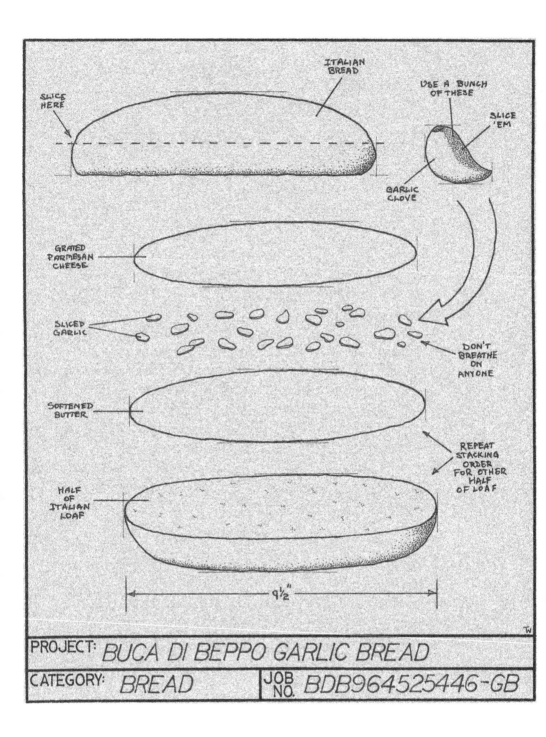

SLICE HERE

ITALIAN BREAD

USE A BUNCH OF THESE

SLICE 'EM

GARLIC CLOVE

GRATED PARMESAN CHEESE

SLICED GARLIC

DON'T BREATHE ON ANYONE

SOFTENED BUTTER

REPEAT STACKING ORDER FOR OTHER HALF OF LOAF

HALF OF ITALIAN LOAF

9½"

PROJECT: *BUCA DI BEPPO GARLIC BREAD*

CATEGORY: *BREAD*

JOB NO. *BDB964525446-GB*

mately ¼ cup of softened butter on the faces of each half of the loaf.

3. Arrange about 3 cloves of sliced garlic on each face of the bread.

4. Sprinkle about 1½ tablespoons of Parmesan cheese over the butter and garlic on each half.

5. If you are making the mozzarella version, sprinkle 1 cup of mozzarella cheese on top. (Skip this step for the plain recipe.)

6. Bake bread on a baking sheet for 10 to 12 minutes, until top begins to brown. Slice and serve.

• MAKES 8 SERVINGS.

TIDBITS

The older version of this garlic bread had a little oregano on it. If you like that recipe simply sprinkle about ½ teaspoon of dried oregano on each half of bread before baking.

•   •   •   •

BUCA DI BEPPO
CHICKEN LIMONE

MENU DESCRIPTION: *"Chicken breasts lightly sautéed and topped with lemon butter sauce and capers."*

Buca di Beppo's most popular chicken dish was deliciously simple to reverse-engineer. I asked the server to check on what kind of dairy is used in the sauce and whether or not white wine is cooked into it. After getting the information I needed, I ordered the dish to go with the sauce on the side and got to work back in the lab. Several versions hit the sink as I unsuccessfully experimented with various amounts of wine, butter, and cream. It was only after I decided to chill the sauce that I got the information I needed. The sauce formed a firm solid in the fridge, which indicated that I needed a lot more butter than I first estimated. I made the proper adjustments and the sauce that sat in my pan was a perfect match that could surely stand up to a blindfolded taste test. The rest of the secret technique required pounding the chicken breast halves until thin. This tenderized the chicken and made each piece the same size as the original. A quick sauté later, I was arranging the chicken on a serving platter, adding capers, spooning on plenty of sauce, and I had before me a beautiful culinary carbon copy indistinguishable from the favorite on the menu at the 73-unit Italian chain owned by Planet Hollywood.

LEMON BUTTER SAUCE

½ cup white wine
2 teaspoons minced garlic
½ cup (1 stick) butter

½ cup heavy cream
⅛ teaspoon salt
1 lemon

2 skinless chicken breast fillets,
   halved
¼ cup all-purpose flour

¼ cup extra light olive oil
1½ tablespoons capers

1. Prepare the lemon butter sauce by combining the wine and garlic in a small saucepan over medium heat. When the wine begins to boil, reduce the heat to a simmer and cook for 3 to 4 minutes, or until the wine has reduced by about half. Pour the wine into a strainer over a bowl to remove the garlic.
2. While the wine drips through the strainer, rinse out the saucepan and place it back over medium heat. Add the butter.
3. When the butter has completely melted, pour the strained wine back into the pan along with the heavy cream and salt.
4. Slice two wedges out of the lemon for use later as a garnish, then juice the rest of the lemon. Add 1½ teaspoons of the juice to the sauce. When it comes to a boil, reduce the heat and simmer for 10 to 12 minutes, or until thick and creamy. Cover and remove from the heat.
5. While the sauce simmers, prepare the chicken by heating the olive oil in a large sauté pan over medium/high heat until the oil is shimmering.
6. Cover each piece of chicken with plastic wrap and pound on it with a mallet until each chicken breast half is about ½-inch thick.
7. Pour the flour onto a plate. Coat each side of each chicken breast with a light dusting of flour. Shake off any excess.
8. Carefully slide each piece of chicken into the oil and sauté for 4 minutes per side, or until lightly browned.
9. Arrange the chicken pieces side by side on a serving platter.

Sprinkle the capers over the top of the chicken, then spoon on a generous amount of the lemon butter sauce. Place a lemon wedge at each end of the platter and serve.

- SERVES 2.

• • • •

BUFFALO WILD WINGS ASIAN ZING SAUCE

MENU DESCRIPTION: *"Sweet meets heat: A chili pepper, soy, and ginger sauce."*

Here's a clone for one of the newer sauces that the wing masters at Buffalo Wild Wings added to the menu. When I get over to BWW, I order up a tall Foster's on tap and 12 boneless wings covered in this great sauce. It's sweet-and-sour with a kick, and the kick is what the beer's for. Next time you're at the market, grab yourself some chili garlic sauce in the aisle with the other Asian foods. That's the crucial ingredient that gives this sauce its heat, along with its deep red color. Once this sauce is made it'll store for weeks in a sealed container in your fridge. Now you've got a quick dip for eggrolls, wontons, and spring rolls. Cook up some wings, nuggets, or breaded tenders and toss 'em in the gooey goodness until well coated, then serve hot. And don't forget the beer.

2 teaspoons cornstarch
4 teaspoons rice wine vinegar
½ cup light corn syrup
⅓ cup granulated sugar
¼ cup chili garlic sauce
    (sambal)

1 tablespoon soy sauce
1 teaspoon lemon juice
¼ teaspoon ground ginger
¼ teaspoon salt
¼ teaspoon minced garlic

1. Dissolve cornstarch in rice wine vinegar in a small bowl.
2. Combine the vinegar solution with the remaining ingredients in a small saucepan over medium/low heat. Heat mixture, stirring often, until the sauce reaches a boil, then remove it from the heat. Cool, cover, and chill the sauce until needed.
3. To use the sauce, pour ¼ cup over 12 cooked chicken wings, breaded tenders, or chicken nuggets and toss gently until coated.

• MAKES ¾ CUP SAUCE, ENOUGH TO COAT 36 WINGS.

• • • •

BUFFALO WILD WINGS PARMESAN GARLIC SAUCE

MENU DESCRIPTION: *"Roasted garlic and Parmesan sauce with Italian herbs."*

Buffalo Wild Wings had a record day on Super Bowl Sunday 2007 when the chain sold 3.4 million wings! One year later the chain announced the opening of its 500th store. As the biggest buffalo wing chain in the country continues to grow, so does its selection of delicious sauces. Creamy and slightly spicy, this Parmesan Garlic Sauce is one of several new sauces BWW added to its menu. Our *Top Secret* clone starts by roasting a few peeled garlic cloves in your oven. Add mayo and Parmesan cheese to the soft roasted garlic plus some corn syrup, lemon juice, red pepper flakes, and an assortment of dried herbs and you've got yourself an addictive sauce that's as good on finger food as it is on a salad. Bake up some breaded chicken nuggets or fry up some wings, then simply toss 'em in some of this delicious sauce and serve.

4 cloves garlic, peeled
1 teaspoon olive oil
½ cup mayonnaise
2 tablespoons light corn syrup
5 teaspoons grated Parmesan
    cheese

1 tablespoon white vinegar
1 teaspoon lemon juice
½ teaspoon salt
½ teaspoon crushed red pepper
    flakes
¼ teaspoon dried basil

¼ teaspoon dried marjoram
¼ teaspoon dried oregano
¼ teaspoon dried thyme
⅛ teaspoon ground black pepper

1. Preheat oven to 350 degrees F.
2. Toss garlic cloves with oil in a small oven-safe dish, and then bake in the preheated oven for 20 minutes or until the cloves soften and begin to turn light brown. Cool garlic and then run the cloves through a garlic press or finely mince with a sharp knife.
3. Combine garlic and remaining ingredients in a small bowl and stir well. Cover and chill for several hours or overnight before using.
4. To use sauce, pour ¼ cup over 12 cooked chicken wings, breaded tenders, or chicken nuggets and toss gently until coated.

• MAKES ¾ CUP SAUCE, ENOUGH TO COAT 36 WINGS.

•   •   •   •

CALIFORNIA PIZZA KITCHEN THE ORIGINAL BBQ CHICKEN CHOPPED SALAD

MENU DESCRIPTION: *"Chopped lettuce, black beans, sweet corn, jicama, cilantro, basil, crispy corn tortilla strips, and Monterey Jack cheese tossed together in our herb ranch dressing. Topped with chopped BBQ chicken breast, diced tomatoes, and scallions."*

It was probably the popularity of CPK's BBQ chicken pizza that inspired this twist on the Original Chopped Salad. I think the herb ranch dressing that's made here is much better than any ranch dressing you can buy in bottles in your local supermarket, but you can always use one of those, if you prefer. You might also consider substituting ingredients listed here with lower-fat ingredients, such as low-fat mayonnaise and sour cream and fat-free milk. As with any clone, consider this formula as your springboard into a custom dish that suits your specifications. That's the fun part.

HERB RANCH DRESSING

⅔ cup mayonnaise

¼ cup sour cream

¼ cup buttermilk (or whole milk)

1 tablespoon white wine vinegar

1 teaspoon granulated sugar

½ teaspoon lemon juice

¼ teaspoon salt

½ teaspoon minced fresh parsley
½ teaspoon minced fresh dill
¼ teaspoon onion powder

¼ teaspoon garlic powder
⅛ teaspoon ground black pepper

2 skinless chicken breast fillets
¼ cup Bull's-Eye barbecue sauce
two 6-inch yellow corn tortillas
2 cups vegetable oil or peanut oil
4 cups chopped iceberg lettuce
4 cups chopped romaine lettuce
⅔ cup diced jicama
½ cup frozen sweet white corn
   kernels, thawed

½ cup shredded Monterey Jack
   cheese
2 teaspoons chopped cilantro
2 teaspoons chopped basil
2 tomatoes, chopped
2 green onions, chopped (green
   part only)

1. Make herb ranch dressing by whisking together all ingredients in a medium bowl. Cover and chill.
2. Preheat grill to high. Cover chicken fillets with plastic wrap, and use a kitchen mallet to pound them to about ½-inch thick. Rub some vegetable oil on each fillet, and sprinkle each with salt and pepper. Grill chicken for 3 to 5 minutes per side, until done. When cool, chop chicken into ½-inch cubes, mix with barbecue sauce, and chill.
3. Heat oil in a medium saucepan over medium heat. Slice tortillas into thin strips. Drop 1 strip into the oil as a test—it should bubble and fry to a nice golden brown in 2 to 3 minutes. When your oil is hot enough, fry all of the tortilla strips until golden brown, then drain them on paper towels.
4. Assemble each salad by combining 2 cups of iceberg lettuce, 2 cups of romaine lettuce, ⅓ cup jicama, ¼ cup corn, ¼ cup Monterey Jack cheese, 1 teaspoon cilantro, and 1 teaspoon basil in a large mixing bowl. Add ¼ cup to ⅓ cup dressing to each salad and toss well. Spoon each salad onto a serving

plate, top with half the chicken, a chopped tomato, and sprinkle with green onion.

- Makes 2 large salads.

• • • •

CALIFORNIA PIZZA KITCHEN ORIGINAL CHOPPED SALAD

MENU DESCRIPTION: *"Chopped lettuce, basil, salami, chilled roast turkey breast, diced tomatoes, and mozzarella cheese tossed in our herb-mustard Parmesan vinaigrette topped with scallions."*

The ingredients in the salad are no big secret; it's really that delicious herb-mustard Parmesan vinaigrette that makes it all so good. And since freshly made dressings are way better than anything you'll buy in a store, here's a great clone for vinaigrette that you can use either on the chopped salad clone here, or on any salad you assemble with ingredients on hand. After heating up these vinaigrette ingredients for a couple minutes, let the mixture cool, and then drizzle a thin stream of olive oil into the dressing as you blend it with an electric mixer on high speed. This will create an emulsion to thicken the vinaigrette and hold all the ingredients together even as the dressing chills.

HERB-MUSTARD PARMESAN VINAIGRETTE

⅓ cup red wine vinegar
3 tablespoons grated Parmesan
   cheese
4 teaspoons granulated sugar

2 tablespoons Grey Poupon Dijon
   mustard
1 teaspoon minced garlic
1 teaspoon minced fresh parsley
1 teaspoon lemon juice

½ teaspoon salt
½ teaspoon coarse grind black
   pepper
½ teaspoon dried tarragon

½ teaspoon dried oregano
⅛ teaspoon dried thyme
¾ cup light olive oil

SALAD

4 cups chopped iceberg lettuce
4 cups chopped romaine lettuce
1 cup strips of thinly sliced salami
1 cup diced cooked turkey breast
   (cold)
½ cup shredded mozzarella
   cheese

2 tomatoes, chopped
2 teaspoons sliced basil
2 green onions, sliced
   (green part only)

1.   Make the herb-mustard Parmesan vinaigrette by combining all dressing ingredients except oil in a small saucepan over medium heat. When the mixture begins to bubble, reduce heat and simmer for 2 minutes, then take the pan off the heat and let it cool for about 10 minutes. When vinaigrette mixture has cooled, pour it into a medium bowl. Using an electric mixer, mix dressing while slowly drizzling the olive oil into the bowl. This will create an emulsion that will hold the oil and the other ingredients together. Continue to mix dressing with the mixer until it's thick, then store it in a covered container in the refrigerator.

2.   When the vinaigrette has chilled, make each salad separately by combining 2 cups iceberg lettuce, 2 cups romaine, ½ cup salami, ½ cup turkey breast, ¼ cup cheese, 1 chopped tomato, and 1 teaspoon of basil in a large bowl. Add ¼ cup to ⅓ cup vinaigrette to the salad and toss until it's well coated. Spoon each dressed salad onto a serving plate, then sprinkle each with the green onion, and serve.

• MAKES 2 LARGE SALADS.

•   •   •   •

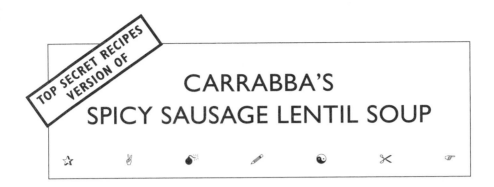

CARRABBA'S
SPICY SAUSAGE LENTIL SOUP

It's not served every day at Carrabba's Italian Grill, but when this amazing soup is on the menu, consider yourself lucky and snag a bowl. It's chock-full of lentils and other good bits of vegetables and herbs, plus there are big chunks of spicy Italian sausage in every bite. Best of all, it's a cinch to clone. Most of the work here is just chopping stuff up, including a small ham steak that you can find where the bacon is sold in your market. If you can't find a ham steak, you can slice up some deli ham. Get everything in a pot and let it simmer. In 1 hour you'll have enough hot, chunky soup for at least a dozen cup-size servings.

2 tablespoons olive oil
1 cup minced onion
¾ cup grated and minced carrot
1 tablespoon minced garlic
1 pound uncooked hot Italian
   sausage
2 ounces diced ham (about ½
   cup, cut from a ham steak)
7 cups water
5 cups chicken broth
1 pound dry lentils
1 medium tomato, diced

2 tablespoons white wine vinegar
1 tablespoon minced fresh basil
1 tablespoon minced fresh parsley
2 bay leaves
1½ teaspoons salt
½ teaspoon ground black
   pepper
½ teaspoon dried thyme
½ teaspoon dried oregano
½ teaspoon crushed red pepper
   flakes

1. Heat up the olive oil in a Dutch oven or large saucepan over medium heat. Add onion, carrot, and garlic. Remove the sausage from its casing and add it to the pan. Sauté for 8 minutes, stirring often. Break up the sausage into bite-size bits as it cooks. Add ham and cook for an additional minute.
2. Add the remaining ingredients to the pot, bring to a boil, then reduce heat and simmer for 1 hour.
3. Serve 1 cup for a "cup" portion or 2 cups for a "bowl" serving.

- MAKES 12 TO 13 CUPS.

• • • •

CARRABBA'S CHICKEN BRYAN

MENU DESCRIPTION: *"Grilled chicken breast topped with goat cheese, sundried tomatoes, and a basil lemon butter sauce."*

Carrabba's number one chicken dish is simple to clone once you duplicate the delicious basil lemon butter sauce. Preheat your grill to high and pound the chicken breasts with a mallet so that they'll cook evenly. Use the sun-dried tomatoes that come in a bag rather than those that come bottled in oil. To rehydrate them, you simmer the sun-dried tomatoes in a small pan of water for about 4 minutes, then slice them. The goat cheese used at the chain is called Caprino cheese, which is a very smooth and creamy goat cheese. If you can't find Caprino, using any available goat cheese from your market still makes for a great clone.

BASIL LEMON BUTTER SAUCE

½ cup (1 stick) butter
1 teaspoon minced garlic
2 teaspoons lemon juice
1 tablespoon white wine

⅛ teaspoon salt
⅛ teaspoon white pepper
¼ cup heavy cream
6 to 7 basil leaves, sliced

4 skinless chicken breast fillets
vegetable oil
salt
freshly cracked black pepper

½ ounce sun-dried tomatoes (⅓ cup reconstituted and sliced)
4 slices Caprino cheese (or other goat cheese)

1. Preheat a barbecue grill to high.
2. Make the basil lemon butter sauce by melting the butter in a small saucepan over medium/low heat. Add the garlic and slowly sauté (sweat) it for 5 minutes. Add the lemon juice and wine and cook for another 5 minutes. Add the salt, pepper, and cream and reduce the heat to low. Cook the sauce for 15 to 20 minutes over low heat until thick, stirring often, while you grill the chicken.
3. Use a kitchen mallet to flatten the thick part of the chicken breasts so that they will cook evenly. Rub each chicken breast with oil, then sprinkle each with salt and pepper.
4. Grill the chicken for 3 to 5 minutes per side, or until done.
5. While chicken is cooking, simmer the sun-dried tomatoes in a small saucepan of boiling water for 3 to 4 minutes. Strain the tomatoes, then slice into strips.
6. When the chicken is done, place each chicken breast on a plate and place a slice of cheese on top of each chicken breast. Divide the sun-dried tomatoes and place a pile on top of the chicken on each plate. Stir the sliced basil leaves into the sauce, then spoon the sauce over the chicken and serve.

• SERVES 4.

•   •   •   •

CHEESEBURGER IN PARADISE SWEET POTATO CHIPS

MENU DESCRIPTION: *"Fried sweet potato chips, dusted with our seasoning blend."*

The same company that runs Outback Steakhouse operates this 39-outlet chain inspired by the Jimmy Buffett song of the same name. As you would guess, the freshly ground beef burgers here are great. But you'll also find many Caribbean island–inspired dishes on the menu such as BBQ Jerk Ribs, Tropical Tilapia, St. Barts Citrus Chicken, and amazing island cocktail creations served at the Tiki Bar. One of the specialties of the house is the Sweet Potato Chips that are fried to a golden brown, sprinkled with a secret sweet/salty seasoning, and served alongside the joint's sandwich selections or ordered as an appetizer. For a home version, sweet potatoes are sliced thin using a vegetable slicer that is set on $1/16$ inch, and the slices are fried in canola oil. After a sprinkling with the special seasoning blend, you'll have a big bowl of sweet, crispy chips that will serve 4 or more people. And these go great as a side with the BBQ Jerk Ribs clone on page 75.

SEASONING BLEND

1 teaspoon salt
1 1/4 teaspoons granulated sugar
3/4 teaspoon ground black pepper
3/4 teaspoon paprika

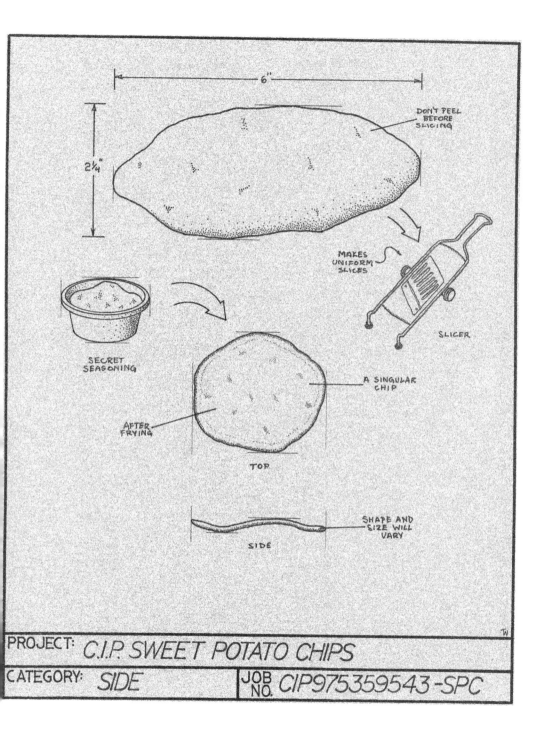

6"

2¼"

DON'T PEEL
BEFORE
SLICING

MAKES
UNIFORM
SLICES

SLICER

SECRET
SEASONING

A SINGULAR
CHIP

AFTER
FRYING

TOP

SHAPE AND
SIZE WILL
VARY

SIDE

PROJECT: *C.I.P. SWEET POTATO CHIPS*

CATEGORY: *SIDE*

JOB NO. *CIP975359543-SPC*

73

¼ teaspoon onion powder
¼ teaspoon garlic powder
⅛ teaspoon ground cayenne
    pepper

⅛ teaspoon ground coriander
pinch ground cinnamon

2 medium sweet potatoes
6 to 10 cups canola oil (as
    required by your fryer)

1. Combine ingredients for seasoning in a small bowl.
2. Slice potatoes to ¹⁄₁₆-inch thick with a vegetable slicer or man-
    doline. Soak potato slices in cold water for 10 to 15 minutes,
    then pat slices dry on a towel.
3. Heat canola oil in a deep fryer to 325 degrees F. When oil
    is hot, fry potato slices in batches for 4 to 5 minutes, until
    chips become light brown. Occasionally stir slices gently while
    they fry. Be careful not to overcook, since the chips will con-
    tinue to brown after you remove them from the oil. Remove
    chips to paper towels to cool, and sprinkle with the seasoning
    blend.

• Makes 4 to 6 servings.

• • • •

CHEESEBURGER IN PARADISE BBQ JERK RIBS

MENU DESCRIPTION: *"Slow-cooked marinated domestic pork ribs lightly seasoned with Jerk spices and basted with BBQ sauce."*

I love the flavor of smoked pork ribs, but ribs cooked this way often end up on the tough side. The best racks I've ever had are those pumped with smokiness and other flavors, and with meat that practically falls off the bone. The clone recipe right here will produce just that. An island taste in the secret jerk paste formula permeates the ribs as they slow-cook in low heat. Halfway through cooking, the ribs are wrapped in foil to begin a braising process that tenderizes the meat. And finally, for a big finish, the racks are tossed on the grill just before serving to add charring and then they're slathered with a smoky sauce. Follow the grilling instructions here and you won't lose any meat from your ribs sticking to the barbecue grate. Start by grilling the ribs bony side down so that some of the fat from the ribs melts onto your grill. Now when you flip the racks over onto the meaty side the grill is well lubricated, giving you beautiful grill marks on the good part, and no sticking. And don't freak on that whole habanero pepper included in the jerk paste. Sure, it may be one of the world's hottest peppers, but the paste goes a long way, and you'll only detect a hint of heat on the finished product. In fact, I'll usually add a couple habaneros to my paste. That's how we roll in the Southwest. Serve up these babies with a

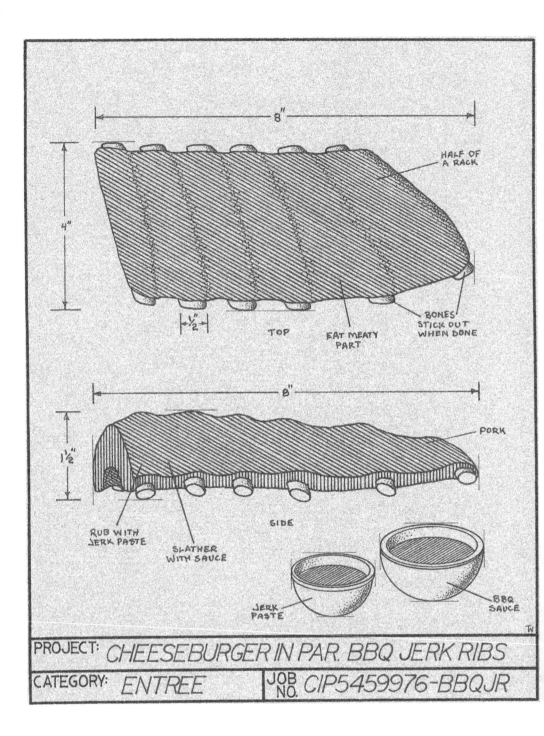

8"

HALF OF
A RACK

4"

1/2"

TOP

EAT MEATY
PART

BONES
STICK OUT
WHEN DONE

8"

PORK

1½"

RUB WITH
JERK PASTE

SLATHER
WITH SAUCE

SIDE

JERK
PASTE

BBQ
SAUCE

TW

PROJECT: *CHEESEBURGER IN PAR. BBQ JERK RIBS*

CATEGORY: *ENTREE*

JOB NO. *CIP5459976-BBQJR*

side of the Sweet Potato Chips clone from page 72 for the complete CIP taste experience.

JERK PASTE

⅓ cup plus 1 tablespoon red wine vinegar
1 habanero pepper (scotch bonnet), coarsely chopped
¼ cup dark brown sugar
4 cloves garlic, quartered
2 green onions, chopped
1 tablespoon chopped parsley
1 tablespoon lemon juice
2 teaspoons ground allspice

2 teaspoons paprika
2 teaspoons salt
1¼ teaspoons ground black pepper
1 teaspoon dried thyme
¼ teaspoon ground cinnamon
¼ teaspoon ground cloves
¼ teaspoon ground ginger
¼ teaspoon ground coriander
½ cup (1 stick) salted butter

4 racks pork baby back ribs

BBQ SAUCE

1 cup ketchup
¾ cup red wine vinegar
½ cup dark brown sugar
¼ cup molasses
2 teaspoons hickory-flavored liquid smoke
½ teaspoon salt

1 teaspoon ground black pepper
1 teaspoon ground mustard
½ teaspoon garlic powder
½ teaspoon onion powder
½ teaspoon paprika
¼ teaspoon ground cayenne pepper

1. Make jerk paste by combining all ingredients except butter in a food processor or blender and blend until no big chunks of garlic are visible. Pour mixture into a medium saucepan and add butter. Cook over medium heat until bubbling, then reduce heat and simmer for 2 minutes. Brush jerk paste on

underside (bony side) of ribs, then flip 'em over and brush paste on the meaty side.

2. Preheat oven to 250 degrees F. Place ribs on baking sheets with the meaty side up and bake for 1½ hours. Flip each rack over onto a large piece of aluminum foil and wrap tightly. Be sure the meaty side is down now, and bake for another 1 to 1½ hours until the meat is tender. The cut ends of the bones should now be sticking out about ¼ inch.

3. While your ribs are cooking make the BBQ sauce by combining all ingredients in a medium saucepan. Bring to a boil, then reduce heat, and simmer sauce for 30 minutes. Cool, cover, and chill until you are ready to grill your ribs.

4. When the ribs are done, remove them from the oven and let them cool in the foil for 15 to 20 minutes. Preheat your grill to medium/high. Use tongs to remove the ribs from the foil and place them on the grill with the bony side facing the heat (ribs curving down). Cook for 2 to 3 minutes, until browned, then flip ribs over onto the meaty side. Brush the grilled bony side (now face up) with BBQ sauce, and cook for another 2 to 3 minutes until grill marks develop on the meat. Flip the ribs over onto a serving platter when you remove them from the heat and brush the just-grilled meaty side with BBQ sauce.

• Makes 4 large servings.

•　•　•　•

CHEESEBURGER IN PARADISE
EL CUBANO SANDWICH

MENU DESCRIPTION: *"Ham, salami, pork, Swiss cheese, mayo, mustard, and pickles, pressed until golden brown."*

This chain of island-themed restaurants features a delicious Cuban sandwich as one of the menu's specialty items. A variety of meats are stacked on a crusty sandwich roll along with some pickles, then the sandwich is pressed until warm and flattened on a plancha grill. While there are many different ways to build a Cuban sandwich, the traditional recipe does not include mayonnaise, tomatoes, lettuce, or onions. Cheeseburger in Paradise breaks tradition a bit by spreading some mayonnaise on the bread, but that's okay since it tastes great, and other than that this recipe stays true to the classic formula. Marinated pork is the superstar in this sandwich, so we must make that from scratch using a marinade made from a mixture of juices plus lots of garlic, onion, and oregano. We'll marinate the pork for a couple hours just as the restaurant does, then bake it in a slow oven. When the pork is ready and sliced, you stack it on the sandwich with other sliced deli meats, some Swiss cheese, and pickles, and then it's ready to be pressed and browned. I don't expect you'll have a plancha grill handy, but you can use a hot skillet with another very heavy pan, such as a cast-iron skillet, to press down on top of the sandwich. I also like to put a brick in the skillet on top to help flatten the sandwich even more. For a true Cuban experience, serve these along with a pitcher of mojitos and have everyone do their best Ricky Ricardo impression.

MARINADE

1 ¼ cups vegetable oil
1 small onion, chopped
20 cloves garlic, sliced in half
    lengthwise
1 teaspoon dried oregano
1 teaspoon whole black
    peppercorns

2 cups orange juice
¾ cup pineapple juice
¼ cup lemon juice
2 tablespoons lime juice
1 tablespoon salt

3- to 4-pound pork shoulder

4 crusty 8-inch sandwich rolls
8 ounces sliced Swiss cheese
8 ounces sliced salami
8 ounces sliced ham
salt

8 long dill pickle slices (sliced
    lengthwise, such as Vlasic
    Stackers)
mayonnaise
spicy brown mustard

1. Combine the oil with the onion, garlic, oregano, and pepper-corns in a medium saucepan and place it over medium heat. When the oil begins to bubble, cook for 3 minutes, then remove from the heat.
2. Combine the orange juice, pineapple juice, lemon juice, lime juice, and salt in a large bowl. Pour the oil mixture into the juice mixture and stir until the salt has dissolved. Pour this marinade over the pork shoulder in a large storage container or zip-top bag. Cover and chill for 2 hours. Flip the pork over in the marinade after about an hour.
3. Preheat the oven to 300 degrees F.
4. Place the pork in a roasting pan. Pour 2 cups of the marinade

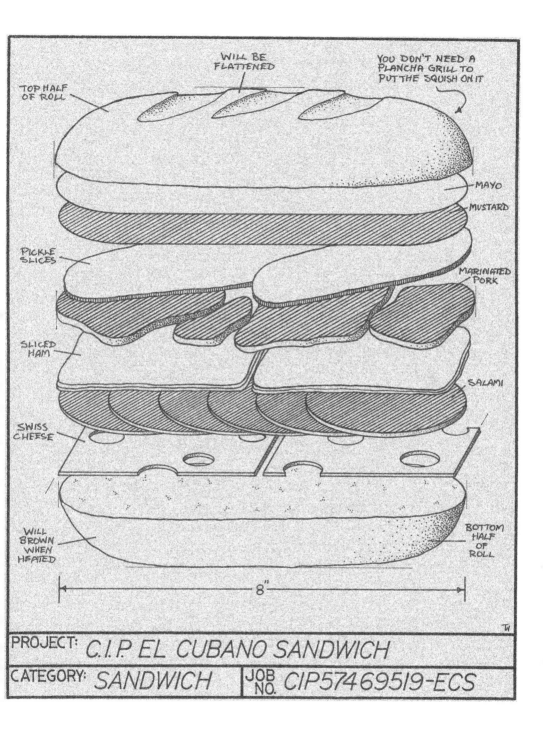

WILL BE
FLATTENED

YOU DON'T NEED A
PLANCHA GRILL TO
PUT THE SQUISH ON IT

TOP HALF
OF ROLL

MAYO

MUSTARD

PICKLE
SLICES

MARINATED
PORK

SLICED
HAM

SALAMI

SWISS
CHEESE

WILL
BROWN
WHEN
HEATED

BOTTOM
HALF
OF
ROLL

8"

PROJECT: C.I.P EL CUBANO SANDWICH

CATEGORY: SANDWICH   JOB NO. CIP57469519-ECS

over the roast and bake the pork for 2½ to 3 hours, or until the internal temperature is 170 degrees F.

5. Allow the pork to sit for 20 minutes after it comes out of the oven, then thinly slice it.

6. When you are ready to build your sandwiches, preheat a large skillet over medium/low heat. You will also need a large heavy skillet, such as a cast-iron skillet to place on top of the sandwiches while they are browning. You can also use a panini press, but I found a heavy skillet will make the sandwich flatter (more like a plancha press) and a real Cuban sandwich doesn't have lines in it.

7. Build each sandwich by placing 2 ounces of Swiss cheese on the bottom of the sandwich roll. Slice the cheese to fit on the bread.

8. Pile 2 ounces of salami on the cheese followed by 2 ounces of ham. Fold the meats to fit on the sandwich. If your sliced meats are cold, heat them for 20 to 30 seconds in your microwave oven until warm.

9. Place 3 to 4 ounces of the sliced pork on the ham.

10. Lay two pickle slices on the pork. Use a spatula or a butter knife to spread mayonnaise on the top half of the sandwich roll, then spread an equal amount of brown mustard over the mayo.

11. Place the sandwich in the hot skillet and press a heavy skillet on top of the sandwich. Cook for 3 to 4 minutes, or until the bread has browned, then flip the sandwich over and brown the top. You can also use a panini press for this step.

12. Slice the warm sandwich through the middle at a slight angle and serve.

• MAKES 4 SANDWICHES.

•   •   •   •

CHEESECAKE FACTORY PINEAPPLE PISCO SOUR

MENU DESCRIPTION: *"Our version of the 150-year-old classic with pisco and pineapple juice. Served on the rocks."*

If you aren't familiar with this drink, you soon will be. I predict that we'll see variations of the pisco sour added to an increasing number of chain restaurant menus in the coming years, similar to growth in popularity of the mojito. Pisco is a South American grape brandy produced in Peru and Chile; and both countries claim to have invented the original version of this cocktail, which is made with pisco, simple syrup, lime juice, egg white, and bitters. You could say it's South America's margarita. Cheesecake Factory, however, has added other juices plus sweet-and-sour to the mix, and swapped out the egg white for Frothee (look for this drink-foaming ingredient at liquor stores and bar supply outlets). Shake up all the ingredients with flair until foamy and pour the drink into a wine glass (or martini glass) to serve.

1 ½ ounces pisco
1 ½ ounces pineapple juice
1 ½ ounces sweet-and-sour mix
¾ ounce grapefruit juice

¾ ounce lime juice
¾ ounce simple syrup
2 or 3 squirts Frothee

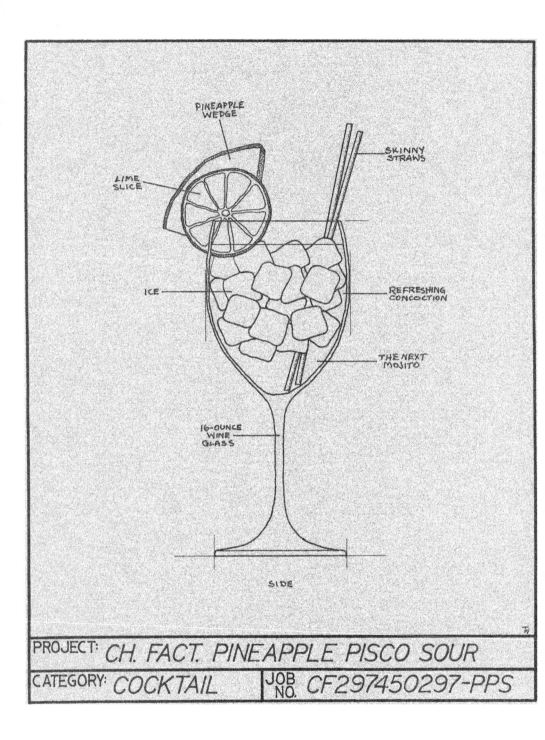

PINEAPPLE
WEDGE

SKINNY
STRAWS

LIME
SLICE

ICE

REFRESHING
CONCOCTION

THE NEXT
MOJITO

16-OUNCE
WINE
GLASS

SIDE

PROJECT: *CH. FACT. PINEAPPLE PISCO SOUR*

CATEGORY: *COCKTAIL* JOB NO. *CF297450297-PPS*

GARNISH

pineapple wedge
lime slice

1. Fill a 16-ounce wine glass with ice, then pour the ice into a cocktail shaker.
2. Add all drink ingredients to the shaker and shake well.
3. Pour contents of shaker back into the wine glass.
4. Garnish with a wedge of fresh pineapple and a lime slice on the rim of the glass. Add a straw and serve.

•   MAKES 1 DRINK.

•   •   •   •

CHEESECAKE FACTORY THAI LETTUCE WRAPS

MENU DESCRIPTION: *"Create your own Thai lettuce rolls! Satay chicken strips, carrots, bean sprouts, coconut curry noodles, and lettuce leaves with three delicious spicy Thai sauces—peanut, sweet red chili, and tamarind-cashew."*

Cheesecake Factory's number one appetizer is finally fauxed, and I've got every secret component for an impressive knockoff here in one recipe: delicious duplicates of the three amazing dipping sauces, perfect sweet-and-sour cucumber slices, and an easy coconut curry marinade clone for the chicken that also doubles as a sauce for the noodles. Get ready to blow everyone away when you unveil this build-it-yourself Thai-inspired lettuce wrap kit at the table. The final dish will serve twice as many people as the restaurant version, and you'll most likely have enough leftover sauces to serve it again if you want to get more chicken.

SWEET-AND-SOUR CUCUMBER SLICES

1 medium cucumber
¼ cup thinly sliced red onion
2 tablespoons granulated sugar

2 tablespoons rice vinegar
¼ teaspoon salt

COCONUT CURRY CHICKEN MARINADE AND NOODLE SAUCE

1 ½ cups coconut milk
1 tablespoon yellow curry powder

1 tablespoon fish sauce
1 teaspoon ground coriander

1 pound chicken breast
tenderloins (about 10 strips)

PEANUT SAUCE

⅓ cup crunchy peanut butter
⅓ cup water
¼ cup dark brown sugar
2 tablespoons soy sauce
2 tablespoons rice vinegar

4 teaspoons chili garlic sauce
(sambal)
½ teaspoon paprika
¼ teaspoon sesame oil
1 tablespoon lime juice

SWEET RED CHILI SAUCE

⅓ cup dark brown sugar
2 tablespoons hot water
2 tablespoons soy sauce
4 teaspoons chili garlic sauce
(sambal)
1 tablespoon minced ginger
1 clove garlic, quartered

1 teaspoon lime juice
1 teaspoon rice vinegar
½ teaspoon sesame oil
⅛ teaspoon ground black
pepper
¼ teaspoon white sesame
seeds

TAMARIND-CASHEW SAUCE

½ cup coarsely chopped cilantro
2 green onions, chopped
2 tablespoons chopped cashews
1 clove garlic

1 teaspoon ground cumin
¼ teaspoon yellow curry powder

½ teaspoon ground black
   pepper
½ cup honey
4 teaspoons rice vinegar
2 tablespoons water

1 tablespoon granulated sugar
1 teaspoon tamarind paste
1 teaspoon balsamic vinegar
3 tablespoons vegetable oil

3 ounces Japanese-style noodles
   (somen—see Tidbits)
½ head red cabbage
1 cup bean sprouts

1 cup julienned carrots
1 head butterhead (Bibb) lettuce
⅓ cup coarsely chopped cilantro

GARNISH

1 teaspoon sesame seeds (see
   Tidbits)

1 tablespoon chopped peanuts

1. Use a peeler to remove just a few strips of the peel from a medium-size cucumber. You want about half of the peel to stay on there. Now slice the cuke in half lengthwise, then use a teaspoon to scoop out the seeds. Slice the two halves of cucumber into very thin slices using a mandoline or other thin-slicing device. In a medium bowl, combine 2 tablespoons granulated sugar with 2 tablespoons rice vinegar, and ¼ teaspoon salt. Stir until sugar is dissolved, then add sliced cucumber and sliced red onion to bowl and stir. Cover and chill 2 to 4 hours. Stir every hour or so.
2. Make the coconut curry chicken marinade by combining coconut milk, yellow curry powder, fish sauce, and coriander. Reserve ¼ cup of this sauce for the noodles, and pour the rest over the chicken strips in a zip-top plastic bag or covered container. Seal up the bag or container and park the chicken in your refrigerator for at least 2 hours.
3. Make peanut sauce by combining all ingredients except lime

juice in a small saucepan over medium heat. Stir often as mixture comes to a boil, then reduce heat and simmer for 3 minutes. Let mixture cool for a bit, then add lime juice and pour mixture into blender. Blend on medium speed for 20 seconds. Make sure to hold the lid on the blender with a dish towel so that the top doesn't pop off as the hot liquid is blended. Pour this sauce into a covered container and let it chill out in the fridge.

4. Make sweet red chili sauce by dissolving brown sugar in hot water and soy sauce. Pour this solution, plus remaining ingredients, except sesame seeds, into a food processor (or blender), and blend on high speed until ginger is pureed. Stir in sesame seeds, cover, and chill.

5. Make tamarind-cashew sauce by combining cilantro, green onions, cashews, garlic, cumin, curry powder, and black pepper in a food processor and blending until fine. Combine honey, water, rice vinegar, sugar, tamarind paste, and balsamic vinegar in a small mixing bowl. Heat mixture in microwave oven for 30 to 60 seconds, until hot, then stir to dissolve sugar and honey. Pour this into the food processor and mix for 5 seconds, then pour the mixture back into the bowl and stir in oil. Cover and chill.

6. Cook noodles following directions on the package (cook for 3 to 5 minutes in boiling water, drain, and rinse with cold water). Coarsely chop the noodles so that they'll be easier to handle when building the wraps, then mix noodles with ¼ cup of the leftover coconut curry sauce and let them kick it in the fridge until go-time.

7. When you're ready to assemble the dish, preheat your grill to high, and grill the chicken strips for 3 to 4 minutes per side, until done. Just before the chicken is done, brush each piece with some reserved peanut sauce.

8. All of the components for the wraps will be presented on one plate, so you'll need a large platter. Spoon some of the remaining peanut sauce, sweet red chili sauce, and tamarind-

cashew sauce into small dishes and arrange them in the center of the platter.

9. Make 4 "bowls" by slicing half a head of red cabbage in half. Peel off 4 outside leaves from cabbage to use as bowls for the components.

10. Use your hands to load the noodles into one cabbage bowl, the bean sprouts into another, the carrots into the third one, and sliced cucumber into the last one. Arrange these ingredients around the sauces, on the left and right sides of the platter.

11. Peel the rest of leaves off of the lettuce and fan them out at the top of the plate, above the sauces. Place 1 lettuce leaf at the bottom of the plate, below the sauces, and stack the chicken strips on top of this leaf.

12. Pile chopped cilantro between the chicken and the sauces.

13. Sprinkle sesame seeds over the cucumber and noodles, sprinkle chopped peanuts over the chicken, and serve.

• MAKES 4 APPETIZER SERVINGS.

TIDBITS

You can find these thin white noodles where Asian foods are stocked in your market. If you can't find somen noodles, you can also use the slightly thicker chow mein noodles. Just be sure to chop the noodles up a bit after they are cooked so that you aren't wrangling long strands when building the wraps.

The restaurant chain uses a blend of black and white sesame seeds. Black sesame seeds, or a blend of the two, can be hard to find. So, if you can't track down the stronger-tasting black sesame seeds, white seeds on their own work just fine here.

• • • •

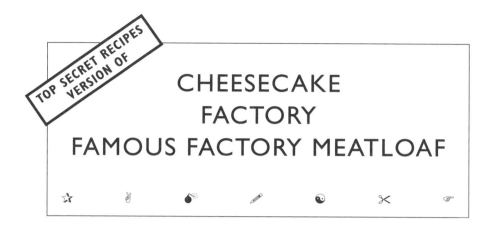

CHEESECAKE FACTORY FAMOUS FACTORY MEATLOAF

Filled with carrots, onions, garlic, bell peppers, and herbs—this is definitely the most flavorful meatloaf I have cloned so far, and it's one of Cheesecake Factory's signature dishes. While most meatloaf creations are coated with a tomato-based sauce, such as ketchup or barbecue sauce, this one is doused with rich mushroom gravy, and then topped with a pile of caramelized onions (those secret formulas are included here as well). This recipe will yield exactly three ginormous dinner-size portions—that's three thick slices of meatloaf at the restaurant. But you could easily fill the bellies of four or more famished folks with more reasonable serving sizes from the huge meatloaf you unveil.

1 tablespoon vegetable oil
2 tablespoons minced green bell pepper
2 tablespoons minced red bell pepper
½ cup minced red onion
⅓ cup shredded and minced carrot
5 teaspoons minced garlic
3 eggs, beaten
1½ pounds ground sirloin
1 pound ground pork

1 tablespoon minced Italian parsley
1 tablespoon granulated sugar
2 teaspoons salt
1½ teaspoons dried thyme
1 teaspoon ground black pepper
1 teaspoon dried oregano
1 teaspoon rubbed (ground) sage
½ teaspoon paprika
¾ cup whole milk
¾ cup bread crumbs

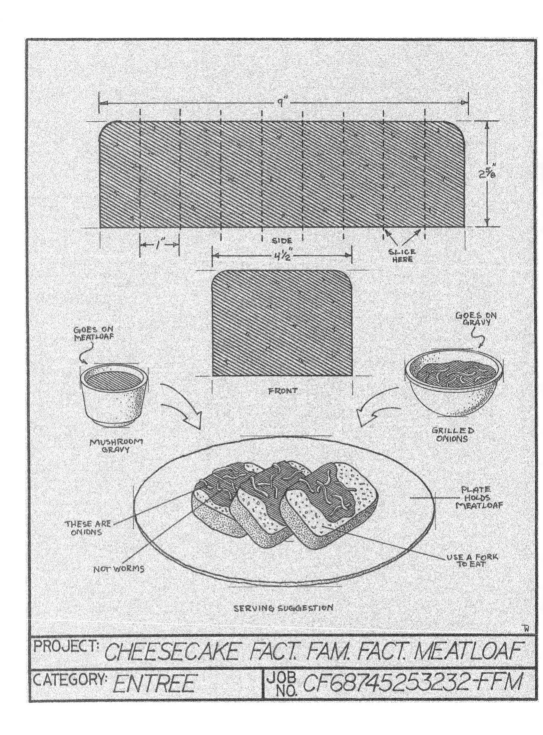

9"

2⅝"

←—1"—→   SIDE   SLICE HERE

4½"

FRONT

GOES ON MEATLOAF

MUSHROOM GRAVY

GOES ON GRAVY

GRILLED ONIONS

THESE ARE ONIONS

NOT WORMS

PLATE HOLDS MEATLOAF

USE A FORK TO EAT

SERVING SUGGESTION

PROJECT: *CHEESECAKE FACT. FAM. FACT. MEATLOAF*

CATEGORY: *ENTREE*

JOB NO. *CF68745253232-FFM*

GRILLED ONIONS

1 medium onion, sliced
2 tablespoons butter
¼ teaspoon salt
¼ teaspoon ground black pepper

MUSHROOM GRAVY

2 tablespoons butter
1 teaspoon minced garlic
2 tablespoons all-pupose flour
one 14-ounce can beef broth
   (1¾ cups)
1½ cups sliced mushrooms
1 teaspoon minced Italian parsley
¼ teaspoon salt
¼ teaspoon ground black
   pepper
¼ teaspoon dried thyme
¼ teaspoon rubbed (ground)
   sage

1. Preheat oven to 350 degrees F.
2. Heat up 1 tablespoon of oil in a medium sauté pan over medium/low heat. Sweat (slowly sauté) the minced green and red bell pepper in the oil for 5 minutes. Add the minced onion, carrot, and garlic and cook for an additional 5 minutes. You just want the veggies to soften, not to get browned.
3. Beat the eggs in a large bowl. Add the ground beef, pork, sautéed vegetables, and remaining ingredients except bread crumbs. Mix well with your hands until everything is combined, then work in the bread crumbs a little bit at a time. Press meatloaf into a 9 x 5-inch loaf pan and bake for 1 hour. Remove meatloaf from the oven and cool for 30 minutes. If you cut the meatloaf now a lot the juices will run out, so give it a rest before diving in.
4. As meatloaf rests, make grilled onions by melting butter in a medium sauté pan over medium/low heat. Add onions, salt, and pepper and cook for 20 to 25 minutes, stirring often, until onions are light brown.
5. Make gravy by melting butter over medium/low heat. Add garlic and sauté for 1 minute. Whisk in flour and cook for 2

to 3 minutes, until mixture begins to turn light brown. Add remaining ingredients and simmer for 10 to 15 minutes, until sauce is thick.

6. To prepare meatloaf for serving, preheat broiler to high. Remove meatloaf from the loaf pan and slice it into nine 1-inch-thick slices. Arrange slices to be served on a baking sheet and place under the broiler for 2 to 3 minutes, until hot. Place slices of meatloaf on serving plate, spoon gravy over the meatloaf, and then top with grilled onions.

*   MAKES 3 OR MORE SERVINGS.

• • • •

CHEESECAKE FACTORY MISO SALMON

MENU DESCRIPTION: *"Fresh miso marinated salmon served with snow peas, white rice, and a delicious miso sauce."*

Presented beautifully on top of white rice and surrounded by sake butter sauce is a baked salmon fillet that tastes like candy. Miso is a salty fermented soybean paste that combines well with sweet brown sugar and sake for a syrupy marinade that makes salmon taste so good that even salmon haters will devour it. Look for red miso in a refrigerator in your market. You can also find it in Asian markets and some health food stores. After cooking up your marinade, you should allow the salmon fillets to soak in it for up to 6 hours, so start this dish early in the day and plan to scarf out at dinnertime. The cool presentation starts by pressing cooked rice into a lightly greased 5-inch ramekin or small cake pan, and then turning it out onto the center of your serving plate. Add a moat of sake reduction sauce, a few steamed snow pea pods, and you will have re-created a dish that looks and tastes exactly like the number one fish dish at The Factory.

MISO MARINADE

½ cup red miso
¾ cup sake
¾ cup light brown sugar
I tablespoon rice vinegar

I tablespoon soy sauce
I teaspoon minced garlic
¼ teaspoon minced ginger

four 8-ounce salmon fillets
2 cups uncooked white rice
(converted or jasmine rice)

SAKE BUTTER SAUCE

I cup sake

I tablespoon minced shallot

I teaspoon minced ginger

½ cup (I stick) unsalted butter

2 tablespoons all-purpose flour

I cup heavy cream

¼ teaspoon kosher salt

20 lightly steamed snow pea
pods
4 green onions, julienned

1. Combine marinade ingredients in a medium saucepan over medium heat. Whisk to break up the miso. When the mixture begins to bubble, reduce heat and simmer for 15 to 20 minutes, until thick. While the marinade is still hot, pour it through a strainer to filter out the chunks of garlic and ginger. When this strained sauce is cool pour all but ¼ cup of marinade over the 4 salmon fillets in a large zip-top plastic bag. Seal and chill the salmon for 4 to 6 hours. Keep the reserved marinade parked in the fridge as well.

2. When your salmon has marinated, preheat oven to 425 degrees F. Remove the salmon from marinade (ditch this marinade), and bake salmon fillets on a baking sheet for 20 to 22 minutes, until the edges and top of each fillet begin to brown. This is also a good time to cook the white rice following the cooking instructions on the package. For 6 cups of cooked rice you should cook 2 cups uncooked rice in 4 cups of water for about 20 minutes.

3. Make sake butter sauce by combing sake, shallots, and ginger in a small saucepan. Reduce over medium/low heat for 10 to 12 minutes or until liquid reduces by half. Pour sake through

a strainer to remove shallots and ginger. In a separate medium pan melt butter over medium heat, and then whisk in flour. When butter and flour begins to bubble, cook for 1 minute, then whisk in the cream. Keep stirring the sauce as it cooks for another minute, then add reduced sake and salt. Cook the sauce for another minute or so, until thick.

4.   To plate each dish, rub some melted butter around the inside of a 5-inch ramekin or cake pan. Press 1½ cups of cooked white rice into the dish, and then flip it over onto the center of a serving plate. The rice should slip out of the mold and hold its cylindrical shape on the plate. Spoon sake butter sauce around rice on the plate, and then place 5 steamed snow pea pods in a spoke-like fashion around the rice. Use a spoon to drop approximately ¼ teaspoon of the reserved miso glaze between each of the snow pea pods.

5.   Use a spatula to carefully position a salmon fillet onto the center of the rice, add a pile of julienned green onion onto the center of the salmon and serve.

• MAKES 4 SERVINGS.

•   •   •   •

CHEESECAKE FACTORY FRESH BANANA CREAM CHEESECAKE

MENU DESCRIPTION: *"Banana cream cheesecake topped with Bavarian cream and fresh sliced bananas."*

I've learned a lot about cheesecakes over the last couple decades in the process of duplicating a variety of popular versions for the *Top Secret Recipes* cookbooks, and I've made a lot of mistakes. But the best technique to help produce picture-perfect cheesecakes has to be using a water bath in the oven. By baking the cheesecake in a pan filled with just a little water, you add moisture to the oven, thereby allowing the top of the cheesecake to expand as it cooks without developing what looks like an aerial view of the San Andreas Fault. If you don't overmix your filling and use a water bath, you'll bake a restaurant-quality cheesecake every time. You also need a good recipe to start with of course, and I think you'll find this one is amazing—especially if you love banana cream pie. This cheesecake, with banana flavor in every layer, has quickly become a top choice at the restaurant chain. And everyone knows that Nilla Wafers go great with bananas, so these ground-up cookies make the perfect crust.

CRUST
3 cups (5 ½ ounces) Nilla Wafers
¼ cup (½ stick) butter, melted

CHEESECAKE FILLING
four 8-ounce packages cream
    cheese
1 ⅓ cups granulated sugar
4 eggs

¼ cup sour cream
2 teaspoons vanilla extract
¼ teaspoon banana flavoring

BAVARIAN CREAM
¾ cup whole milk
¾ cup heavy cream
3 egg yolks
⅓ cup granulated sugar

1 teaspoon unflavored gelatin
2 tablespoons cold water
½ teaspoon vanilla extract
¼ teaspoon banana flavoring

BANANA WHIPPED
CREAM TOPPING
2 cups heavy cream
½ cup granulated sugar
¼ teaspoon banana flavoring

½ teaspoon cream of tartar
dash salt

GARNISH
6 bananas, sliced

1. Preheat oven to 350 degrees F. Fill a pan that is larger than the springform pan with ½ inch of water and place it into the center of the oven.
2. Line the inside of a 9-inch springform pan with parchment paper. Wrap a sheet of aluminum foil around the outside of

the pan so that water cannot get into the pan when it's submerged into the water bath in the oven.

3. Use a food processor to crush the Nilla Wafers to a fine crumb. The crumbs should be the consistency of sand with no chunks. Mix the melted butter with the cookie crumbs and press the crumbs into the bottom of the springform pan and up the side 1 to 1½ inches. Place the pan into your freezer while you make the cheesecake filling.

4. Make the filling by combining the softened cream cheese with the sugar using an electric mixer on high speed. When the mixture is smooth, add the eggs, sour cream, vanilla, and banana flavoring and beat well. Use a spatula to pour all of the filling into the springform pan. Smooth the top, then gently place the pan into the water bath in the oven and bake for 70 minutes, or until the cheesecake filling does not jiggle in the middle when moved.

5. Cool the cheesecake, then cover and chill it while you make the Bavarian cream.

6. Make the Bavarian cream by heating the milk in a medium saucepan over medium heat until boiling. Remove from the heat. Use an electric mixer on high speed to beat the egg yolks with the sugar in a medium bowl until the mixture is pale yellow, about 1 minute. Add hot milk a little bit at a time to the eggs while beating. Pour the mixture back into the pan and heat over low heat, stirring often until the mixture thickens just enough to coat the back spoon, about 8 minutes. Be sure that the mixture does not boil or the eggs will curdle. Pour back into the medium bowl. Dissolve the gelatin in cold water, let it sit for 1 minute, then mix it into the Bavarian cream with an electric mixer on high speed, along with the vanilla and banana flavoring. Chill the Bavarian cream for 1 hour, then spread it over the top of the cheesecake. Re-cover and chill the cheesecake.

7. Make the banana whipped cream topping by combining all the ingredients in a medium bowl. Beat with an electric mixer

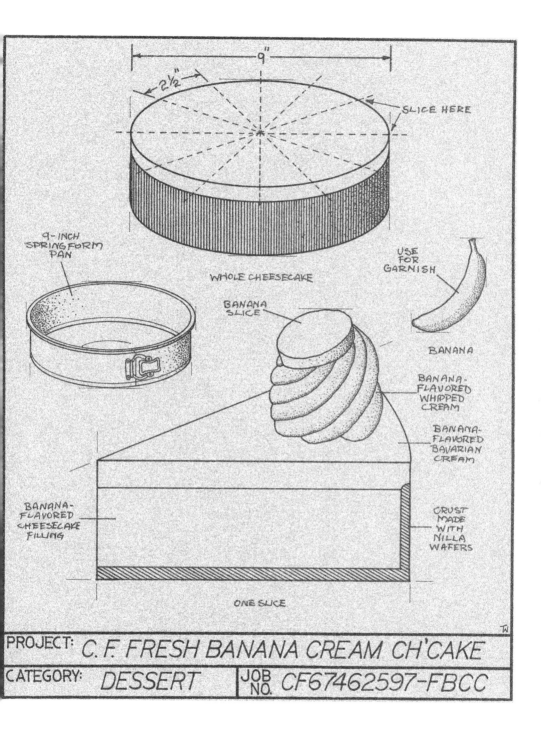

9"

2½"

SLICE HERE

9-INCH
SPRINGFORM
PAN

WHOLE CHEESECAKE

USE
FOR
GARNISH

BANANA

BANANA
SLICE

BANANA-
FLAVORED
WHIPPED
CREAM

BANANA-
FLAVORED
BAVARIAN
CREAM

BANANA-
FLAVORED
CHEESECAKE
FILLING

CRUST
MADE
WITH
NILLA
WAFERS

ONE SLICE

PROJECT: *C. F. FRESH BANANA CREAM CH'CAKE*

CATEGORY: *DESSERT*   JOB NO. *CF67462597-FBCC*

on high speed until the cream forms stiff peaks. Cover and chill.

8. When the cheesecake has completely chilled out, after about 4 hours, cut it into 12 slices and serve each with a dollop of the banana whipped cream on top, with 1 slice of banana on top of the whipped cream and a half of a banana, sliced up, on the side of each serving.

• MAKES 12 SERVINGS.

• • • •

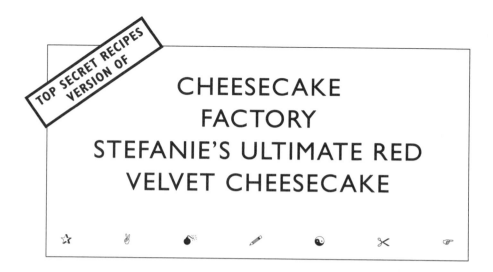

CHEESECAKE FACTORY STEFANIE'S ULTIMATE RED VELVET CHEESECAKE

MENU DESCRIPTION: *"Moist layers of red velvet cake and our Original Cheesecake covered with our special Cheesecake Factory cream cheese frosting."*

To make the best red velvet cheesecake like the great version that is made at Cheesecake Factory, we have to start with a good red velvet cake recipe. I studied several versions and eventually created an original red velvet formula that is moist, with the perfect color and size to layer into a 9-inch springform pan between a no-bake cheesecake filling. When the cheesecake sets up in a few hours, remove it from the pan and apply the delicious cream cheese frosting. The white chocolate curls pressed into the side of the cake can be made easily by dragging a peeler over the edge of a white chocolate bar. One 4-ounce bar will give you more than enough of the curls, but that's okay, since many will fall off in the process of pressing them onto the side of the cake.

RED VELVET CAKE

¾ cup butter (1 ½ sticks), softened
1 ¼ cups granulated sugar
2 eggs

2 tablespoons vegetable oil
1 teaspoon vanilla extract
¾ cup buttermilk
2 tablespoons red food coloring

1 ¾ cups cake flour
5 teaspoons cocoa powder

½ teaspoon baking soda
½ teaspoon salt

CHEESECAKE FILLING

½ cup heavy cream
three 8-ounce packages cream
   cheese, softened

1 cup granulated sugar
1 ½ teaspoons vanilla extract
1 teaspoon cream of tartar

CREAM CHEESE
FROSTING

½ cup (1 stick) butter, softened
8 ounces cream cheese, softened
2 ½ cups powdered sugar

1 tablespoon whole milk
¾ teaspoon vanilla extract

GARNISH

one 4-ounce bar white chocolate

1. Preheat the oven to 350 degrees F.
2. Make the red velvet cake by mixing the butter with the sugar in a large bowl for 1 minute using a mixer on high speed. Add the eggs, oil, and vanilla and mix until smooth. Mix in the buttermilk and red coloring.
3. In a separate medium bowl, sift together the flour, cocoa powder, baking soda, and salt. Pour the dry ingredients into the wet mixture and blend with an electric mixer for about 30 seconds. Pour the batter into a buttered nonstick or parchment paper–lined 9-inch cake pan and bake for 35 to 40 minutes, or until a toothpick stuck into the center of the cake comes out clean. Cool completely.
4. When the cake has completely cooled, remove it from the pan. Slice the domed top off the cake and discard. Then slice the cake through the middle. Place the bottom of the cake into the

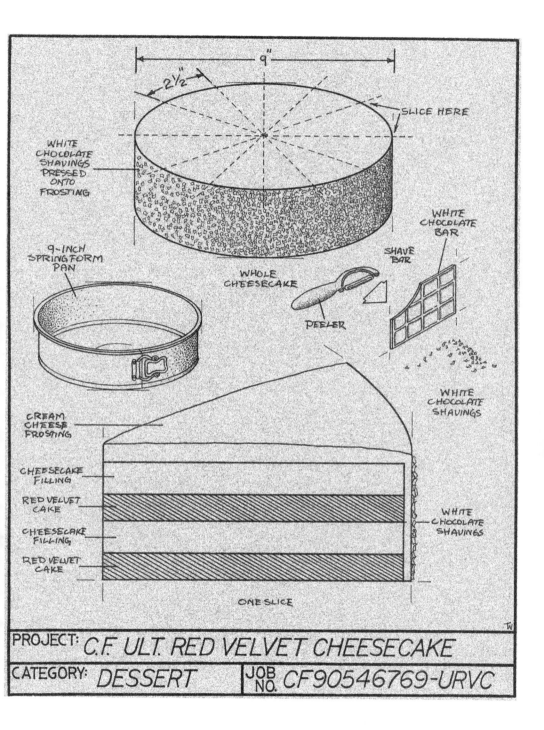

9"

2½"

SLICE HERE

WHITE CHOCOLATE SHAVINGS PRESSED ONTO FROSTING

9-INCH SPRINGFORM PAN

WHOLE CHEESECAKE

SHAVE BAR

PEELER

WHITE CHOCOLATE BAR

WHITE CHOCOLATE SHAVINGS

CREAM CHEESE FROSTING

CHEESECAKE FILLING

RED VELVET CAKE

CHEESECAKE FILLING

RED VELVET CAKE

WHITE CHOCOLATE SHAVINGS

ONE SLICE

PROJECT: *C.F. ULT. RED VELVET CHEESECAKE*

CATEGORY: *DESSERT*

JOB NO. *CF90546769-URVC*

bottom of a 9-inch springform pan. Place the pan into the freezer. Place the other half of the cake onto a plate and put it into the freezer as well. This will help to prevent the cake from contributing red crumbs to the white cheesecake filling.

5. Make the cheesecake filling by whipping the heavy cream with an electric mixer in a medium bowl until it forms stiff peaks. Mix in the softened cream cheese, sugar, vanilla, and cream of tartar until smooth and creamy. Use a spatula to spread half of this filling over the red velvet cake in the bottom of the springform pan. Carefully place the other half of the cake over the filling, then spread the rest of the filling on top of the cake. Chill for several hours.

6. When the cheesecake has completely chilled, make the cream cheese frosting by combining the butter and cream cheese in a large mixing bowl with an electric mixer on high speed. Add the powdered sugar, milk, and vanilla and beat for 2 minutes, or until smooth and fluffy.

7. Remove the cheesecake from the springform pan. Use a spatula to completely cover the top and sides of the cake with the cream cheese frosting. Use 2 to 3 times as much icing on the top as on the sides.

8. Use a carrot peeler to make small curls from the white chocolate bar by turning the bar on its side and dragging the peeler over the edge of the bar. Shave most of the bar into curls, then press the white chocolate shavings onto the icing on the side of the cake all the way around. Chill the cake for a couple hours.

9. To serve the chilled cake, slice into 12 slices and serve.

• Makes 12 slices.

•   •   •   •

CHILI'S
CRISPY HONEY-CHIPOTLE
CHICKEN CRISPERS

MENU DESCRIPTION: *"Tossed in our honey-chipotle sauce."*

After cloning the plain version of these breaded chicken fingers in *Top Secret Restaurant Recipes 2*, I received many requests to knockoff this more flavorful sweet and spicy version. If you like big flavor and some heat, this is the clone for you. The breading technique is the big secret: first using a wet batter and then tossing the tenders in a dry breading. When the chicken tenders are fried to a golden brown, they are gently tossed in the secret honey-chipotle sauce and served either as an appetizer or with corn on the cob and French fries as an entrée.

HONEY-CHIPOTLE SAUCE

⅔ cup honey
¼ cup water
¼ cup ketchup

1 tablespoon white vinegar
2 teaspoons ground chipotle chile
½ teaspoon salt

6 to 10 cups shortening or vegetable oil (in a fryer or large saucepan)

BATTER

1 egg, beaten
½ cup whole milk
½ cup chicken broth (Swanson)
1 ½ teaspoons salt

¼ teaspoon ground black pepper
¼ teaspoon paprika
¼ teaspoon garlic powder
¾ cup all-purpose flour

BREADING
1 ½ cups all-purpose flour
1 ½ teaspoons salt

¾ teaspoon paprika
½ teaspoon ground black pepper
½ teaspoon garlic powder

10 to 12 chicken tenderloins

1. Make the honey-chipotle sauce by combining all the ingredients in a small saucepan and heating over medium heat until boiling. Reduce the heat and simmer for 2 minutes. Remove from the heat.
2. Heat the shortening or oil in fryer or a large saucepan to 350 to 360 degrees F.
3. Whisk together all ingredients for the batter, excluding the flour, in a shallow bowl. Continue whisking for about 30 seconds to dissolve the salt. Whisk in the flour.
4. Make the breading by combining all the ingredients in another shallow bowl or a pie pan.
5. When you are ready to fry the chicken, dip each piece of chicken into the batter. Lift the chicken out of the batter and let some of the batter drip off, then toss the chicken into the dry breading. Completely coat the chicken with breading and let it sit for a bit in the breading while you batter and bread 2 or 3 more pieces. Carefully drop the breaded chicken into the hot oil and fry for 4 minutes, or until golden brown. Remove the chicken from the hot oil onto paper towels while you fry the remaining pieces.
6. When all the chicken is done, drop it into a large glass or metal bowl, pour the sauce over the top, and toss gently until all the chicken is coated with sauce.

• Serves 4 as an appetizer or 2 as an entrée.

• • • •

CHILI'S
QUESADILLA EXPLOSION
SALAD

MENU DESCRIPTION: *"Fajita-marinated chicken, corn relish, mixed cheese, cilantro, diced tomato and crispy tortilla strips. Garnished with a chipotle-ranch drizzle and cheese quesadilla wedges. Served with our citrus-balsamic dressing."*

I'm a happy camper on a Saturday afternoon when I dive into one of these big salads, served up with a Presidente Margarita to help relieve my hangover from a long Friday night hoo-ha. For the last several years, this has been the go-to salad when you're dining at Chili's. The chicken marinade is delicious, the corn relish is a great touch, and the citrus-balsamic vinaigrette totally rocks. And where else can you get a salad that includes slices of cheese quesadilla on the side? I love it. If you're a fan of the original, this 4-serving clone will bring it home.

4 skinless chicken breast fillets

FAJITA MARINADE

2½ cups water
2 tablespoons soy sauce
2 tablespoons granulated sugar
2 teaspoons salt

1½ teaspoons ground cumin
1 teaspoon garlic powder
1 teaspoon onion powder

½ teaspoon ground cayenne
   pepper

½ teaspoon ground black pepper

½ teaspoon hickory-flavored
   liquid smoke

CORN RELISH

1 cup frozen yellow corn kernels,
   thawed

½ cup canned black beans,
   drained and rinsed

2 tablespoons shredded carrot

2 tablespoons minced green bell
   pepper

2 teaspoons cilantro

1 teaspoon lime juice

½ teaspoon granulated sugar

¼ teaspoon salt

⅛ teaspoon ground cayenne
   pepper

pinch ground black pepper

CHIPOTLE-RANCH DRIZZLE

½ cup Hidden Valley Ranch Salad
   dressing

⅛ teaspoon ground chipotle chile

CITRUS-BALSAMIC VINAIGRETTE

1 cup canola oil

¼ cup balsamic vinegar

3 tablespoons granulated sugar

2 tablespoons Grey Poupon Dijon
   mustard

2 tablespoons lemon juice

1 teaspoon minced garlic

1 teaspoon lime juice

½ teaspoon salt

¼ teaspoon ground black pepper

CRISPY TORTILLA STRIPS

6 corn tortillas

2 cups canola oil

CHEESE QUESADILLAS

eight 7-inch flour tortillas
1 cup shredded cheddar cheese

1 cup shredded Monterey
    Jack cheese
butter

8 cups chopped iceberg lettuce
    (about 1 head)
8 cups chopped romaine lettuce
    (about 1 head)
½ cup shredded cheddar cheese

½ cup shredded Monterey Jack
    cheese
1 cup diced tomatoes (about 2
    tomatoes)
4 teaspoons minced cilantro

1. The chicken will need to marinate for 2 hours, so we'll get that going first. To ensure that the chicken breasts cook evenly, pound the fat end of the chicken fillets with a kitchen mallet. Whisk the marinade ingredients together in a medium bowl, and then pour it over the chicken in a zip-top plastic bag. Park the bag in your refrigerator for 2 to 2½ hours.

2. While the chicken marinates you'll have plenty of time to make the corn relish, dressings, and crispy tortilla strips. To make the corn relish, simply combine all of the ingredients in a medium bowl, then cover and chill.

3. Make the chipotle-ranch drizzle by combining ground chipotle pepper with Hidden Valley or your favorite ranch dressing— you can even use low-fat ranch dressing, if you like.

4. Make the citrus-balsamic vinaigrette by combining all the in-gredients in a blender on medium speed for 30 seconds or until thick. Cover and chill.

5. Make the crispy tortilla strips by slicing 6 corn tortillas into thin strips. Heat oil in a medium saucepan over medium heat until 1 strip dropped into the oil bubbles and fries to a crunchy golden brown in about a minute. When the oil is hot, fry the tortilla strips in batches until crispy, and then drain on paper towels.

6.	When the chicken has marinated for a couple hours, preheat the barbecue grill to high. Arrange the chicken breasts on a plate and coat them with a little oil so they won't stick to the grill. When your grill is hot, cook the chicken for 5 to 6 minutes per side, until done.

7.	As the chicken cooks, make the quesadillas by heating a medium sauté pan over medium/low heat. Combine I cup shredded cheddar cheese and I cup Monterey Jack cheese, then spread ½ cup of this cheese blend on top of a flour tortilla. Cover with another tortilla. Melt some butter into the sauté pan, then brown the quesadilla for I minute on each side or until light brown. Repeat for the other 3 quesadillas, and then slice each quesadilla into quarters with a knife or pizza wheel.

8.	Build each salad by combining 2 cups iceberg lettuce with 2 cups romaine lettuce and arranging the greens on a large serving plate. Sprinkle the lettuce with about ½ cup of the crispy tortilla strips. Spoon ⅓ cup of corn relish on next. Slice each grilled chicken breast into thin strips and arrange the chicken on the corn relish, followed by about ¼ cup of the cheddar–Jack cheese blend. Arrange ¼ cup of diced tomato on next, with I teaspoon of cilantro piled on top. Drizzle some of the chipotle-ranch drizzle over the salad using a squirt bottle or a spoon, and serve the citrus-balsamic vinaigrette in a small bowl on the side. Arrange 4 slices of quesadilla around the edge of the salad and serve.

• MAKES 4 LARGE SALADS.

TIDBITS

Save a little time and money by using a blend of shredded cheddar–Monterey Jack cheese for your salads and quesadillas. It's found near the other preshredded cheeses in most stores.

•   •   •   •

CHILI'S
CAJUN RIBEYE

MENU DESCRIPTION: *"12 oz. ribeye steak seasoned with Cajun spices and topped with roasted herb jus & spicy Cajun butter."*

Three secret formulas must be decoded before we can consider this steak a culinary clone of Chili's signature Cajun Ribeye. The Cajun seasoning, the herb jus, and the Cajun butter comprise the flavorful hat trick that earns this dish its signature item status. We'll make each component from scratch ingredients—with the exception of canned beef broth—and everything is pretty easy. Sprinkle the seasoning on the steak before it's grilled, and then add the jus and herb butter just before serving. That's it. So rustle up some ribeyes from your favorite butcher and fire up the grill. Once you've assemble these three simple secret recipes below, you're just minutes away from an impressive, flavor-filled steak.

CAJUN SEASONING

1 teaspoon salt
1 teaspoon coarse grind black
    pepper
1 ½ teaspoons paprika
½ teaspoon onion powder
½ teaspoon garlic powder

¼ teaspoon dried thyme
¼ teaspoon ground coriander
¼ teaspoon dried oregano
¼ teaspoon crushed red pepper
⅛ teaspoon ground cayenne
    pepper

CAJUN BUTTER

¼ cup salted butter, softened
½ teaspoon garlic powder

¼ teaspoon salt
¼ teaspoon Cajun seasoning

HERB JUS

one 14-ounce can beef broth
  (1¾ cups)
½ teaspoon dried parsley
⅛ teaspoon dried thyme

⅛ teaspoon dried oregano
⅛ teaspoon salt
⅛ teaspoon dried rosemary
pinch ground black pepper

four 12-ounce ribeye steaks

1. Make Cajun seasoning by combining all ingredients in a small bowl.
2. Make Cajun butter by combining softened butter with garlic powder, salt, and ¼ teaspoon of the Cajun seasoning blend made in step #1. Chill butter until 20 to 30 minutes before grilling the steaks.
3. Make the herb jus by combining all ingredients in a small saucepan over medium heat. When the mixture begins to boil, reduce heat and simmer for 10 minutes.
4. To prepare your steaks, sprinkle steaks with Cajun seasoning, then let them sit out at room temperature for 20 to 30 minutes. Preheat your barbecue grill to high. Grill on high heat to create crisscross grill marks on both sides of the steaks, then reduce heat and cook steaks until desired doneness. If your steaks are thicker than 1 inch, close the cover of the grill.
5. Serve each steak by spooning 2 tablespoons of herb jus over the top, and then spooning a heaping teaspoon of herb butter onto the center.

• MAKES 4 STEAKS.

• • • •

CHILI'S
FIRECRACKER TILAPIA

MENU DESCRIPTION: *"A grilled tilapia fillet brushed with a sweet and spicy glaze and garnished with red chili tapenade, cilantro, and sesame seeds."*

Here's a great way to prepare that next batch of fresh fish fillets when you're contemplating a new taste. If you and your diners love spicy food this is the perfect clone, since the *Top Secret* glaze and tapenade recipes I've included here both come packing heat. You can make the sauces several hours—or even days—ahead of time, and then when you're ready to eat, the fish will cook up in less than 10 minutes. Chili's calls this "grilled" tilapia on the menu, but don't expect to find grill marks on the fish. It appears the restaurant uses a flat griddle or sauté pan to cook the fish, since the tender tilapia would fall through the grate on a barbecue grill (also, restaurants must avoid contributing any fishy tastes to their grilled burgers and ribs). Don't limit this recipe to tilapia. The intense glaze and tapenade will perk up a variety of fish fillets, from sea bass to salmon.

SWEET AND SPICY GLAZE

1 teaspoon minced garlic
1 teaspoon vegetable oil
⅓ cup dark brown sugar
2 tablespoons water
¼ cup Kikkoman hoisin sauce

2 tablespoons chili paste
1 teaspoon minced cilantro
¼ teaspoon soy sauce
2½ tablespoons rice vinegar

RED CHILI TAPENADE

1 ½ teaspoons minced garlic
¼ cup minced red bell pepper
2 tablespoons chopped white
    onion
2 tablespoons chopped green
    onion
1 tablespoon vegetable oil
½ cup bottled pimentos
    (sliced or diced), with liquid

1 ½ cups water
3 tablespoons apple cider vinegar
2 teaspoons chili paste
1 ½ teaspoons dark brown sugar
1 ½ teaspoons soy sauce
½ teaspoon sesame seeds
¼ teaspoon salt
¼ teaspoon dried parsley
⅛ teaspoon ground black pepper

4 tilapia fillets

2 tablespoons melted butter

GARNISH

sesame seeds
minced cilantro

1. Make sweet and spicy glaze by sautéing garlic for 1 minute in 1 teaspoon of oil over medium/low heat in a small saucepan. Add all the remaining ingredients except rice vinegar and simmer for 5 minutes, or until thick. Add rice vinegar, and then remove the sauce from the heat. Cover until needed.
2. Make red chili tapenade by sautéing garlic, red bell pepper, and onions in the oil over medium/low heat for 2 to 3 minutes. Combine bottled pimentos with ½ cup water in a blender and blend on high speed until smooth. Add pureed pimentos, plus remaining ingredients (including leftover 1 cup of water) to the saucepan and simmer for 45 minutes or until liquid has cooked off and mixture is a thick paste. Cover and cool.
3. Heat a large sauté pan or skillet over medium heat. Brush both sides of tilapia fillets with melted butter, then sprinkle fish with a little salt and pepper. Cook fillets in preheated pan for 4 to 5 minutes per side, until golden brown. When the fish

is done, use a spatula to place each fillet on a serving plate and brush top of each fillet with the glaze. Spoon a couple teaspoons of tapenade onto the center of each fillet, and sprinkle with sesame seeds and minced cilantro. Serve fish with rice and vegetables, or your choice of sides.

• Makes 4 servings.

• • • •

CHILI'S
NACHO BURGER

MENU DESCRIPTION: *"Nacho Ordinary Burger! Shredded lettuce, tortilla strips, chili queso & green onions. Served open faced w/sour cream, guacamole, jalapeños & pico de gallo."*

I created this cool hamburger clone way back in 1997 for the original *Top Secret Recipes* Web site, but when the site was redesigned in 2005 the recipe was left off. I had planned to include it in *Top Secret Restaurant Recipes 2*—I even drew up a blueprint for it—as a tribute to the great burger that Chili's was no longer offering on its menu, until I realized there were already 13 Chili's clones in that book, and the poor Nacho Burger once again failed to make the cut. Too bad really, since this recipe is made up of several smaller recipes for popular garnishes and sides offered at the chain that folks are often interested in cloning: Chili's Chili Queso, Chili's Pico de Gallo, and Chili's Guacamole. Now, in this one recipe, you'll learn how to clone all three components from scratch, and then you pile everything on a hamburger with some jalapeños, crunchy tortilla chips, and chopped green onion and serve it open-faced with extra guacamole and queso on the side. After you taste this delicious long-lost clone that tastes like a hamburger crashed into a plate of nachos, you'll wonder why Chili's retired the original to the Land of the Dead Foods.

PICO DE GALLO

2 medium tomatoes, diced
½ cup diced onion
1 tablespoon minced fresh
   cilantro

2 teaspoons chopped fresh
   jalapeño pepper, seeded and
   deribbed
   juice of ½ lime
⅛ teaspoon salt

GUACAMOLE

1 large Hass avocado
¼ cup diced tomato
1 tablespoon sour cream
½ teaspoon diced jalapeño

½ teaspoon chopped fresh
   cilantro
½ teaspoon lime juice
⅛ teaspoon salt

CHILI QUESO

one 16-ounce box Velveeta
   cheese
one 15-ounce can Hormel Chili
   (no beans)
1 cup milk

4 teaspoons chili powder
2 teaspoons paprika
1 tablespoon lime juice
½ teaspoon cayenne pepper
½ teaspoon ground cumin

4 large sesame seed buns
1 pound ground beef
salt and pepper
2 cups shredded iceberg lettuce
16 to 20 tortilla chips

1 green onion, chopped
2 tablespoons mayonnaise
2 to 3 fresh jalapeño peppers,
   sliced

1. First make the pico de gallo by combining all of the ingredients for the pico in a small bowl. Cover the bowl and chill the pico in the refrigerator.
2. Make the guacamole by smashing up the avocado in a small bowl. Add the remaining ingredients for the guacamole to

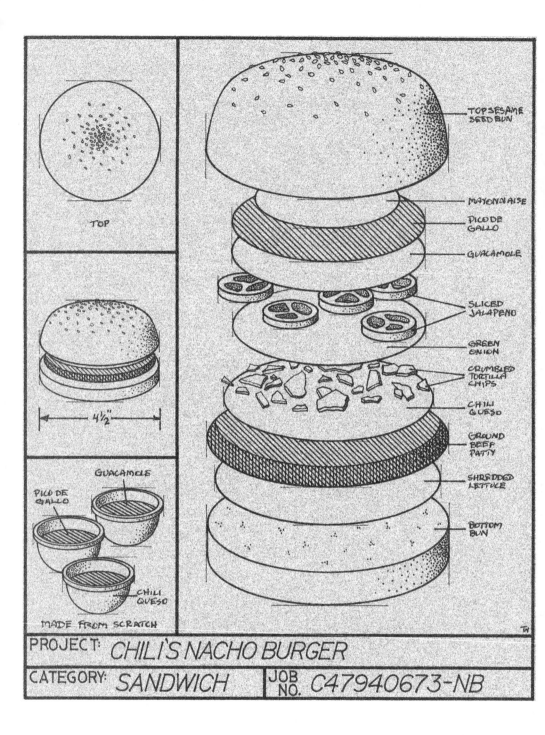

TOP

TOP SESAME SEED BUN

MAYONNAISE

PICO DE GALLO

GUACAMOLE

SLICED JALAPENO

GREEN ONION

CRUMBLED TORTILLA CHIPS

CHILI QUESO

GROUND BEEF PATTY

SHREDDED LETTUCE

BOTTOM BUN

4½"

GUACAMOLE

PICO DE GALLO

CHILI QUESO

MADE FROM SCRATCH

PROJECT: *CHILI'S NACHO BURGER*

CATEGORY: *SANDWICH*   JOB NO. *C47940673-NB*

the avocado and mix well. Cover the bowl and chill in the refrigerator, next to the pico.

3. Make the chili queso by cutting the Velveeta into cubes. Combine the cheese with the remaining queso ingredients in a medium saucepan over medium heat. Stir frequently until the cheese melts, then reduce the heat and simmer for 20 minutes.

4. Preheat a griddle or large skillet over medium heat. Lightly butter the face of each bun and brown the buns facedown on the heat.

5. Separate the ground beef into four ¼-pound portions. Roll each portion of meat into a ball and then pat the meat down into a circular patty slightly larger in diameter than the hamburger buns. Cook the hamburger patties for 3 to 5 minutes per side, until done. Lightly salt and pepper each burger patty.

6. Build each burger open-faced in the following order starting with the bottom bun:

ON BOTTOM BUN

½ cup shredded lettuce   *4 or 5 crumbled tortilla chips*
cooked hamburger patty   *2 teaspoons chopped green onion*
2 tablespoons chili queso

ON TOP BUN

½ tablespoon mayonnaise   *2 tablespoons guacamole*
2 tablespoons pico de gallo   *4 jalapeño slices*

Serve the burgers with extra chili queso and guacamole on the side.

• MAKES 4 BURGERS.

•   •   •   •

CHILI'S
WHITE CHOCOLATE
MOLTEN CAKE

MENU DESCRIPTION: *"Topped with vanilla ice cream under a white chocolate shell."*

After the success of the Molten Chocolate Cake, Chili's chefs went back into the development kitchen and emerged with this incredible white chocolate variation that has become the new go-to meal ender. Just as with my clone for the Molten Chocolate Cake in *Top Secret Restaurant Recipes 2*, I found that an instant cake mix is the perfect solution to quickly and easily knockoff this seriously awesome dessert. It just so happens that Duncan Hines Moist Deluxe Butter Recipe Golden Cake Mix produces a butter cake that matches perfectly to the moist, buttery cake used in the Chili's original. For the molten white chocolate inside the cake, we mix melted white chocolate chips with a little cream and then spoon the mixture into a hole cut into each cake. Pop the filled cakes into your refrigerator, and when you're ready to serve the dessert, nuke each one in the microwave to heat up the molten filling, add ice cream and a little white chocolate on top, and serve. This is a great make-ahead dish, since the loaded cakes can be stored in your refrigerator for a couple days (even longer in your freezer), and when you're ready to plate the dessert, each serving takes only a minute or two to set up.

one 18.25-ounce box Duncan
    Hines Moist Deluxe Butter
    Recipe Golden Cake Mix
⅔ cup water
½ cup (1 stick) butter, softened
3 eggs
18 ounces (3 cups) white
    chocolate chips

¼ cup plus 2 teaspoons heavy
    cream
one 16-ounce box frozen
    strawberries in syrup (sugar
    added), thawed
8 scoops vanilla ice cream

1. Preheat the oven to 350 degrees F.
2. Make the cake batter following directions on the box and pour ½ cup of batter into the greased cups of a large (Texas-size) muffin pan. If your pan has six cups, bake the cakes in two batches of 4 cakes each. Bake for 25 to 30 minutes in the preheated oven, or until a toothpick stuck into the center of one cake comes out clean. Let the cakes cool for 15 minutes, then turn all of the cakes out of the pan.
3. While the cakes cool, measure 9 ounces or 1½ cups of white chocolate chips into a microwave-safe glass or ceramic bowl. Add the heavy cream and microwave on high temperature for 30 seconds. Stir, then microwave for 30 seconds more. Let this cool for 15 to 20 minutes to thicken.
4. The cakes will be served upside down, so you may have to slice a bit of the domed top off each cake to help it lay flat when inverted. A serrated knife works best for this. After you've flipped over all of the cooled cakes, use a sharp paring knife to cut out a 1½-inch diameter cylindrical chunk in the center of the bottom (now the top) of each cake. The hole should be about 1½ inches deep. After cutting straight down into the cake in a circle, scoop out the chunk of cake with a teaspoon and discard (or eat) the piece. This is where you will hide the white chocolate filling.
5. Spoon 2 to 3 tablespoons of white chocolate filling into each of the holes you've made in the cakes, then store the cakes in a sealed container in the refrigerator.

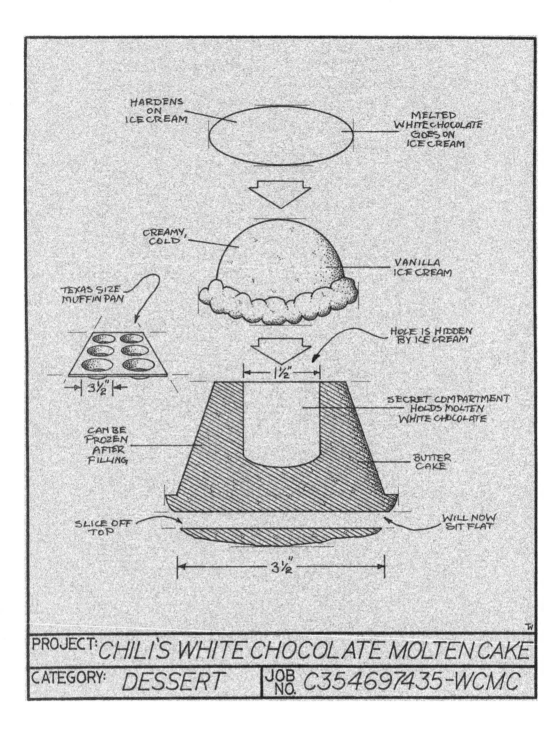

HARDENS ON ICE CREAM

MELTED WHITE CHOCOLATE GOES ON ICE CREAM

CREAMY, COLD

VANILLA ICE CREAM

TEXAS SIZE MUFFIN PAN

3½"

HOLE IS HIDDEN BY ICE CREAM

1½"

SECRET COMPARTMENT HOLDS MOLTEN WHITE CHOCOLATE

CAN BE FROZEN AFTER FILLING

BUTTER CAKE

SLICE OFF TOP

WILL NOW SIT FLAT

3½"

PROJECT: *CHILI'S WHITE CHOCOLATE MOLTEN CAKE*

CATEGORY: *DESSERT*

JOB NO. *C354697435-WCMC*

6. Make the strawberry sauce by pureeing the strawberries with syrup in a blender until smooth.
7. When you're ready to serve, pour the remaining 9 ounces (1½ cups) of white chocolate chips into a medium microwave-safe glass or ceramic bowl. Microwave the white chocolate for 30 seconds, then stir, and microwave for 30 seconds more.
8. Heat up each cake in the microwave on high power for 40 to 45 seconds, or until you see the filling bubble.
9. Drizzle the strawberry sauce onto each serving plate with a spoon, or use a squirt bottle.
10. Place a warm cake on the strawberry sauce, then place a scoop of vanilla ice cream on top of the cake, concealing the hole. Drizzle approximately 1½ tablespoons of melted white chocolate over the ice cream and serve right away with a spoon. Repeat for each dessert.

- Makes 8 desserts.

• • • •

CRACKER BARREL
COLE SLAW

Similar to cloning the cole slaw at KFC, the secret technique for duplicating Cracker Barrel's delicious slaw starts with slicing the cabbage into very small pieces. A mandoline works great for this (or use whatever slicing contraption you have). Slice the heads of green and red cabbage on the thinnest setting, and then chop those strips into small bits. The carrot can be shredded using a cheese grater. Mix it all up and then let the cole slaw chill out for several hours so the mixture can get its flavor on. An overnight chill is even sweeter.

½ cup mayonnaise
⅓ cup granulated sugar
¼ cup whole milk
¼ cup buttermilk
4 teaspoons lemon juice
1 teaspoon white vinegar

¼ teaspoon salt
¼ teaspoon celery seed
8 cups finely shredded green
    cabbage
1 cup finely shredded red cabbage
1 cup shredded carrots

1. Whisk together mayonnaise, sugar, milk, buttermilk, lemon juice, vinegar, salt, and celery seed in a large bowl until sugar is dissolved.
2. Stir in cabbages and shredded carrots. Cover and chill for at least 4 hours. Stir before serving.

• MAKES 6 SERVINGS.

•   •   •   •

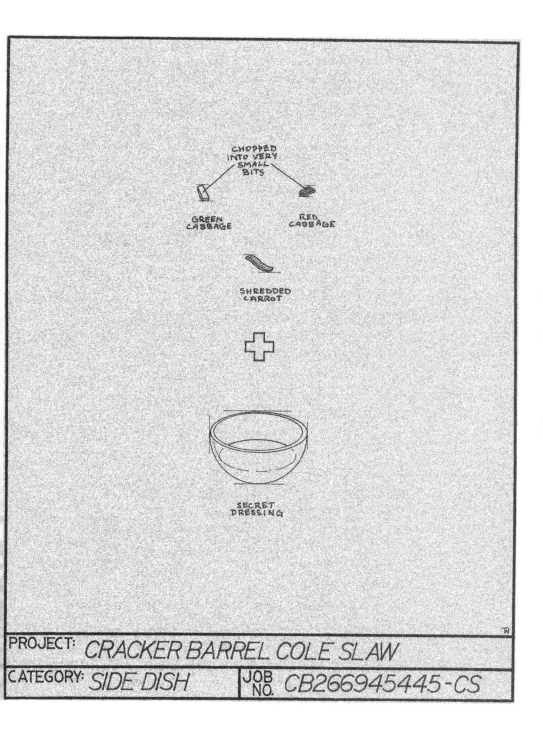

CHOPPED
INTO VERY
SMALL
BITS

GREEN
CABBAGE

RED
CABBAGE

SHREDDED
CARROT

SECRET
DRESSING

PROJECT: *CRACKER BARREL COLE SLAW*

CATEGORY: *SIDE DISH*

JOB NO. *CB266945445-CS*

CRACKER BARREL MACARONI N' CHEESE

No mix that comes in a box tastes as good as macaroni and cheese that's made from scratch. It seems crazy that these boxed mixes are so popular when making really good mac n' cheese the old-fashioned way is so doggone easy. I say we get on down right now with a clone that's been garnering many requests at *TSR* Central over the years. The 594-unit Cracker Barrel Old Country Store restaurant chain serves up an awesome version that's offered as a side dish with any meal. We'll whip up this cool clone in a 10-inch skillet and then brown it just a bit on top under the broiler before presenting it to our hungry masses.

¾ cup elbow macaroni pasta
3 tablespoons salted butter
3 tablespoons all-purpose flour
2¼ cups whole milk

½ teaspoon salt
⅛ teaspoon coarse grind black
    pepper
2½ cups shredded Colby cheese

1. Preheat broiler to high.
2. Cook pasta in 4 cups of boiling water for 8 minutes or until tender, then drain off the water.
3. Melt the butter in a 10-inch oven-safe skillet over medium heat. Whisk in flour and continue whisking until bubbly. Add milk, salt, and black pepper and stir until the milk begins to bubble. Add cheese, and then turn off the heat. Whisk the sauce until the cheese is melted and the sauce is smooth.

4. Stir in cooked elbow macaroni, and then set the skillet under the preheated broiler for 2 to 3 minutes, until several browned spots appear on the surface. Remove the pan from the oven (careful—it's hot!), and let it sit for 5 minutes before serving. The cheese sauce will thicken as it rests.

*   MAKES 4 TO 6 SIDE SERVINGS.

•   •   •   •

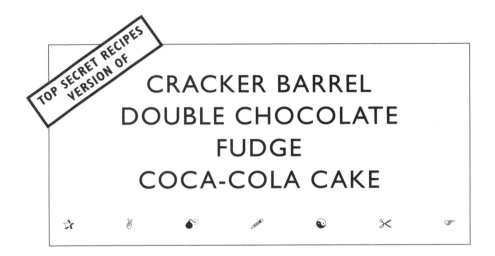

CRACKER BARREL DOUBLE CHOCOLATE FUDGE COCA-COLA CAKE

MENU DESCRIPTION: *"A Cracker Barrel tradition. Our rich, chocolate cake made with real Coca-Cola is baked right in our own kitchen. It's served with premium vanilla bean ice cream and makes for a warm treat on a cool day."*

Cracker Barrel's signature dessert is moist and chocolaty, with just a hint of Coke flavor. Coca-Cola is added to the batter for our clone, and we'll double up on the chocolate by using melted semi-sweet chocolate chips and cocoa powder. A little more Coke goes into the creamy chocolate icing that's also made by melting chocolate chips. Be sure to slide on down to the Tidbits at the end of the recipe for a great way to easily get the cake out of your baking pan in one piece.

CAKE

¼ cup (½ stick) salted butter
6 ounces semisweet chocolate
    chips (1 cup)
3 eggs
1⅔ cups granulated sugar
⅔ cup vegetable oil
1 teaspoon vanilla extract

1½ cups Coca-Cola
2 cups all-purpose flour
⅓ cup unsweetened cocoa
1½ teaspoons baking powder
½ teaspoon baking soda
¾ teaspoon salt

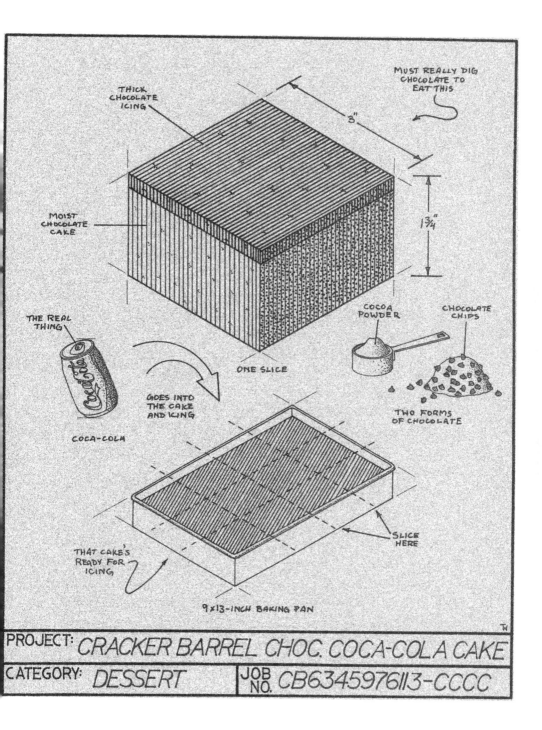

MUST REALLY DIG CHOCOLATE TO EAT THIS

THICK CHOCOLATE ICING

MOIST CHOCOLATE CAKE

8"

1¾"

THE REAL THING

GOES INTO THE CAKE AND ICING

COCA-COLA

ONE SLICE

COCOA POWDER

CHOCOLATE CHIPS

TWO FORMS OF CHOCOLATE

SLICE HERE

THAT CAKE'S READY FOR ICING

9×13-INCH BAKING PAN

PROJECT: CRACKER BARREL CHOC. COCA-COLA CAKE

CATEGORY: DESSERT

JOB NO. CB6345976113-CCCC

ICING

8 ounces semisweet chocolate
   chips (1 ⅓ cups)
6 tablespoons (¾ stick) butter
1 teaspoon vanilla extract

⅛ teaspoon salt
2 cups powdered sugar
⅓ cup Coca-Cola

12 scoops of vanilla ice cream

1. Preheat oven to 350 degrees F.
2. Melt butter and 1 cup chocolate chips in a large bowl in your microwave on high for 1 minute. Stir until smooth.
3. In a medium bowl, beat the eggs and granulated sugar for 30 seconds with a mixer on medium speed. Mix in the oil and vanilla. Pour this mixture into the chocolate mixture, then add Coca-Cola and blend for 30 seconds.
4. Combine flour, cocoa, baking powder, baking soda, and salt in a medium bowl. Pour this dry mixture into the wet stuff, and mix with electric mixer until well combined. Pour batter into a buttered 13 x 9-inch baking pan and bake cake for 35 to 38 minutes, until a toothpick stuck into the center of the cake comes out clean.
5. Make the icing while the cake cools by combining 1 ⅓ cup chocolate chips and 6 tablespoons butter in a medium mixing bowl. Microwave the butter and chocolate for 1 minute or until the chocolate softens. Use an electric mixer on low to blend the chocolate with the butter, and then add 1 teaspoon vanilla and ⅛ teaspoon salt. Blend in powdered sugar one cup at a time, add ⅓ cup Coca-Cola, and mix for 1 minute, until smooth and creamy. Use a spatula to frost the entire surface of the cake with the icing.
6. To serve the cake, slice it into 12 squares. Serve each slice with a scoop of vanilla ice cream.

• MAKES 12 SERVINGS.

TIDBITS

For easy removal of the cake, line the pan with a "sling" of parchment paper that hangs over the long edges of the pan. When cake is cool, you can easily pull up on the parchment paper to remove the cake.

•   •   •   •

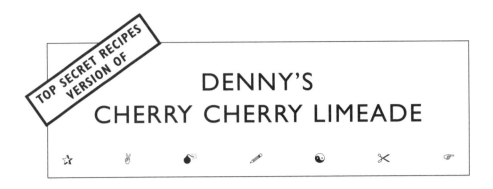

DENNY'S
CHERRY CHERRY LIMEADE

MENU DESCRIPTION: *"One part lime. Two parts cherry. All blended with ice-cold Sprite."*

Denny's Fusion Favorites are creative drink mixes blended from the chain's soda fountain with a variety of added fruit flavors. The secret ingredients in these trademarked drinks are the flavored syrups dispensed from giant squirt bottles next to the soda machines, but I discovered that we can easily re-create these syrups using Kool-Aid drink mix powder. For this drink that is the top choice on the Fusion Favorite menu, dissolve the Kool-Aid mix into a little lime juice for a cherry-lime syrup that can be stirred into a refreshing blend of Sprite and Minute Maid lemonade over ice. And if you want to significantly reduce the calories in this drink, use diet Sprite and light Minute Maid lemonade and you won't even be able to taste the difference.

I teaspoon cherry-flavored Kool-Aid drink mix (sweetened)	¾ cup cold Sprite lemon-lime soda
I tablespoon lime juice	¾ cup cold Minute Maid lemonade

1. Dissolve the Kool-Aid mix in the lime juice in a small bowl.
2. Fill a 16-ounce glass with ice.

3.   Pour the Sprite, lemonade, and cherry-lime mix into the glass. Add a straw and serve.

• MAKES ONE 16-OUNCE DRINK.

•   •   •   •

DENNY'S
BROCCOLI CHEESE SOUP

This soup is only served on Mondays at the Denny's near my house and it's not on the menu, but of all the soups served at one of America's largest diner chains, this one comes in at the top of the list for cloning requests we get here at *Top Secret Recipes* Headquarters. A home clone for this popular soup is beautifully simple: Make a roux with flour and butter, add milk, shredded cheddar cheese, chicken broth, and broccoli, and simmer until thick. The only suggestion I would make is to shred the cheddar yourself rather than using the preshredded stuff. I find that in soups like this, freshly shredded cheese melts much better, giving the soup a creamier and less grainy consistency.

¼ cup (½ stick) butter
¼ cup all-purpose flour
1 ½ cups whole milk
3 cups (7 ounces) shredded mild
   cheddar cheese

2 ¼ cups chicken broth
4 cups (7 ounces) chopped
   broccoli florets
¼ teaspoon salt
⅛ teaspoon white pepper

1. Melt the butter in a medium saucepan over medium heat. Stir in the flour and cook for 1 minute, stirring often.
2. Whisk the milk into the roux, then add the cheese and stir often until the cheese is melted.
3. Stir in the remaining ingredients and continue cooking over medium heat until the soup begins to bubble. Reduce the

heat to low and slowly simmer the soup, stirring often, for 60 minutes, or until the broccoli is tender.

• MAKES FOUR 1-CUP SERVINGS.

•   •   •   •

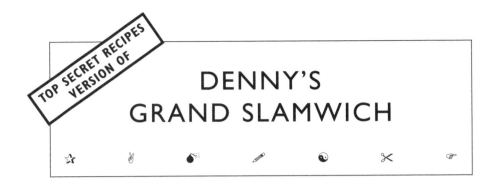

DENNY'S GRAND SLAMWICH

MENU DESCRIPTION: *"Two scrambled eggs, seasoned sausage, crispy bacon, shaved ham, mayonnaise, and American cheese grilled on potato bread with a maple spice spread."*

After a successful Super Bowl promotion when Denny's gave away over 2 million Grand Slam Breakfast platters in February 2009, the chain revealed its next generous publicity stunt the following April by offering a free serving of its new Grand Slamwich with every purchase of a Grand Slam Breakfast. This entire breakfast-in-a-sandwich features everything you'd want in a hearty day starter, including 2 eggs, bacon, sausage, ham, and cheese, all on potato bread that fills in for the hash browns one might find on a traditional breakfast platter. It seems that the taste buds of Denny's corporate chefs were influenced by the maple-flavored buns used on McDonald's McGriddle sandwich when they got the idea to brush the bread on each Grand Slamwich with a maple-infused buttery spread. Regardless of the inspiration, it's a recipe that works great, and now it's one that you can make at home anytime you like.

1 ½ tablespoons butter, softened
½ teaspoon maple syrup
2 slices potato bread
2 eggs

2 pieces cooked bacon, crumbled
2 links breakfast sausage,
    removed from casings and
    cooked

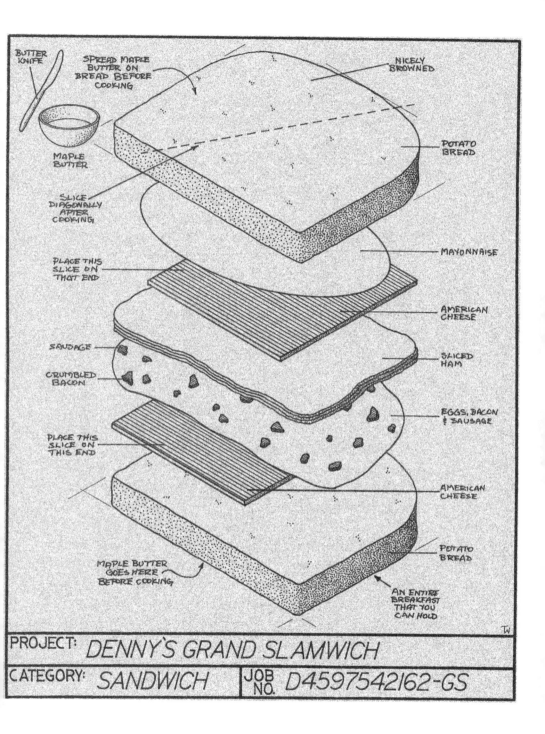

BUTTER
KNIFE

SPREAD MAPLE
BUTTER ON
BREAD BEFORE
COOKING

NICELY
BROWNED

MAPLE
BUTTER

POTATO
BREAD

SLICE
DIAGONALLY
AFTER
COOKING

MAYONNAISE

PLACE THIS
SLICE ON
THAT END

AMERICAN
CHEESE

SAUSAGE

SLICED
HAM

CRUMBLED
BACON

EGGS, BACON
& SAUSAGE

PLACE THIS
SLICE ON
THIS END

AMERICAN
CHEESE

POTATO
BREAD

MAPLE BUTTER
GOES HERE
BEFORE COOKING

AN ENTIRE
BREAKFAST
THAT YOU
CAN HOLD

PROJECT: *DENNY'S GRAND SLAMWICH*

CATEGORY: *SANDWICH* **JOB NO.** *D4597542162-GS*

pinch salt and pepper
2 teaspoons mayonnaise

2 slices American cheese
4 slices thinly sliced deli ham

1. Preheat a large sauté pan or griddle pan over medium heat. Also, preheat a small (6-inch) omelet pan over medium heat.
2. Combine 1 tablespoon of the softened butter with the maple syrup in a small bowl, and spread it on one side of each slice of bread.
3. Beat the eggs in a medium bowl. Drop the remaining ½ tablespoon butter into the hot omelet pan, and then pour in the beaten eggs. Add the cooked bacon and sausage to the eggs, along with a pinch of salt and pepper. When the eggs begin to solidify on the bottom, use a fork to swirl the eggs in the pan. Allow the eggs to cook a little more, then swirl again with a fork so that the uncooked egg on top runs onto the pan. When the eggs are fully cooked, fold the scrambled omelet in half in the pan, fold the ends in toward the middle, and turn off the heat. The egg should be folded into the approximate shape and size of the bread.
4. Place one slice of bread on the preheated sauté pan, buttered-side down. Spread the mayo on the side of the bread facing up, then place a slice of cheese on one end of the bread, followed by the ham. Use a spatula to slide the eggs on top of the ham, then position the final piece of cheese on the eggs at the end opposite from where you placed the first slice of cheese. Top off the sandwich with the second slice of bread, being sure that the buttered side is facing up.
5. After a minute or two, when the bread has browned on the bottom, flip the sandwich over and cook for another minute or so, until the bread on the bottom has turned a nice golden brown. Remove the sandwich to a plate, let it cool for 1 minute, then slice diagonally through the middle and serve.

*   SERVES 1.

• • • •

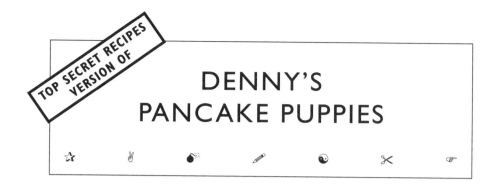

DENNY'S PANCAKE PUPPIES

The original version of these bite-size hush puppy–style breakfast snacks made with extra-thick pancake batter and coated with cinnamon sugar are so popular at the diner chain that chefs at Denny's went back to work in the development kitchen to come up with another version that has blueberries and white chocolate in it. Initially I thought I could use an instant blueberry pancake mix to clone the new flavor, such as the mix made by Krusteaz. But those "blueberries" in there aren't even real blueberries—they're blueberry-flavored bits. Blech! The best solution for the best clone is to add chopped-up dried blueberries to an extra-thick batter, along with some chopped-up white chocolate chips. I found that the thick batter was easy to portion out using a 1¾–inch cookie scoop that's been dipped in oil, but you could also use a tablespoon measure as long as you don't scoop up too much. Keep your batter balls about 1½ inches in diameter or they may not cook all the way through. Here are clones for the original Pancake Puppies as well as the new blueberry & white chocolate chip version.

ORIGINAL

6 to 10 cups vegetable shortening or oil, plus extra oil for coating the scoop

1 cup Aunt Jemima Original Pancake Mix

⅓ cup whole milk

1 egg

2 tablespoons granulated sugar

¾ teaspoon ground cinnamon

BLUEBERRY & WHITE CHOCOLATE CHIP

6 to 10 cups vegetable shortening or oil, plus extra oil for coating the scoop

1 cup Aunt Jemima Original Pancake Mix

⅓ cup whole milk

1 egg

½ cup dried blueberries, chopped

1 tablespoon white chocolate chips (or ¼ ounce from a bar), finely chopped

powdered sugar

ON THE SIDE

maple syrup

1. Preheat the shortening or oil in a deep fryer or a large saucepan to 325 degrees F.

2. Combine the pancake mix, milk, and egg in a medium bowl and beat with an electric mixer on high speed. If you are making the blueberry & white chocolate chip version, add the chopped dried blueberries and chopped white chocolate to the batter and mix just until blended in. Set the batter aside for 10 minutes.

3. When your oil is hot and the batter has rested, dip a cookie dough scoop (a 1½- to 1¾-inch scoop) or a tablespoon measure into a small bowl filled with oil before scooping up each ball of batter and carefully dropping it into the oil. Cook for 2½ to 3 minutes, or until the batter is dark brown. You can fry about 6 balls of batter at a time, but first test the cooking time using one ball so that you can make sure the dough is cooking all the way through. Remove the fried batter balls to paper towels to drain.

4. If you are making the original version, combine the cinnamon and sugar in a small bowl. Place all of the cooked batter balls into a large bowl, sprinkle with cinnamon-sugar, then toss until coated.

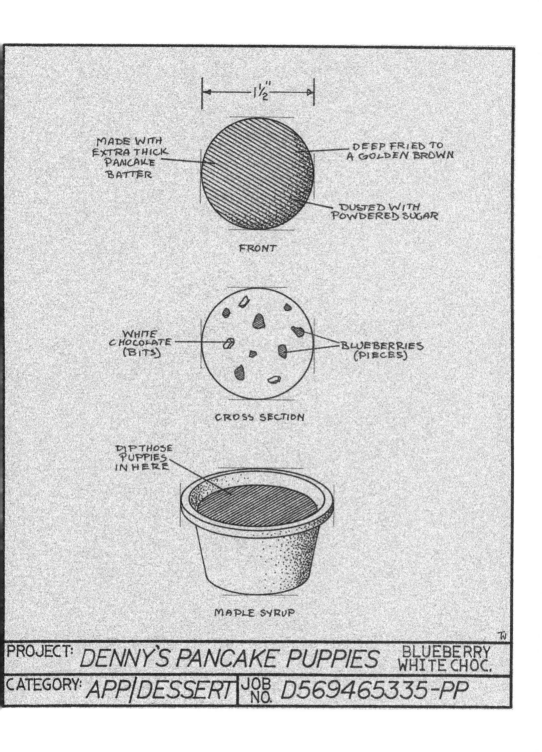

1½″

MADE WITH
EXTRA THICK
PANCAKE
BATTER

DEEP FRIED TO
A GOLDEN BROWN

DUSTED WITH
POWDERED SUGAR

FRONT

WHITE
CHOCOLATE
(BITS)

BLUEBERRIES
(PIECES)

CROSS SECTION

DIP THOSE
PUPPIES
IN HERE

MAPLE SYRUP

PROJECT: DENNY'S PANCAKE PUPPIES   BLUEBERRY WHITE CHOC.

CATEGORY: APP/DESSERT   JOB NO. D569465335-PP

5. If you are making the blueberry & white chocolate version, shake a little powdered sugar over the top.
6. Serve the Pancake Puppy clones with a small bowl of maple syrup for dipping.

- MAKES 16 TO 18 PUPPIES.

• • • •

FAMOUS DAVE'S CORN MUFFINS

Each entrée at this popular barbecue joint is served with one of these delicious, freshly baked corn muffins that I believe is the best I've ever had. They're cakey and perfectly sweet with just the right amount of cornmeal. Some of the secrets to making great corn muffins like these are found in restaurant founder Dave Anderson's cookbook. His recipe for corn muffins includes a small box of yellow cake mix and the addition of stone-ground cornmeal. However, I found that the cake mix made the muffins taste too much like yellow cake, so I opted for a completely scratch recipe with elements borrowed from my clone recipe for Duncan Hines Yellow Cake Mix. And since stone-ground cornmeal is difficult to find, we can run regular cornmeal through a food processor for 5 minutes to pulverize many of the granules to powder. After baking 120 muffins over several days and making a few other adjustments to the cookbook recipe, I can now share with you this original *Top Secret Recipe* that will produce a dozen corn muffins that taste identical to the restaurant version.

1 ¾ cups cornmeal
1 ¾ cups all-purpose flour
2 teaspoons baking powder
¾ teaspoon salt
¼ teaspoon baking soda
2 eggs
¾ cup granulated sugar

¼ cup shortening
½ teaspoon vanilla extract
¾ cup whole milk
¼ cup buttermilk
⅓ cup vegetable oil
3 tablespoons honey

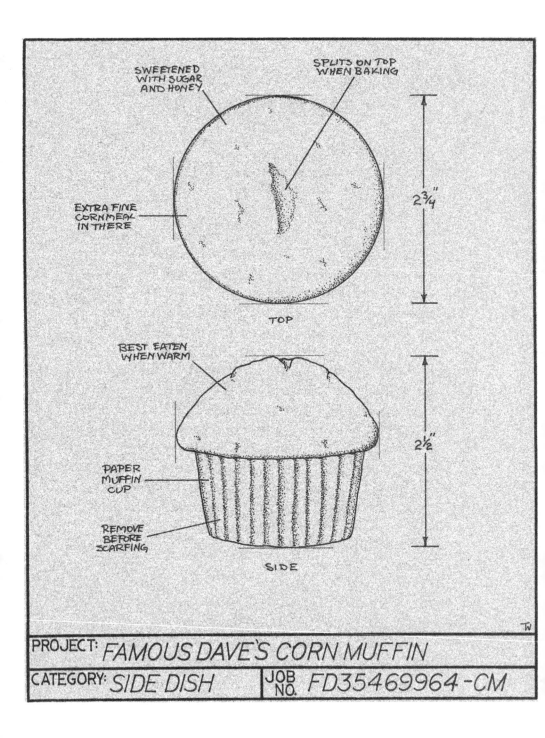

SWEETENED
WITH SUGAR
AND HONEY

SPLITS ON TOP
WHEN BAKING

EXTRA FINE
CORN MEAL
IN THERE

$2\frac{3}{4}$"

TOP

BEST EATEN
WHEN WARM

$2\frac{1}{2}$"

PAPER
MUFFIN
CUP

REMOVE
BEFORE
SCARFING

SIDE

PROJECT:	*FAMOUS DAVE'S CORN MUFFIN*	
CATEGORY: *SIDE DISH*	JOB NO.	*FD35469964-CM*

146

1. Preheat the oven to 400 degrees F.
2. Grind the cornmeal at high speed in a food processor for 5 minutes, or until some of it has become flour. Pour all of the ground cornmeal into a large bowl with the flour, baking powder, salt, and baking soda and mix.
3. Use an electric mixer on medium speed to cream together the eggs, sugar, shortening, and vanilla.
4. Pour the wet ingredients into the dry stuff. Add the remaining ingredients and mix well with an electric mixer on high speed until the batter is smooth.
5. Line a 12-cup muffin pan with paper muffin cups. Fill each muffin cup with batter, then bake the muffins for 20 to 25 minutes, or until browned.

• MAKES 1 DOZEN.

•　•　•　•

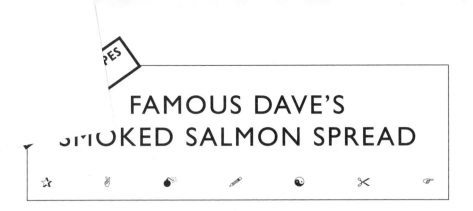

FAMOUS DAVE'S SMOKED SALMON SPREAD

MENU DESCRIPTION: *"Our own hickory-smoked salmon, cream cheese, capers, and chipotle peppers makes this a spread worth swimming upstream for. Served with fire-grilled flatbread."*

Famous Dave's is famous for making pork ribs so good you forget you're wearing an embarrassing bib. But before your face is smeared with BBQ sauce, you may be kicking off your meal with this top pick from the chain's appetizer menu. And if you're a fan of the version at the restaurant, you're going to love this clone. Start with 4 ounces of the best smoked salmon you can find—it should be very smoky if you want to duplicate the same taste of the original. If you can't find salmon that's smoky enough, don't worry. I found that adding a little hickory liquid smoke to the mix works perfectly to punch up the spread so that it tastes just like Dave's version. You'll end up with twice the amount of spread as the original, which makes this a great appetizer for a small party. You can even prepare the flatbread ahead of time, then wrap it up in foil and reheat it in an oven before serving.

8 ounces cream cheese, softened
4 ounces smoked salmon
4 teaspoons minced capers

¼ teaspoon ground chipotle chile
¼ teaspoon hickory liquid smoke (optional)

SEASONING BLEND
FOR FLATBREAD

1 tablespoon paprika
½ teaspoon salt
½ teaspoon ground black pepper
½ teaspoon garlic powder

¼ teaspoon cayenne pepper
¼ teaspoon dried thyme
¼ teaspoon dried oregano

2 tablespoons butter, melted
¼ teaspoon garlic powder
4 to 6 flatbreads (or naan)

1. Preheat a barbecue grill or a grill pan over high heat.
2. Combine the cream cheese with 3 ounces of the smoked salmon, the capers, and chipotle chile. If the salmon has only a mild smoky taste, stir in the liquid smoke. Spoon the salmon spread into a small bowl and crumble the remaining 1 ounce of salmon over the top of the spread.
3. Combine the ingredients for the seasoning blend in a small bowl.
4. Combine the melted butter with garlic powder in another small bowl.
5. Brush one side of each flatbread with a light coating of garlic butter. Place the bread, buttered-side down, onto the grill or grill pan. Cook for 30 seconds to 1 minute, or until grill marks form on the bread. Flip the bread over, sprinkle the seasoning on the buttered side, and continue to grill the bread for another 30 seconds or so.
6. After all the flatbread is grilled, slice each one like a pizza into 4 to 6 slices each, and arrange the slices around the salmon spread that has been placed onto the center of a serving platter.

• SERVES 8 AS AN APPETIZER.

• • • •

FAMOUS DAVE'S
WILBUR BEANS

MENU DESCRIPTION: *"Baked beans loaded with smoked pork, brisket, hot link sausage, and jalapeño peppers."*

David Anderson published a recipe for Wilbur Beans in his cookbook *Famous Dave's Backroads & Sidestreets*, but the recipe isn't a perfect clone for the beans that are now served as a side dish in each of the 170 restaurants across the country. For example, the recipe in the book (the same recipe is also found abundantly across the Internet) requires strip steak, which is an ingredient not found in the restaurant dish. The barbecue pork and brisket have been left out, and the book recipe requires that you use Famous Dave's barbecue sauce but is not specific about which variety of Dave's sauce to use, nor does it offer a nearly identical alternative if you can't find that particular brand. After several visits to my local Famous Dave's and chatting with the store manager, I gathered enough information to create this recipe with more accurate and specific ingredients, plus alternatives to help you whip up a spot-on clone for a dish that I not only love to eat, but that I felt destined to replicate once I saw the name.

6 slices bacon
8 ounces smoked pork sausage
   (2 links if using Farmer John's)
4 ounces cooked beef brisket
   (Tyson or Lloyd's works great)

4 ounces cooked pulled pork
   (Lloyd's or Jack Daniel's works
   great)
1 cup minced white onion
¼ cup minced red bell pepper

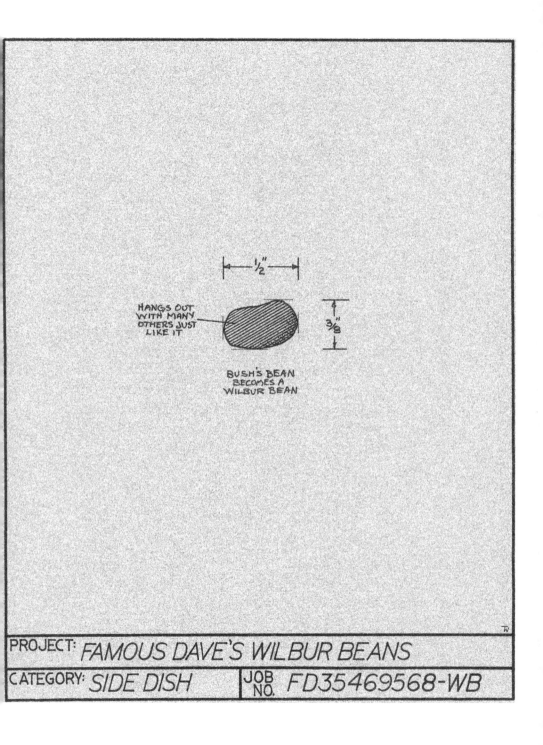

HANGS OUT
WITH MANY
OTHERS JUST
LIKE IT

BUSH'S BEAN
BECOMES A
WILBUR BEAN

PROJECT: *FAMOUS DAVE'S WILBUR BEANS*

CATEGORY: *SIDE DISH* JOB NO. *FD35469568-WB*

*2 tablespoons minced jalapeño
    pepper*
*two 28-ounce cans Bush's Best
    Original Baked Beans*

*1 ¾ cups Famous Dave's Rich &
    Sassy Barbecue Sauce or
Hunt's Original Barbecue Sauce*

1. Preheat the barbecue grill to high heat.
2. Cook the bacon and save the fat. You'll need 3 tablespoons of fat, so you can toss out any extra.
3. Grill the sausage until the surface is mostly charred, about 20 minutes. This will add smoky flavor to the beans. When the sausage is almost done (after about 15 minutes), toss the brisket on the grill and give it a little charring as well.
4. Preheat 3 tablespoons of bacon fat in a large saucepan over medium/low heat. Add the onion and peppers to the fat and sauté for 5 minutes, or until the onion begins to turn translucent.
5. Dice the bacon, sausage, brisket, and pulled pork and add it the pan. Crank the heat up to medium, and cook for 2 minutes, then add the beans (with the liquid) and barbecue sauce. Bring the mixture to a boil, stirring occasionally, then reduce heat and simmer uncovered for 15 minutes.

• MAKES 8 CUPS.

TIDBITS

In his book Dave claims that the flavor of the beans will improve if you store them for 8 to 10 hours in your refrigerator after cooking them, then reheat the beans before serving.

•   •   •   •

FLEMING'S PRIME STEAKHOUSE WICKED CAJUN BARBECUE SHRIMP

Before diving into a juicy steak, many diners at Fleming's Prime Steakhouse start their meal with this small shrimp dish that is the number one appetizer at the chain. Even though it says "barbecue" in the name, there is no grilling here. Barbecue refers to the Cajun-style flavors in the butter sauce that the shrimp are sautéed in. The shrimp are finished under a broiler for a couple minutes until the tails have browned, and the dish is served bubbling hot. The clone here requires 4 shrimp, just as in the original dish, but you can bump that up to 6 large shrimp and the recipe will still work great.

BARBECUE BUTTER

¼ cup (½ stick) butter, softened
½ teaspoon minced garlic
½ teaspoon Tabasco pepper sauce
¼ teaspoon paprika
⅛ teaspoon coarsely ground black pepper
⅛ teaspoon dried thyme
⅛ teaspoon cayenne pepper

SHRIMP SEASONING

¼ teaspoon paprika
⅛ teaspoon medium ground black pepper
⅛ teaspoon dried thyme
⅛ teaspoon cayenne pepper

¼ cup (½ stick) butter
1 teaspoon minced garlic
4 large shrimp, peeled, with tails left on

2 tablespoons white wine

GARNISH

slice of bread
lemon wedge

1. Preheat the broiler.
2. Make the barbecue butter by combining the ¼ cup softened butter with the other ingredients in a medium bowl and set aside.
3. Combine the shrimp seasoning ingredients in a small bowl. Sprinkle this blend over both sides of the shrimp in a medium bowl.
4. Melt ¼ cup butter in a medium saucepan over medium/low heat and add the 1 teaspoon garlic. When the butter begins to bubble, add the shrimp and sauté for 2 to 2½ minutes per side, or until done. Remove the shrimp from the pan, and add the barbecue butter. When the butter begins to bubble, add the white wine and cook the sauce for about a minute.
5. Pour the butter sauce into a shallow oven-safe dish or ramekin, and then place the shrimp in the sauce, with the tails pointing up. Broil the shrimp for 2 minutes, or until the tails begin to brown.
6. Add a slice of crusty bread to the sauce and serve with a lemon wedge on the side.

- SERVES 2 AS AN APPETIZER.

• • • •

FLEMING'S PRIME STEAKHOUSE CHIPOTLE CHEDDAR MACARONI & CHEESE

I've never met macaroni and cheese I didn't like—even the stuff that comes in a box with fluorescent orange cheese powder is pretty darn good. Some restaurants bring this common side dish to a higher level with creative variations on the basic formula. I've had mac and cheese made with a variety of cheese blends, and some that come drizzled with truffle oil. Good stuff. I've had the dish made with green pepper, and onion, and parsley, and bacon—it all tastes great to me. As for the macaroni and cheese served at Fleming's Prime Steakhouse, chipotle is the star. The smoky jalapeño flavor sets this macaroni and cheese apart from the others and makes this one of the top side dishes at the upscale steakhouse chain. For our clone we start with a cheese sauce made using smoked cheddar. There's some minced jalapeño and green onion in there, plus a little ground chipotle chile. A nice finishing touch comes from the bread crumb topping that's made with Japanese bread crumbs, called panko, and flavored with more ground chipotle. As for the pasta used at Fleming's, it's called cellentani, which looks like long corkscrews. I had no trouble tracking some down at a local Vons, but you can also use cavatappi pasta, which is shaped like shorter corkscrews. Or just go for the traditional elbow macaroni, which can be found pretty much anywhere, including your local mini-mart.

2 tablespoons butter

2 tablespoons finely minced seeded jalapeño pepper

1 tablespoon finely minced green onion (white and light green part only)

2 tablespoons all-purpose flour

1 cup whole milk

1 cup heavy cream

3 cups shredded smoked cheddar cheese

¼ heaping teaspoon salt

⅛ teaspoon ground chipotle chile

½ pound uncooked cellentani pasta

CHIPOTLE BREAD CRUMB TOPPING

¼ teaspoon ground chipotle chile

dash salt

1 tablespoon butter, melted

2 tablespoons panko (Japanese bread crumbs)

GARNISH

minced parsley

1. Melt the butter in a large saucepan over medium/low heat. Add the jalapeño and green onion and sweat (sauté slowly) for 5 minutes. You want the jalapeño and green onion to only soften, not turn brown.
2. Whisk in the flour and continue to cook over medium/low heat for another 5 minutes.
3. Add the milk, cream, cheese, salt, and ground chipotle. Continue cooking over medium/low heat for 10 to 15 minutes, stirring often, until thick.
4. While cheese sauce is thickening, cook the pasta in 6 to 8 cups of boiling water for 11 minutes, or until soft.
5. Make the bread crumb topping by stirring ¼ teaspoon ground chipotle and a dash of salt into the 1 tablespoon of melted butter. Measure 1 teaspoon of this mixture into the 2 tablespoons of panko, and stir until the panko is well coated.

You can toss out the rest of the chipotle butter, or use it for another dish.

6. Drain the pasta when it's done, then combine it with the cheese sauce. Spoon the macaroni and cheese into a serving dish, then top it with the chipotle bread crumb topping, and sprinkle with minced parsley.

• SERVES 4 TO 6 AS A SIDE DISH.

• • • •

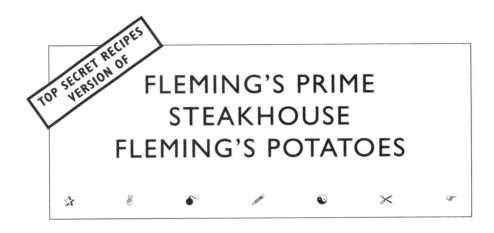

FLEMING'S PRIME STEAKHOUSE
FLEMING'S POTATOES

MENU DESCRIPTION: *"Our house specialty with cream, jalapeños, and cheddar cheese."*

These slightly spicy au gratin potatoes are cooked at a low heat several hours in advance of the dinner house's evening opening. When an order for the signature side comes into the kitchen a generous serving of the potatoes is portioned out, topped with grated sharp cheddar cheese, and baked again at a higher temperature until browned. The real trick here is to slice the potatoes very thin—$\frac{1}{16}$ of an inch to be exact—and the only way to do that is with a slicing contraption such as a mandoline. The rest of the prep involves making a basic béchamel sauce using cream, and then carefully layering the sauce and sliced potatoes in the baking dish. In the restaurant the potatoes are baked for 2 hours and then chilled, so this can be a great make-ahead dish for entertaining. Although you can also serve the potatoes immediately by topping them with cheese, cranking up the oven, and heading straight into the second baking step.

¼ cup (½ stick) butter
¼ cup minced jalapeño pepper
    (seeded and deribbed)
¼ cup chopped green onion
3 tablespoons all-purpose flour

2½ cups heavy cream
1½ teaspoons salt
¾ teaspoon ground black
    pepper

4 russet potatoes
2 cups shredded sharp cheddar
   cheese

GARNISH

1 teaspoon minced fresh parsley

1. Preheat the oven to 300 degrees F and butter a 9 x 9-inch baking dish.
2. Melt the butter in a medium saucepan over medium/low heat. Add the minced jalapeño and green onion and sauté for 3 minutes. Whisk in the flour and simmer for 2 minutes. Keep the heat low so the mixture doesn't brown.
3. Add the cream, salt, and pepper and simmer for 5 minutes, or until thick.
4. Peel the potatoes, and then use a slicer to slice the potatoes into $\frac{1}{16}$-inch-thick slices.
5. Arrange a single layer of sliced potatoes onto the bottom of the buttered baking dish. Drizzle a little cream sauce over the top of the potatoes and then lay another layer of potatoes on top. Repeat this layering process using all of the potato slices and cream sauce. After the last layer of potatoes is laid into the dish, spread the remaining sauce over the top layer of potatoes so that the potatoes are fully coated.
6. Bake the potatoes for 2 hours.
7. To complete the dish, remove the potatoes from the oven and crank it up to 425 degrees F. Cover the potatoes with the shredded cheddar cheese and bake for 12 to 14 minutes, or until the cheese is bubbling and the potatoes are browned around the edges. Sprinkle with minced parsley before serving.
8. If you are planning to serve the potatoes later, remove them from the oven before adding the shredded cheddar cheese and cool for 1½ to 2 hours. Spread the shredded cheddar

cheese over the top, cover, and chill. When you are ready to prepare the dish, preheat the oven to 450 degrees F. Bake the potatoes for 18 minutes, or until the cheese is melted and potatoes are browned around the edges. Sprinkle the minced parsley over the top and serve hot.

• SERVES 8.

•   •   •   •

FUDDRUCKERS
HAMBURGER SEASONING

For more than 25 years Fuddruckers has been serving up huge, cooked-when-ordered beef patties on freshly baked buns. The rest is up to you, as you decorate your hamburger creation with sliced tomato, onions, lettuce, pickles, peppers, relish, and whatever else is offered up at the toppings bar. Because of this garnishing freedom everyone's hamburger is unique, yet the company claims these are "The World's Greatest Hamburgers." So what makes them so good? Fuddruckers proudly boasts that it uses only 100 percent USDA Choice aged ground beef. But, what Fuddruckers won't tell you is exactly what secret ingredients make up the delicious burger seasoning used on each of those beef patties, and that's what really makes these hamburgers special. So, after analyzing a sample of the blend used in the shakers back by the griddle, I've come up with this simple clone that you can now mix up at home in a flash, and pour into an empty shaker bottle. Sprinkle it onto ⅓- or ½-pound ground beef patties as they grill, and snag yourself some fresh buns in the bakery section of your store. Add your choice of other fresh toppings, and in no time you'll have a great hamburger clone that tastes just like those served at the more than 260 Fuddruckers joints.

2 teaspoons paprika
1 ½ teaspoons ground black
   pepper

1 ¼ teaspoons salt
½ teaspoon dark brown sugar
¼ teaspoon garlic powder

¼ teaspoon onion powder
¼ teaspoon ground cayenne
　　pepper

Combine all ingredients in a small bowl. Sprinkle on hamburger patties before cooking.

• MAKES 2 TABLESPOONS.

• • • •

GORDON BIERSCH RASPBERRY ICED TEA COCKTAIL

This cocktail is a creative riff on the old-school Long Island Iced Tea, although it's not quite as potent. I think this version tastes way better than the classic drink, so if you're into Long Island Iced Teas, you should definitely try this variation.

½ ounce Stoli Razberi vodka
½ ounce Tanqueray gin
½ ounce Captain Morgan
    Original Spiced Rum

3 ounces sweet-and-sour mix
½ ounce Chambord Liqueur
    Royale
splash Sprite

GARNISH
lemon wedge

1. Fill a 12-ounce glass with ice.
2. Pour ingredients into glass in the order listed.
3. Add a lemon wedge to the rim of the glass and serve with a straw.

• MAKES 1 DRINK.

• • • •

GORDON BIERSCH CRAN BLUEBERI LEMONADE COCKTAIL

Here's a good way to use the blueberry-flavored vodka that's collecting dust in your liquor cabinet. All you need is a little sweet-and-sour mix, some cranberry juice, and 3 blueberries, and you'll have a perfect re-creation of the signature drink from this growing 40-unit brewery chain.

CRAN BLUEBERI LEMONADE
1 ½ ounces Stoli Blueberi vodka
2 ounces sweet-and-sour mix
2 ounces cranberry juice cocktail

GARNISH
3 blueberries

1. Fill a 12-ounce glass with ice.
2. Pour ingredients into glass in the order listed.
3. Drop 3 blueberries into the glass and serve with a straw.

MAKES 1 DRINK.

• • • •

GORDON BIERSCH
GARLIC FRIES

Don Gordon and Dean Biersch's vision of a fun place for delicious food and great beer became a reality in Palo Alto, California in 1988. Now there are more than 40 Gordon Biersch locations in 19 states serving custom-brewed beer and an extensive menu of entrées and appetizers including these easy-to-clone flavorful French fries. No need to make the fries from scratch. Just grab a bag of frozen French fries at your local supermarket, and bake or fry a pound of 'em following the directions on the bag. When the fries are done, simply toss them with the secret garlic mixture and serve.

1 pound frozen French fries
1 tablespoon light olive oil
2 teaspoons finely minced garlic
2 teaspoons finely minced parsley

¼ teaspoon coarse grind black
    pepper
⅛ teaspoon salt

1. Bake or fry French fries until crispy following directions on the package.
2. As the fries are cooking, combine remaining ingredients in a small bowl.
3. Pour cooked French fries into a large bowl and spoon garlic

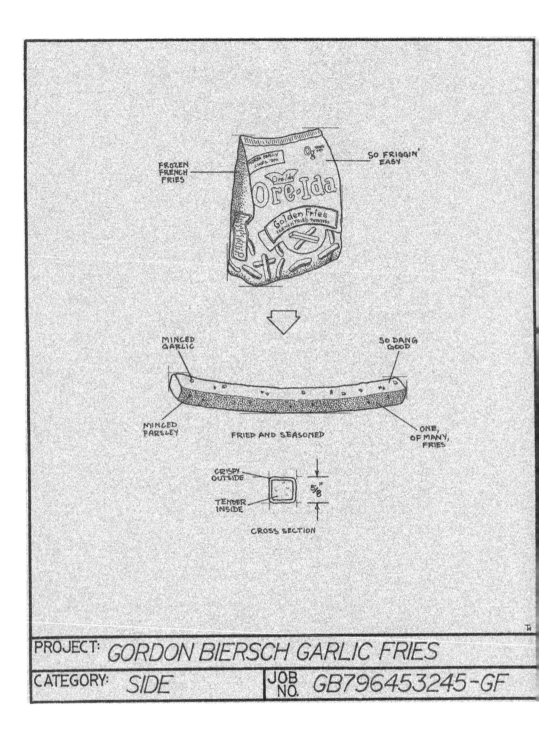

FROZEN FRENCH FRIES

SO FRIGGIN' EASY

MINCED GARLIC

SO DANG GOOD

MINCED PARSLEY

FRIED AND SEASONED

ONE, OF MANY, FRIES

CRISPY OUTSIDE

5/8"

TENDER INSIDE

CROSS SECTION

PROJECT: GORDON BIERSCH GARLIC FRIES

CATEGORY: SIDE

JOB NO. GB796453245-GF

blend over them. Toss well until French fries are coated with garlic, then serve.

- MAKES 2 TO 4 APPETIZER SERVINGS.

• • • •

GORDON BIERSCH
WARM APPLE
BREAD PUDDING

MENU DESCRIPTION: *"With vanilla ice cream and sticky bun caramel sauce."*

Lately I've been searching for the restaurant chain with the best bread pudding recipe, and I think I've found it here at Gordon Biersch. This small, yet growing, microbrewery chain serves great beer, awesome pizza, and a bread pudding that is downright amazing. It could be described as what would materialize out the other side if Jeff Goldblum threw an apple pie, some bread pudding, and a cinnamon roll into his teleportation machine from *The Fly*. The sautéed apples laid into the middle of the bread pudding make other bread puddings I eat now seem like they're missing something. And the homemade caramel sauce, with just a little brown sugar thrown into our clone version, adds a sticky bun flavor you'll have dreams about. No matter how big your dinner feast was, everyone will still somehow find room for this treat. The original at the restaurant is baked in a deep pan, and the pudding is sliced and served on its side, so you'll want to use the biggest loaf pan you can find. I used a 3-inch-deep 10 x 5-inch loaf pan, and it was full. If your pan is smaller, you may have to leave a bit out. The pudding will swell up out of the pan as it cooks, but it will shrink back down as it cools. Fun to watch. You may want to make this the day before so that the bread pudding can set up in the fridge. When you are ready to serve, simply nuke a serving for 1 minute until

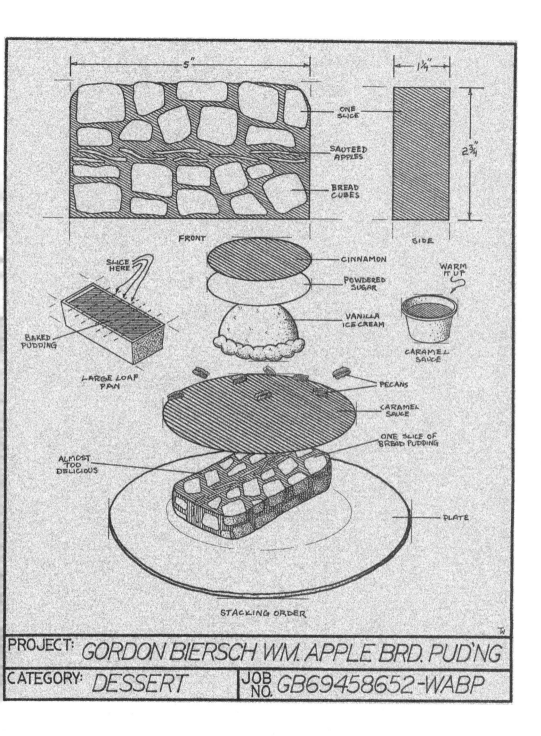

5"

ONE SLICE

SAUTEED APPLES

BREAD CUBES

1¼"

2¾"

FRONT

SIDE

SLICE HERE

BAKED PUDDING

LARGE LOAF PAN

CINNAMON

POWDERED SUGAR

VANILLA ICE CREAM

WARM IT UP

CARAMEL SAUCE

PECANS

CARAMEL SAUCE

ONE SLICE OF BREAD PUDDING

ALMOST TOO DELICIOUS

PLATE

STACKING ORDER

PROJECT: GORDON BIERSCH WM. APPLE BRD. PUD'NG

CATEGORY: DESSERT

JOB NO. GB69458652-WABP

warm, then add sauce and ice cream and a handful of pecans. It appears the restaurant chain uses egg bread in the pudding, but "Texas toast" (thick-sliced white bread) may be easier to find, and it works just as well.

3 whole eggs
1 egg yolk
1 cup granulated sugar
1 ¾ cups whole milk
2 cups heavy cream

2 teaspoons ground cinnamon
1 teaspoon ground nutmeg
¼ teaspoon salt
12 ounces (½ loaf) Texas toast,
    chopped into 1-inch squares

SAUTÉED APPLES

2 tablespoons salted butter
2 Granny Smith apples, peeled
    and sliced thin

2 tablespoons light brown sugar
½ teaspoon ground cinnamon

CARAMEL SAUCE

1 ½ cups granulated sugar
½ cup light brown sugar
1 cup water

½ cup heavy cream, warmed
3 tablespoons salted butter
¼ teaspoon salt

ON TOP

2 cups shelled whole pecans
ground cinnamon

powdered sugar
6 to 8 scoops vanilla ice cream

1. Preheat oven to 350 degrees F.
2. Combine eggs, egg yolk, and 1 cup granulated sugar in a large bowl with electric mixer until the sugar is mostly dissolved. Mix in milk, 2 cups cream, 2 teaspoons cinnamon, nutmeg, and ¼ teaspoon salt. Pour mixture over cubed bread in another

large bowl and gently fold the bread over with your hands until all pieces are moistened. Let bread soak for 30 minutes.

3. As the bread soaks, melt 2 tablespoons butter in a sauté pan. Add the sliced apples, 2 tablespoons brown sugar, and ½ teaspoon cinnamon. Sauté the apples, stirring often, for 10 minutes or until they are beginning to soften. Turn off the heat and let the apples cool until the bread is finished soaking.

4. Butter the inside of a 10 x 5 x 3-inch loaf pan. Use your hands to load half of the soaked bread into the bottom of the pan. Arrange the apple slices in an even layer over the bread. Pour the rest of the pudding mixture into the pan and set it in the oven to bake for 60 minutes or until the top is beginning to brown. When the pudding is finished baking, let it cool for an hour, then cover and chill it. You can also serve it warm at this time, but I found that the pudding sets up better when chilled.

5. As the pudding bakes you can make your caramel sauce by combining 1½ cups granulated sugar, ½ cup brown sugar, and 1 cup water in a medium saucepan over medium heat. When the mixture begins to boil, set your timer to 10 minutes. It will take about this long for the mixture to hit between 230 and 240 degrees F (between the thread and soft ball stage). Use a candy thermometer for this, if you've got one. You can also dribble some of the syrup into cold water, and if it begins to make threads, you're there. When your mixture hits the right temperature, turn off the heat and add ½ cup of warmed heavy cream, 3 tablespoons butter, and ¼ teaspoon salt. When the sauce cools for about 10 minutes, you can use it, or you can chill it and reheat it in the microwave or in a saucepan for serving later.

6. To serve the dessert, slice the bread pudding into 6 to 8 portions, lay each chilled slice on its side on a serving plate, and microwave each one for 45 to 60 seconds, until warm. Spoon hot caramel sauce over and around the bread pudding. Sprinkle a handful of pecans around the pudding onto the caramel, and then sprinkle a dusting of powdered sugar and cinnamon

(tapped through a strainer) around the edge of the plate. Finish off each dessert with a scoop of vanilla ice cream placed onto the center of the bread pudding.

- MAKES 6 TO 8 SERVINGS.

• • • •

HARD ROCK CAFE
TUPELO STYLE CHICKEN

The world's most famous theme restaurant pays tribute to the birthplace of Elvis Presley with this chicken finger appetizer dish, and two great mustard-based dipping sauces. I was a fan of the original version of this appetizer served around ten years ago before they changed the name to Tupelo Chicken Tenders and replaced the apricot dipping sauce with hickory barbecue sauce. With this recipe you can now re-create the classic original version.

6 to 10 cups vegetable oil

HONEY MUSTARD
DIPPING SAUCE

¼ cup mayonnaise
1 ½ teaspoons prepared mustard

2 teaspoons honey
pinch paprika

APRICOT DIPPING SAUCE

2 tablespoons Grey Poupon Dijon mustard

1 tablespoon apricot preserves
2 tablespoons honey

BREADING

1 cup corn flake crumbs	¼ teaspoon onion powder
2 teaspoons crushed red pepper flakes	¼ teaspoon garlic powder
	1 egg
1 ¼ teaspoons cayenne pepper	1 cup milk
1 teaspoon ground cumin	1 cup all-purpose flour
1 teaspoon salt	12 chicken breast tenderloins
½ teaspoon paprika	

1. Heat the oil in a deep fryer to 350 degrees F.
2. Make the honey mustard dipping sauce by combining the ingredients in a medium bowl. Cover and refrigerate. Make the apricot dipping sauce by combing those ingredients in a medium bowl. Cover and refrigerate this sauce as well until your chicken is ready.
3. Prepare the breading by combining the corn flake crumbs, crushed red pepper flakes, cayenne pepper, cumin, salt, paprika, onion powder, and garlic powder in a medium bowl.
4. Beat the egg in a medium bowl, add the milk, and stir.
5. Pour the flour into another medium bowl.
6. When the oil is hot, bread your chicken by first coating each tenderloin with flour. Dip the chicken into the egg-milk mixture and then back into the flour. Dip each chicken tenderloin back in the egg-milk mixture and then into the corn flake crumb mixture. Be sure to coat each chicken piece thoroughly with the corn flake crumbs.
7. Fry 4 to 6 coated chicken tenderloins at a time in the oil for 4 to 5 minutes, or until the chicken is golden brown. Drain and serve the chicken with the dipping sauces on the side.

• SERVES 4 TO 6 AS AN APPETIZER.

• • • •

HARD ROCK CAFE
TWISTED MAC & CHEESE

MENU DESCRIPTION: *"Twisted cavatappi pasta, tossed in a lightly spiced 3-cheese sauce with roasted red peppers, and topped with Parmesan parsley bread crumbs."*

The rock-and-roll theme chain peps up old-school macaroni and cheese with roasted red bell pepper, a bread crumb topping, and a delicious sauce made from 3 cheeses. For a home clone of this hip appetizer, I found that it's best to shred your own cheddar and Monterey Jack cheeses, since the preshredded type sold in bags doesn't melt well and you'll likely end up with grainy sauce. Grainy is not good in a sauce. You can use bottled roasted red bell pepper for convenience, or you can roast your own pepper with the tips provided in Tidbits below. And don't worry about tracking down the hard-to-find cavatappi pasta (twisted tubes). Any pasta shape will do here, and you may just want to go with the universal mac and cheese standard: elbow macaroni.

2 cups uncooked cavatappi pasta
    or elbow macaroni
⅓ cup whole milk
4 ounces Velveeta cheese, diced
½ cup shredded cheddar cheese
½ cup shredded Monterey Jack
    cheese

⅛ teaspoon ground cayenne
    pepper
⅛ teaspoon ground black pepper
¼ cup diced roasted red bell
    pepper
2 teaspoons Italian-style seasoned
    bread crumbs

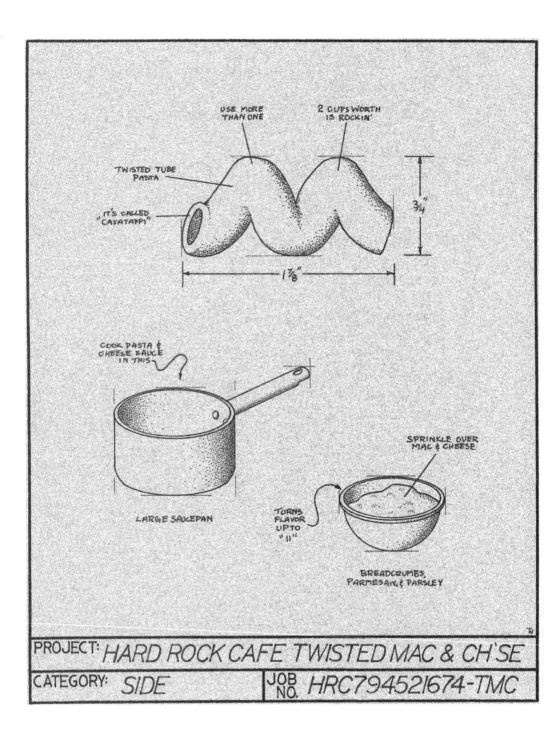

USE MORE THAN ONE

2 CUPS WORTH IS ROCKIN'

TWISTED TUBE PASTA

IT'S CALLED "CAVATAPPI"

3/4"

1 7/8"

COOK PASTA & CHEESE SAUCE IN THIS

LARGE SAUCEPAN

SPRINKLE OVER MAC & CHEESE

TURNS FLAVOR UP TO "11"

BREADCRUMBS, PARMESAN, & PARSLEY

PROJECT: HARD ROCK CAFE TWISTED MAC & CH'SE

CATEGORY: SIDE

JOB NO. HRC794521674-TMC

2 teaspoons grated Parmesan
    cheese
¼ teaspoon finely minced parsley

1. Use a large saucepan to cook pasta following the directions on the package, then drain.
2. Combine milk, Velveeta, cheddar cheese, Jack cheese, cayenne pepper, and black pepper in the same saucepan, and stir over low heat for about 10 minutes until cheese is melted and sauce is smooth. Add pasta and roasted pepper to the pan, and then toss to coat the pasta.
3. Combine the bread crumbs, Parmesan, and parsley in a small bowl.
4. Pour pasta into a serving bowl, and then sprinkle Parmesan breadcrumbs over the top.

• Makes 4 servings.

TIDBITS

You can roast your own red bell pepper by setting it directly over the flame of a gas stove set to medium heat. Turn pepper as skin blisters and chars black. Submerse pepper in ice water, or place the pepper in a bowl and cover it. After a few minutes remove the skin. You can also roast the pepper over a grill set to high heat, or you can slice the pepper in half and roast it under your broiler for 6 to 7 minutes. After you have removed the skin, dice the pepper and measure ¼ cup. Save the rest of the pepper for another dish, such as pizza, pasta, or as a salad topping.

• • • •

HOOTERS
FRIED PICKLES

MENU DESCRIPTION: *"Homemade, fried golden brown and dill-icious. Cut into thin slices and served with dipping sauce."*

Fried Oreos, fried Twinkies, fried bull testicles, fried crickets—just about anything can be battered and fried, but that doesn't always mean it'll taste good. I've tasted many unexpectedly delicious foods out of a fryer, and these are among the tastier surprises. The combination of sour pickles, crunchy breading, and creamy dipping sauce was delicious. It's no wonder these are such a popular pick at the chain known more for its chicken wings, orange short shorts, and belly shirts. After a little sleuthing I discovered that Hooters uses Mrs. Klein's crinkle-cut pickles, but that particular brand can be hard to find. I did a taste test of all popular brands and found that the most similar-tasting pickle slices happen to be one of the most popular brands on the market: Heinz. Find the hamburger dill chips and be sure to blot the pickle slices dry before breading them. The breading recipe here should be enough to coat all the pickle slices in a 16-ounce jar (50 to 55 slices). As for the dipping sauce? That's just a simple matter of stirring a little cayenne pepper into some Hidden Valley Ranch dressing. Done and done.

DIPPING SAUCE
½ cup Hidden Valley Ranch salad
    dressing
⅛ teaspoon cayenne pepper

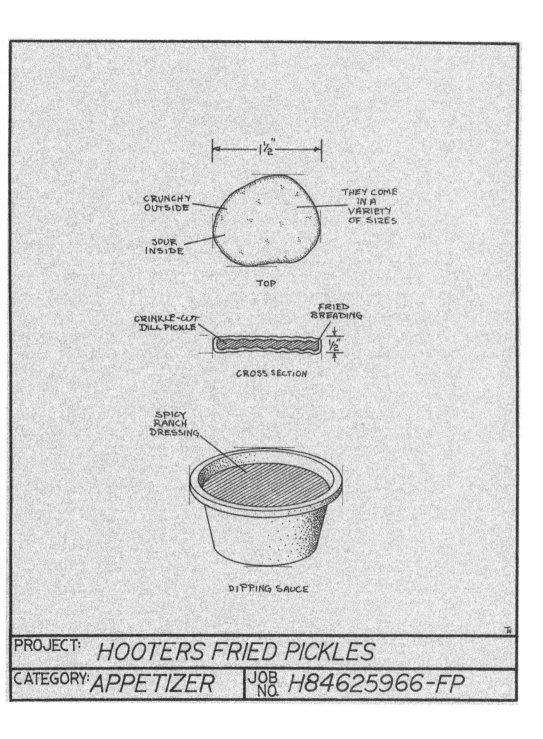

1½"

CRUNCHY
OUTSIDE

THEY COME
IN A
VARIETY
OF SIZES

SOUR
INSIDE

TOP

CRINKLE-CUT
DILL PICKLE

FRIED
BREADING

½"

CROSS SECTION

SPICY
RANCH
DRESSING

DIPPING SAUCE

PROJECT: *HOOTERS FRIED PICKLES*

CATEGORY: *APPETIZER*   JOB NO. *H84625966-FP*

6 to 10 cups vegetable oil for
  frying
one 16-ounce jar Heinz
  hamburger dill chips
1 egg, beaten
¼ cup milk

½ cup all-purpose flour
½ teaspoon salt
½ teaspoon garlic powder
¼ teaspoon paprika
pinch cayenne pepper

1. Make the dipping sauce by combining the ranch dressing and cayenne pepper in a small bowl.
2. Heat the oil to 350 degrees F in a deep fryer or saucepan with a thermometer attached to it.
3. Remove all of the pickle slices from the jar and lay them out flat on paper towels. Use more paper towels to blot the pickles slices until they are dry.
4. Combine the beaten egg and milk in a small bowl.
5. Combine the flour, salt, garlic powder, paprika, and cayenne pepper in a shallow bowl or in a pie pan.
6. Bread each of the pickles slices by first coating with the dry blend, then the egg and milk, then back into the dry stuff. Arrange all of the breaded pickle slices on a baking sheet until they are all breaded.
7. Fry the pickles in the hot oil in batches of 10 to 15 at time for 2 minutes, or until golden brown. Serve with the dipping sauce on the side.

- SERVES 6 TO 8 AS AN APPETIZER.

• • • •

HOUSTON'S
HOUSE VINAIGRETTE

This delicious house vinaigrette is a Houston's favorite, and a home carbon copy is just minutes away. All you'll need are a few basic ingredients, plus tarragon-infused white wine vinegar. If you have trouble tracking down the tarragon vinegar, plain white wine vinegar will work just fine. Use a measuring cup with a spout or a squirt bottle to slowly drizzle the oil into the other ingredients while mixing. This technique will create a thick emulsion that won't separate as your dressing chills out in the fridge.

¼ cup tarragon vinegar or white
    wine vinegar
4 teaspoons granulated sugar
1 tablespoon Dijon mustard
1 teaspoon minced garlic

¼ teaspoon salt
¼ teaspoon ground black pepper
¼ teaspoon Italian herb
    seasoning blend
¾ cup extra virgin olive oil

1. Using an electric mixer on medium speed, combine all ingredients except the oil in a large bowl for approximately 1 minute or until the sugar and salt dissolve.
2. Slowly drizzle in the oil while mixing. Mix for another minute or until the vinaigrette thickens. Cover and chill.

• MAKES 1 CUP.

• • • •

HOUSTON'S COUSCOUS

This cold couscous salad side dish served at this 96-unit chain is unique and seriously delicious. The secret is cooking the couscous in orange juice so that it has a slight sweetness to it. Then you toss in some golden raisins, almonds, radishes, tomatoes, mint, green onion, and parsley, and the flavor party is on. This is a great warm weather side for pool parties and picnics that can be made a day ahead. It's easy. It's tasty. It's finally cloned.

1 cup orange juice
⅓ cup water
1 cup uncooked couscous
¼ teaspoon salt
½ cup sliced radishes
½ cup whole fresh mint leaves
¾ cup golden raisins

6 cherry tomatoes, quartered
¼ cup chopped green onion
⅓ cup raw almonds
2 tablespoons minced fresh
    parsley
⅓ cup extra virgin olive oil

1. Bring the orange juice and water to a boil in a medium saucepan. Add the couscous, cover, and remove from the heat. Keep the couscous covered for 4 minutes.
2. Pour the hot couscous into a large bowl and fluff it with a fork, breaking up any chunks.

3. Add the remaining ingredients except the oil and toss well. Cover and chill for a couple hours, or until cold.
4. Stir in the oil just before serving.

• SERVES 4.

•   •   •   •

IHOP
BANANA MACADAMIA
NUT PANCAKES

MENU DESCRIPTION: *"Two sweet golden pancakes, grilled with fresh sliced banana, drizzled with a rum-butter flavored glaze, and crowned with creamy whipped topping and toasted macadamia nuts."*

This is the best of three varieties of pancakes that IHOP introduced as "Hawaiian Pancakes" in the summer of 2009. The country's largest flapjack house flavors the new pancakes with imitation banana flavoring and a yellow food coloring, since real mashed bananas will eventually oxidize and turn a prepared batter brown. Since we are going to use this batter right away, there's no worry about the batter changing color, so I've included lots of real mashed banana in this recipe. I'm sure you'll agree that real bananas taste much better than banana flavoring. A clone for the delicious rum-butter glaze is also included here, but these pancakes are also great when drizzled with plain old maple syrup if that's what you want to use.

RUM-BUTTER GLAZE

½ cup granulated sugar
¼ cup dark brown sugar
½ cup light corn syrup
⅓ cup water

1 teaspoon butter flavoring
¼ teaspoon imitation rum
    flavoring

PANCAKES

1 ½ cups all-purpose flour
⅓ cup granulated sugar
¾ teaspoon baking soda
¼ teaspoon salt
1 egg
1 ½ cups buttermilk
1 cup mashed banana
    (approximately 2 ripe
    bananas)

¼ cup (½ stick) butter, melted
24 to 27 banana slices (from 1 to
    1 ½ bananas)
6 tablespoons chopped
    macadamia nuts
nonstick spray

GARNISH

6 tablespoons chopped macadamia nuts
canned whipped cream

1. Make the rum-butter glaze by combining the sugars, corn syrup, and water in a small saucepan over medium heat. Stir often until the sugars dissolve and the mixture begins to boil. Continue simmering for 1 minute, then turn off the heat, add the flavorings, and set aside.
2. Combine the flour, sugar, baking soda, and salt in a medium bowl.
3. In a separate large bowl, beat the egg with an electric mixer. Mix in the buttermilk, mashed banana, and butter.
4. Combine the dry ingredients with the wet mixture and mix well until the batter is smooth and no lumps appear.
5. Preheat a griddle or large skillet over medium heat. Spray the cooking surface with a coating of nonstick spray and measure ½ cup portions of batter onto hot griddle. Press three banana slices onto each pancake and then sprinkle on 2 teaspoons of chopped macadamia nuts. Cook the pancakes for 2 minutes, or until the first side is golden brown, then flip and cook for another 1 ½ to 2 minutes, or until done. Serve a

stack of two pancakes, drizzled with rum-butter glaze, and then sprinkle with an additional tablespoon of chopped macadamia nuts, and crown with a swirl of whipped cream.

- SERVES 4 (8 TO 9 PANCAKES).

• • • •

IHOP
CORN CAKE PANCAKES

MENU DESCRIPTION: *"These fluffy, moist, and savory pancakes are made with just the right amount of cornmeal."*

If you like the taste of fresh cornbread, you will definitely dig this new twist on pancakes brought to us from America's largest flapjack factory. Cornmeal plus extra helpings of sugar and butter are added to delicious buttermilk pancake batter for a clone that will turn on the smiles. This new breakfast specialty is easy to make, crazy delicious, and any leftovers will freeze well for several months (check out the Tidbits below).

1 ½ cups all-purpose flour
⅓ cup cornmeal
1 teaspoon baking powder
½ teaspoon baking soda
½ teaspoon salt
2 eggs

⅔ cup granulated sugar
1 cup whole milk
¾ cup buttermilk
⅓ cup salted butter, melted
nonstick spray

ON THE SIDE
butter
maple syrup

1. Combine flour, cornmeal, baking powder, baking soda, and salt in a medium bowl.
2. In another medium bowl, blend together the eggs and sugar

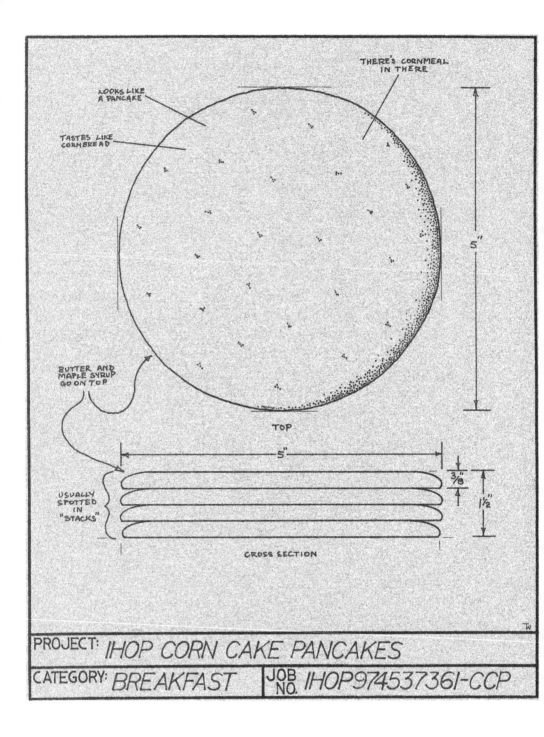

THERE'S CORNMEAL
IN THERE

LOOKS LIKE
A PANCAKE

TASTES LIKE
CORNBREAD

5"

BUTTER AND
MAPLE SYRUP
GO ON TOP

TOP

5"

3/8"

1½"

USUALLY
SPOTTED
IN
"STACKS"

CROSS SECTION

PROJECT: *IHOP CORN CAKE PANCAKES*

CATEGORY: *BREAKFAST*   JOB NO. *IHOP974537361-CCP*

with an electric mixer on medium speed for 30 seconds. Add milk, buttermilk, and melted butter and mix well.

3. Mix the dry ingredients into the wet ingredients with your mixer until smooth. Let the batter sit for 10 minutes.
4. Preheat a large skillet or griddle to medium/low heat.
5. Spray the skillet or griddle with nonstick spray. Spoon $\frac{1}{4}$-cup portions of the batter onto the griddle and cook for 2 to 3 minutes per side, until brown. Serve pancakes hot with butter and maple syrup on the side.

• MAKES 16 TO 18 PANCAKES.

TIDBITS

You can freeze leftover pancakes in stacks of 2 or 3 in sandwich-size zip-top bags. When you're ready to reheat, simply take the frozen stack of pancakes out of the bag, put them on a plate, and microwave for 1 minute on high, or until hot.

• • • •

IHOP
FUNNEL CAKES

International House of Pancake's Funnel Cake Carnival promotion brought the famous fairground food to the masses for a limited time. As you would expect from the name, the first thing you'll need to make proper funnel cakes is, of course, a funnel. The funnel is used to swirl batter into hot oil where it will fry to a happy golden brown in about a minute on each side. Find a funnel with an opening that is at least ½-inch wide so that your funnel cakes will have approximately the same thickness as the IHOP version. For the frying, shortening works the best since that's what IHOP uses, but you can also use vegetable or canola oil. I used a trans fat–free shortening from Smart Balance and it worked great. Load your oil or shortening into a small saucepan with about a 6-inch diameter. This way the batter won't spread out when you funnel it into the oil, and you'll get funnel cakes that are all about the same size. When it's time to serve the dish, arrange 2 funnel cakes on a plate, dust them with powdered sugar, top 'em off with fruit and whipped cream, and enjoy fairground-style funnel cakes without any scary carnies watching you eat.

3 eggs
⅔ cup granulated sugar
1 ¼ cups whole milk
1 teaspoon vanilla extract
½ teaspoon salt

2 cups all-purpose flour
½ teaspoon baking powder
2 to 3 cups vegetable shortening
   or oil

TOPPING

powdered sugar

whipped cream

3½ cups strawberry, blueberry, or
   cinnamon-apple pie filling

1. Combine eggs and sugar with an electric mixer on medium speed. Add milk, vanilla, and salt and mix until the sugar is dissolved.
2. Sift together flour and baking powder and mix into the wet ingredients with an electric mixer for 1 minute. Cover and chill for 1 hour.
3. Heat shortening in a small saucepan over medium heat to 350 degrees F. Spray the funnel with a little nonstick spray and then pour ¼ cup batter into it with your finger over the hole. Tap on the side of the funnel to remove any bubbles from the batter. When the shortening is hot take your finger off the hole and swirl the batter into the oil. Be sure to get the funnel very close to the oil, and keep the funnel moving at a medium speed. If you move the funnel too fast, the dough will come out too thin, and if you move too slowly you'll get big fried clumps of dough. Cook each funnel cake for about 1 minute or until golden brown, then flip it over and cook for 1 minute more. Remove each funnel cake to paper towels or a rack, and cover all of them with foil to keep them warm until you've used up all of the batter. Serve 2 funnel cakes topped with a dusting of powdered sugar, approximately ½ cup of the pie filling of your choice, and whipped cream on top.

• MAKES 14 CAKES, 7 SERVINGS.

TIDBITS

It helps to have a thermometer in the shortening to monitor the temperature. After each funnel cake, the temperature of your shortening may drop as much as 40 degrees F. You may have to wait a few minutes between funnel cakes to get the temperature back up to 350 degrees F. Consider using 2 small saucepans for the frying to speed things up when hungry mouths are drooling nearby.

• • • •

IHOP
SHORTCAKE PANCAKES

MENU DESCRIPTION: *"Biscuit-flavored pancakes layered with your favorite fruit compote and crowned with creamy whipped topping. Choose from blueberry, strawberry, or country apple."*

Since these fruit-covered pancakes are made with the same ingredients that go into biscuits, you won't need any eggs. The batter is like runny biscuit dough, and, when cooked on a hot griddle or in a skillet, you get dense pancakes that have the same flavor as buttermilk biscuits. Way! The fruit compote is just canned pie filling if you are making the blueberry or apple versions. Each can supplies enough fruit for the 3 servings made with this recipe. If it's strawberries you want on top of your pancakes, just thaw out a package of frozen whole or sliced strawberries in syrup. You can also use fresh sliced strawberries that have been mixed in the strawberry glaze that is often found in your market's produce section, usually over by the strawberries.

1 1/3 cups all-purpose flour
1 tablespoon granulated sugar
1/2 teaspoon baking powder
1/2 teaspoon baking soda

1/4 teaspoon salt
1 1/2 cups buttermilk
1/3 cup salted butter, melted

TOPPINGS
(CHOOSE ONE)

one 21-ounce can blueberry pie
    filling

one 21-ounce can apple pie filling
one 16-ounce package frozen
    strawberries in syrup, thawed

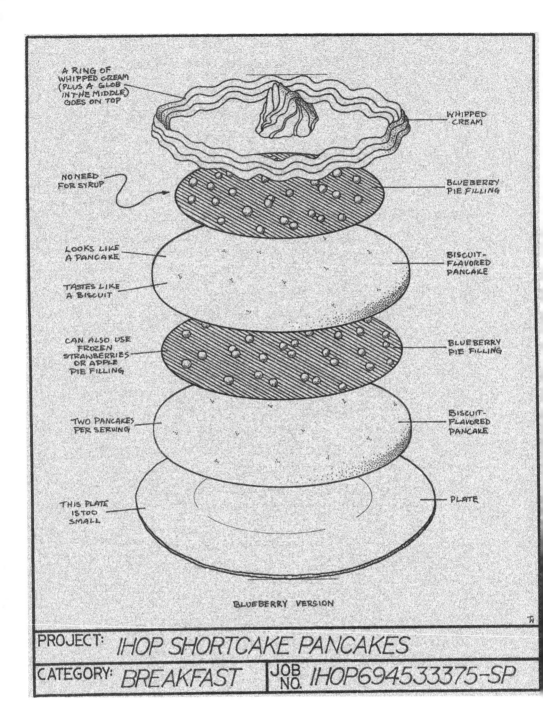

A RING OF
WHIPPED CREAM
(PLUS A GLOB
IN THE MIDDLE)
GOES ON TOP

WHIPPED
CREAM

NO NEED
FOR SYRUP

BLUEBERRY
PIE FILLING

LOOKS LIKE
A PANCAKE

BISCUIT-
FLAVORED
PANCAKE

TASTES LIKE
A BISCUIT

CAN ALSO USE
FROZEN
STRAWBERRIES
OR APPLE
PIE FILLING

BLUEBERRY
PIE FILLING

TWO PANCAKES
PER SERVING

BISCUIT-
FLAVORED
PANCAKE

THIS PLATE
IS TOO
SMALL

PLATE

BLUEBERRY VERSION

PROJECT:	*IHOP SHORTCAKE PANCAKES*	
CATEGORY: *BREAKFAST*	JOB NO.	*IHOP694533375-SP*

194

GARNISH

canned whipped cream

1. Combine flour, sugar, baking powder, baking soda, and salt in a large bowl.
2. Add buttermilk and melted butter to the dry ingredients and mix with an electric mixer for about 30 seconds, or until smooth. Let the batter sit for 3 to 4 minutes before you use it.
3. While the batter sits, heat a griddle to medium/low. Wipe the griddle with a little vegetable oil or use nonstick spray. When the batter has rested, give it a quick stir, then measure ½-cup portions onto the hot griddle. Cook each pancake for 2 to 3 minutes per side, until golden brown.
4. Assemble each serving by spooning about ⅓ cup of the fruit of your choice over the top of one pancake. Place another pancake on top of that one and add another ⅓ cup of fruit. Apply a ring of whipped cream around the edge of the top layer of fruit, and then add a dollop to the center.

• MAKES 3 SERVINGS, 2 PANCAKES EACH.

•　•　•　•

JOE'S CRAB SHACK
CRAB NACHOS

MENU DESCRIPTION: *"Joe's has crossed the border with our take on nachos. Tortilla chips piled high and topped with loads of crab dip, pico de gallo, cheese, and black bean corn relish."*

If you're a nacho freak like I am, you have to love the Crab Nachos at Joe's Crab Shack. The restaurant chain creates this number one appetizer pick by slathering tortilla chips with their awesome crab dip, then adding Jack cheese and popping the whole thing under the broiler. Once the cheese is melted and gooey, the nachos are topped with sliced lettuce and drizzled with a great avocado-lime dressing. I've got all the clones here for the crab dip and the dressing, plus I'm also including perfect re-creations of the black bean corn relish and pico de gallo to finish your pile of nacho greatness. If you don't feel like making the pico de gallo from scratch, you can usually find a good premade version in your local market. This clone creates a bigger serving than the one from the restaurant chain, and there's certainly nothing wrong with that.

AVOCADO-LIME DRESSING

⅓ cup sour cream
¼ cup mashed avocado
¼ cup whole milk
1 tablespoon lime juice
2 teaspoons minced jalapeño pepper

1 teaspoon minced fresh cilantro
1 teaspoon chopped green onion
1 teaspoon minced garlic (1 clove)
½ teaspoon granulated sugar
¼ teaspoon salt

¼ teaspoon MSG (such as
    Ac'cent)
⅛ teaspoon ground cumin

BLACK BEAN CORN RELISH

¼ cup frozen yellow corn, thawed
3 tablespoons canned black
    beans, rinsed and drained
3 tablespoons minced red onion
2 tablespoons minced red bell
    pepper

2 teaspoons minced jalapeño
    pepper
2 teaspoons minced fresh cilantro
1 teaspoon vegetable oil
pinch salt
pinch ground black pepper

PICO DE GALLO

⅓ cup diced tomato
⅓ cup diced white onion
2 teaspoons minced fresh cilantro

2 teaspoons minced jalapeño
    pepper
¼ teaspoon lime juice
pinch salt

CRAB DIP

4 ounces cream cheese
1 cup lump crab meat
1 tablespoon minced green onion
½ tablespoon minced red bell
    pepper
½ tablespoon minced green chile
    (or jalapeño)

¼ teaspoon salt
¼ teaspoon paprika
⅛ teaspoon white pepper
5 to 6 ounces corn tortilla chips
1½ cups shredded Monterey Jack
    cheese
1½ cups sliced iceberg lettuce

1. Make the avocado-lime dressing by combining all the ingre-
    dients in a blender and blending on medium speed for 10
    seconds.

2. Make the black bean corn relish by combining all the ingredients in a small bowl.
3. Make pico de gallo by combining all the ingredients in a small bowl.
4. Make the crab dip by combining all the ingredients in a medium microwave-safe bowl. Cover with plastic wrap and microwave on high for 3 minutes. Stir once halfway through the cooking time.
5. When you're ready to build the plate of nachos, preheat the broiler. Arrange half of the tortilla chips on an oven-safe ceramic plate then spoon on half of the crab dip and sprinkle on half of the cheese. Stack the other half of the tortilla chips on top, and then spread the rest of the crab dip on the chips, followed by the rest of the cheese. Broil the plate on a low rack for 1 to 2 minutes, or until the cheese is melted and some of the chips are beginning to turn brown.
6. Just before serving, stack the lettuce on top of the nachos, and then drizzle on the dressing or apply it with a squirt bottle. Dump the pico de gallo on top of the lettuce, followed by the black bean corn relish, and serve the dish immediately while still warm.

• SERVES 4 TO 6.

•   •   •   •

JOE'S CRAB SHACK
GREAT BALLS OF FIRE

MENU DESCRIPTION: *"Get ready to get fired up! Our jalapeño, shrimp, and crab balls are bound to be our 'hottest' sellers."*

Joe's hit appetizer is not as hard to make as you may think. The secret is in creating a filling that will form easily into a ball and then using a three-step breading process to make sure the balls stay as balls when they're frying. There are jalapeños in there, but the cayenne is where the big heat comes from, so if you want your balls a little less fiery, just reduce the amount of cayenne you put into the mix.

FILLING

2 teaspoons vegetable oil

2 jalapeño peppers, seeded and diced

6 medium raw shrimp, chopped

1 cup lump crabmeat

1 tablespoon shredded Parmesan cheese

¼ teaspoon salt

¼ teaspoon cayenne pepper

⅛ teaspoon garlic powder

⅛ teaspoon white pepper

3 tablespoons cream cheese, plus another 1½ ounces for the centers

2 tablespoons panko (Japanese bread crumbs)

BREADING

2 eggs, beaten

1 cup all-purpose flour

1 cup panko (Japanese bread crumbs)

6 to 10 cups vegetable oil (or the amount required by your fryer)

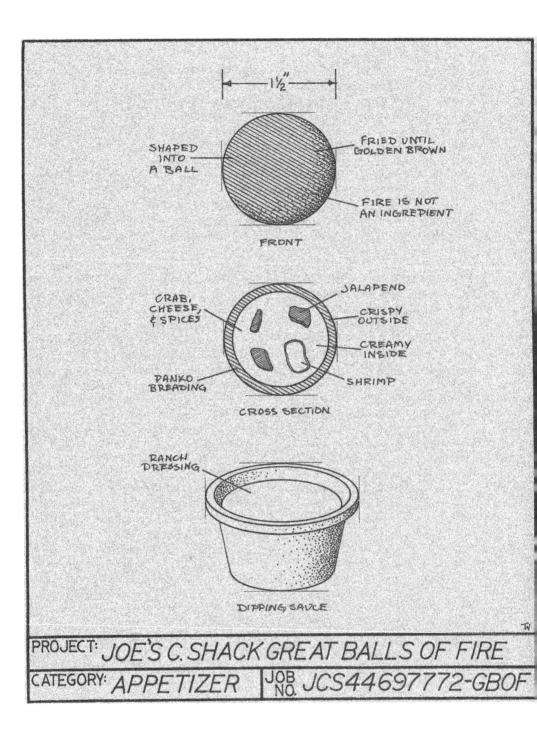

1½"

SHAPED
INTO
A BALL

FRIED UNTIL
GOLDEN BROWN

FIRE IS NOT
AN INGREDIENT

FRONT

CRAB,
CHEESE,
& SPICES

JALAPENO

CRISPY
OUTSIDE

CREAMY
INSIDE

PANKO
BREADING

SHRIMP

CROSS SECTION

RANCH
DRESSING

DIPPING SAUCE

PROJECT: JOE'S C. SHACK GREAT BALLS OF FIRE

CATEGORY: APPETIZER   JOB NO. JCS44697772-GBOF

ON THE SIDE
ranch dressing

1. Heat 2 teaspoons of oil in a sauté pan over medium heat. Add the sliced jalapeños and sauté for 2 minutes. Add the shrimp and cook for another 2 minutes, or until the shrimp is pink.
2. Stir in the crab, Parmesan, salt, cayenne pepper, garlic powder, and white pepper. Cook until the crab is hot, about 1 minute, then remove from the heat and stir in 3 tablespoons of cream cheese and 2 tablespoons of panko. Mix well.
3. Make the crab balls by first beating the eggs in medium bowl. Pour the flour into another bowl, and pour the panko into a third bowl.
4. Form the balls by scooping up a heaping tablespoon of the filling. Press a small marble-size chunk of cream cheese into the center of the filling and form the filling around the cream cheese. This ball should be slightly smaller than a golf ball. Roll the ball in the flour, then in the egg, and back into the flour until it's thoroughly covered with flour. Coat the ball with egg again and then roll it in the panko until completely covered. Repeat with each ball and arrange all of the breaded balls on a plate and chill for 30 minutes.
5. Preheat your oil to 325 degrees F.
6. Drop the balls, 4 to 6 at a time, into the oil and cook for 4 to 5 minutes, or until golden brown. If the cheese begins to squirt out of the balls when they are frying, remove them from the oil immediately. That means they're done!
7. Serve with ranch dressing on the side for dipping.

• SERVES 4 AS AN APPETIZER (MAKES ABOUT 12 BALLS).

• • • •

JOE'S CRAB SHACK
BBQ CRAB

My waitress said that I'd be tempted to lick the shells clean from my order of "BBQ Style" Dungeness crab at Joe's Crab Shack. She was right. Even though it's called "BBQ" on the menu, there's no grilling involved here. Instead, a super-flavorful seasoning paste is brushed on steamed crab of your choice just before it's served to your table. With that bit of knowledge under my belt, the only thing I had to figure out was how to clone that seasoning. When I analyzed a sample of the dark red paste, I first noticed the distinctive flavor of Old Bay. That's a good start. After adding a lot of salt to the blend along with paprika for color I was definitely heading in the right direction. But the taste was missing something until I invited a little MSG to the dance. (You'll find it in the spice aisle of your supermarket under the brand name Ac'cent). After just a bit of sugar and a touch of cayenne pepper for extra zing, I had a dry rub that was a dead ringer for the original blend. Now it was just a matter of adding some vegetable oil to the seasoning to create a paste that could be brushed on Dungeness crab, snow crab, or king crab legs after the crab is fully steamed. Next time you have a crab cookout, give this one a try and you too will serve crab that's "shell lickin' good."

5 teaspoons salt
2 teaspoons Old Bay seasoning
1 teaspoon paprika
1 teaspoon MSG (Ac'cent)

½ teaspoon granulated sugar
¼ teaspoon ground cayenne
  pepper
3 tablespoons vegetable oil

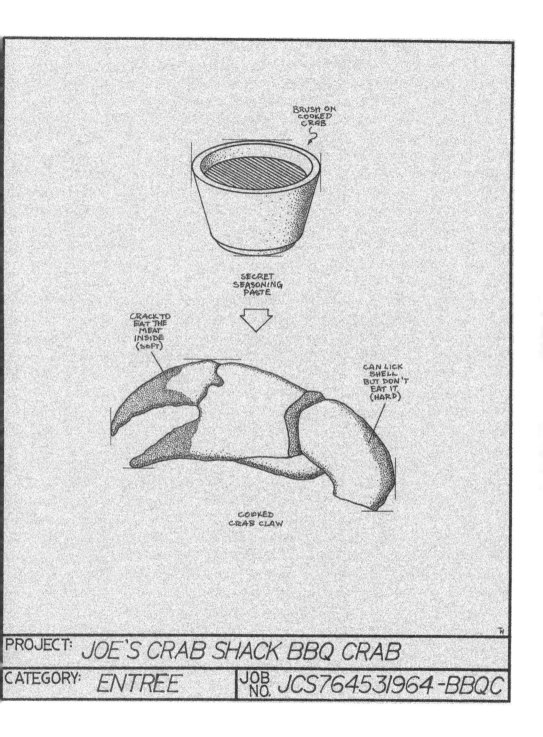

BRUSH ON
COOKED
CRAB

SECRET
SEASONING
PASTE

CRACK TO
EAT THE
MEAT
INSIDE
(SOFT)

CAN LICK
SHELL
BUT DON'T
EAT IT
(HARD)

COOKED
CRAB CLAW

PROJECT: *JOE'S CRAB SHACK BBQ CRAB*

CATEGORY: *ENTREE*   JOB NO. *JCS764531964-BBQC*

1. Stir together all dry ingredients in a small bowl.
2. Add oil and stir well.
3. Brush generously on the shells of cooked crab just before serving.

- MAKES ENOUGH FOR AT LEAST 8 SERVINGS.

• • • •

JOE'S CRAB SHACK
SPICY BOIL

MENU DESCRIPTION: *"Spiced up and smokin' hot!"*

Joe's Crab Shack is known for killer crab that you can order in a variety of flavors, cooked several different ways. For those of us who like biting into food that bites us back, Joe's boils crab in a super-secret spicy seasoning blend along with some corn on the cob and red skin potatoes. This recipe is beautifully simple, and you can use your favorite cooked and frozen crab: Dungeness crab, snow crab, or king crab. After mixing the seasoning, grab a large pot that can hold about 6 quarts of water and bring the water up to a rolling boil. The potatoes take the longest to cook, so they go in first, followed by the seasoning, the corn, and then the crab. The crab is already cooked, so it won't take long—you just want to cook it enough to get the flavor of the seasoning into the meat. The finishing touch is to sprinkle seasoning over the whole pile of goodness after it comes out of the boil and then serve everything up with plenty of napkins, and perhaps a bib or two.

SEASONING BLEND

2 tablespoons Old Bay seasoning
5 teaspoons cayenne pepper
1 tablespoon salt
1 tablespoon paprika

2 teaspoons dehydrated onion
   flakes
2 teaspoons garlic powder
1½ teaspoons ground black
   pepper

5 to 6 quarts water
2 red skin potatoes
2 yellow corn cobs

cooked and frozen crab: 2½ pounds Dungeness crab, or 6 snow crab clusters, or 6 king crab legs

1. Make the seasoning blend by combining all the spices in a small bowl.
2. Bring the water to a boil in a large pot that will hold all the crab, potatoes, and corn.
3. Slice the potatoes in half and drop the halves into the boiling water to cook for 15 minutes.
4. After the potatoes have cooked for 15 minutes, reserve 1½ tablespoons of the seasoning and dump the rest into the water. Drop the corn into the water and cook for 8 to 10 minutes.
5. Add the crab to the seasoned water and boil for 5 minutes. Make sure the water completely covers the crab. Add more hot water if necessary.
6. After 5 minutes, remove the crab, potatoes, and corn from the water and sprinkle with the reserved 1½ tablespoons of seasoning. Serve with shell crackers, napkins, and some cold beverages.

• SERVES 2.

•   •   •   •

JOE'S STONE CRAB GARLIC CREAMED SPINACH

Re-creating the creamy garlic spinach served as a side at Joe's Stone Crab is simple using two boxes of frozen chopped spinach and just a few other ingredients. You'll notice that ground nutmeg is the secret addition that sets this creamed spinach apart from other chains. Use some of this creamed spinach in the following recipe, which clones the famous grilled tomatoes at the chain.

3 tablespoons salted butter
1 tablespoon minced garlic
1 tablespoon all-purpose flour
¾ cup half-and-half

two 10-ounce boxes frozen
    chopped spinach, thawed
½ teaspoon salt
½ teaspoon ground nutmeg
¼ teaspoon ground black pepper

1. Melt the butter in a small saucepan over medium heat. Add the garlic and sauté for about 30 seconds. Whisk in the flour and heat for about 1 minute. Whisk in the half-and-half.
2. Squeeze the water out of the thawed spinach and add the spinach to the saucepan. Add the salt, nutmeg, and black pepper and simmer for 20 minutes over medium-low heat. The spinach will be tender when done.

•   SERVES 4.

•   •   •   •

JOE'S STONE CRAB GRILLED TOMATOES

☆   ✌   ●   ✏   ☯   ✂   ☞

After you've made the delicious creamed spinach from the previous clone recipe, save a little of it and you're only a couple steps away from this famous Joe's Stone Crab side. Bread crumbs and butter are added to ½ cup of the creamed spinach to firm it up, then the mixture is spread on top of thick-sliced beefsteak tomatoes. The restaurant grates a hunk of American cheese to top it all off, but since it's hard to find American cheese that isn't already sliced, you can chop up the sliced stuff and sprinkle it over the tomatoes. Broil the tomatoes until the cheese browns, and you're ready to eat.

4 ½-inch-thick slices of beefsteak tomato
½ cup creamed spinach (from recipe on page 207)
2 tablespoons butter, melted

2 tablespoons seasoned bread crumbs (Progresso brand works well)
3 slices real American cheese (not cheese food)

1. Preheat the broiler to high.
2. Arrange the tomato slices on a baking sheet and lightly salt them.
3. Combine the creamed spinach with the melted butter and bread crumbs in a medium bowl.
4. Spread approximately 2 tablespoons of creamed spinach on top of each tomato. Use up all of the spinach.

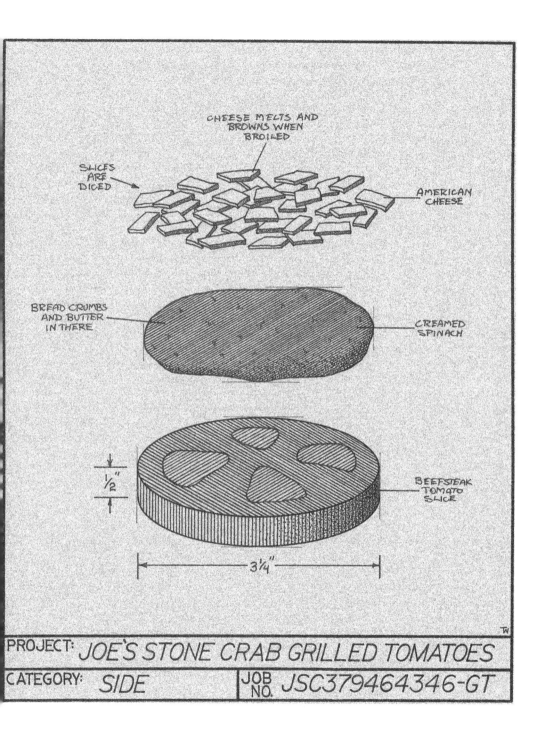

CHEESE MELTS AND BROWNS WHEN BROILED

SLICES ARE DICED

AMERICAN CHEESE

BREAD CRUMBS AND BUTTER IN THERE

CREAMED SPINACH

1/2"

BEEFSTEAK TOMATO SLICE

3¼"

W

PROJECT: *JOE'S STONE CRAB GRILLED TOMATOES*

CATEGORY: *SIDE*

JOB NO. *JSC379464346-GT*

5. Dice the American cheese slices, then pile an equal amount of cheese on top of the spinach on each tomato.
6. Broil the tomatoes for 2 to 3 minutes, or until the cheese melts and browns. Serve hot.

- SERVES 2.

• • • •

JOE'S STONE CRAB JENNIE'S POTATOES

Joe's Stone Crab chefs know how to make mashed potatoes really special. Chunks of fontina cheese are mixed into these creamy potatoes, and the dish comes to your table topped with a golden crust of crispy Asiago bread crumbs. A secret blend of panko (Japanese bread crumbs), butter, and shredded Asiago cheese is patted down onto the potatoes, and then the whole dish is broiled until the top is golden brown.

4 medium russet potatoes
couple of pinches plus 1 teaspoon salt
1 ½ cups half-and-half
¾ cup (1 ½ sticks) salted butter

2 cups (8 ounces) cubed fontina cheese
¼ cup (½ stick) salted butter, cut into cubes
½ cup grated fontina cheese

ASIAGO BREAD CRUMB TOPPING

1 cup panko (Japanese bread crumbs)
⅓ cup shredded Asiago cheese
1 teaspoon paprika

1 tablespoon minced fresh parsley
⅛ teaspoon salt
¼ cup (½ stick) salted butter, melted

1. Peel the potatoes and chop them into quarters. Put the potatoes into a large saucepan and cover them with water. Add a couple pinches of salt. Bring the water to a boil over me-

dium heat, and boil for 20 to 25 minutes, or until potatoes are tender. Strain the potatoes.

2. Push the potato chunks through a ricer back into the saucepan. You can also use a potato masher.

3. Add the half-and-half, butter, and 1 teaspoon of salt to the pan. Cover and set over medium/low heat. Stir occasionally until hot. Stir in the fontina cheese and turn off the heat. Set the oven to broil.

4. Make the bread crumb topping by combining the panko, Asiago cheese, paprika, parsley, and salt in a medium bowl. Stir in the melted butter.

5. Spoon the potatoes into a casserole dish. Smooth the top of the potatoes with a spatula, then spread the ¼ cup cubed butter on top, followed by the ½ cup grated fontina cheese. Use your hands to cover the top of the potatoes with the Asiago bread crumb topping.

6. Set the dish under your broiler for 1 to 2 minutes, or until the bread crumbs turn light brown.

• MAKES 6 TO 8 SERVINGS.

•   •   •   •

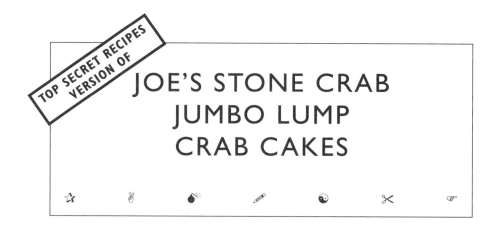

JOE'S STONE CRAB
JUMBO LUMP
CRAB CAKES

Joseph Weiss was living in New York with his wife and son when his doctor told him he would need a change of climate to help his asthma. When he journeyed to Miami, Florida, in 1913 and discovered he was able to breathe again, he quickly moved his family down South and opened his first restaurant, a little lunch counter. Joe's restaurant business exploded in 1921 when he discovered how to cook and serve the stone crabs caught off the coast. Joe boiled the meaty claws and served them chilled and cracked with a secret mustard dipping sauce. (Today only one pincer is removed from each stone crab, and the crab is tossed back into the ocean, where it will regenerate the missing claw in about two years.) The stone crabs, in addition to several other signature items, made Joe's a Miami hot spot, and these days Joe's restaurants can be found in Chicago and Las Vegas. Here is my take on Joe's amazing giant crab cakes, which are made from lump crab meat, and served as an appetizer or entrée at the restaurant. Of course, you can't clone a Joe's crab dish without cloning the secret mustard sauce, so that recipe is here, too.

¼ cup mayonnaise

1 egg

2 teaspoons minced fresh parsley

½ teaspoon Old Bay seasoning

1 teaspoon Worcestershire sauce

1 teaspoon Grey Poupon Dijon
   mustard

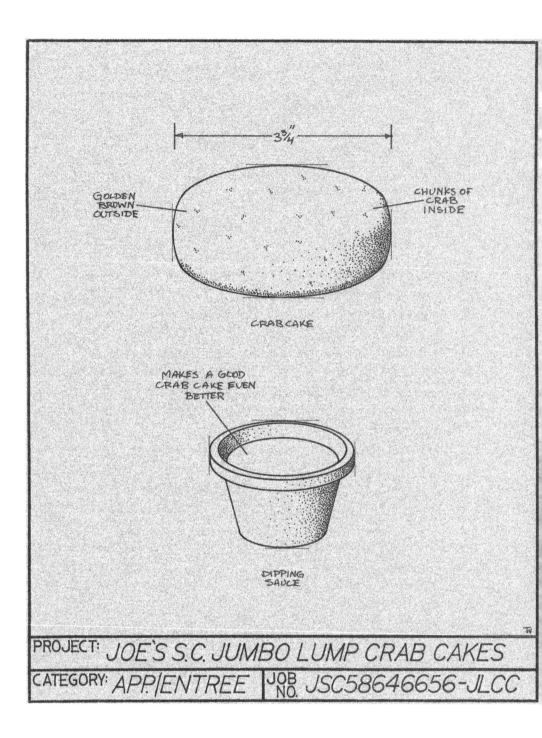

3¾″

GOLDEN BROWN OUTSIDE

CHUNKS OF CRAB INSIDE

CRAB CAKE

MAKES A GOOD CRAB CAKE EVEN BETTER

DIPPING SAUCE

PROJECT:	JOE'S S.C. JUMBO LUMP CRAB CAKES	
CATEGORY: APP./ENTREE	JOB NO.	JSC58646656-JLCC

⅓ cup plain bread crumbs (such as Progresso)

1 pound lump crab meat

½ cup panko (Japanese bread crumbs)

½ cup vegetable oil

¼ cup (½ stick) butter

MUSTARD DIPPING SAUCE

¼ cup mayonnaise

2 teaspoons Grey Poupon Dijon mustard

2 teaspoons milk

½ teaspoon Worcestershire sauce

¼ teaspoon A.1. Steak Sauce

pinch salt

1. Mix the mayonnaise, egg, parsley, Old Bay seasoning, Worcestershire sauce, and Dijon mustard together in a large bowl until smooth. Stir in the bread crumbs. Carefully fold in the crabmeat with a spatula, being careful not to break up the chunks of crabmeat.

2. Pour the panko on a large plate. Form four crab cakes with your hands. Make them into patties that are about 3½ to 4 inches in diameter and about 1 inch thick. Press the patties down on the plate of panko to coat each side of each patty with a layer of crumbs. Arrange the crab cakes on a plate and chill for about 20 minutes. This will help the crab cakes hold together when they are cooked.

3. Make the dipping sauce by combining all the ingredients in a small bowl. Cover and chill until needed.

4. When crab cakes have rested, heat up the vegetable oil and butter in a large skillet over medium/low heat. Preheat the oven to 375 degrees F.

5. When the oil is hot, sauté the crab cakes for 2 to 3 minutes per side, or until golden brown. Slide the crab cakes onto a baking sheet and bake for 8 to 10 minutes in the oven. Serve with the mustard dipping sauce on the side.

• MAKES 4 LARGE CRAB CAKES.

•   •   •   •

LONGHORN STEAKHOUSE FIRECRACKER CHICKEN WRAPS

MENU DESCRIPTION: *"Crispy, fried flour tortillas stuffed with spicy grilled chicken and cheese. Served with cool avocado-lime dipping sauce."*

This *Top Secret Recipes* version of the best-selling signature appetizer dish from the popular steakhouse chain will produce a serving that's two-and-a-half times bigger than the plate you get at the restaurant. That makes this recipe the perfect choice for any big game hoedown or festive holiday shindig where you have set your sights on becoming the event's finger food superstar. You can make the wraps early in the day or even the day before and then fry them off at party time, but I would make the avocado-lime dipping sauce as close to serving time as possible, as the avocado in the sauce will start to brown after a couple hours. For the wraps I found it most convenient to use a shredded cheddar and Monterey Jack cheese blend, which is easy to find in most stores, but if your market doesn't have the blend, simply use ½ cup each of the two shredded cheeses.

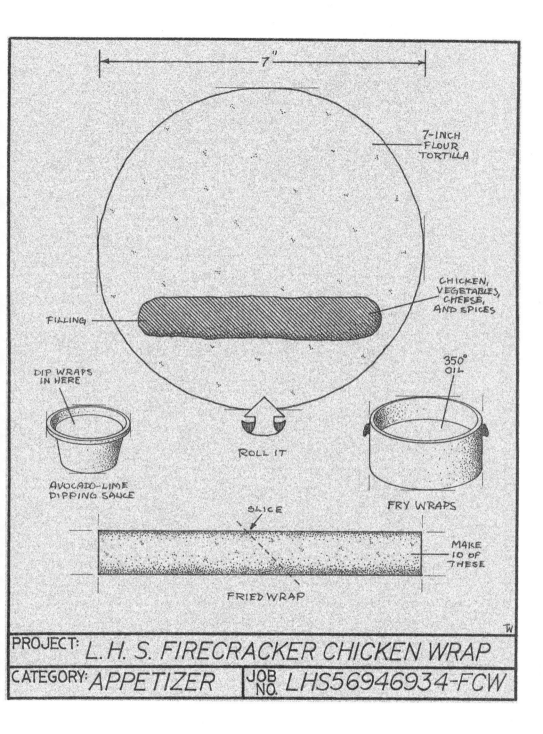

7"

7-INCH
FLOUR
TORTILLA

CHICKEN,
VEGETABLES,
CHEESE,
AND SPICES

FILLING

DIP WRAPS
IN HERE

350°
OIL

ROLL IT

AVOCADO-LIME
DIPPING SAUCE

FRY WRAPS

SLICE

MAKE
10 OF
THESE

FRIED WRAP

PROJECT: *L. H. S. FIRECRACKER CHICKEN WRAP*

CATEGORY: *APPETIZER* **JOB NO.** *LHS56946934-FCW*

AVOCADO-LIME DIPPING SAUCE

1 avocado, smashed
½ cup mayonnaise
½ cup sour cream
¼ cup whole milk
2 tablespoons lime juice
½ teaspoon salt
1½ teaspoons granulated sugar

½ teaspoon ground black pepper
½ teaspoon dried oregano
½ teaspoon ground cumin
½ teaspoon garlic powder
¼ teaspoon onion powder
⅛ teaspoon cayenne pepper

FILLING

one 8-ounce skinless chicken
    breast fillet
1 tablespoon vegetable oil
2 tablespoons diced white onion
1 tablespoon diced red bell
    pepper
1 tablespoon diced jalapeño
    pepper

½ teaspoon minced garlic
1 teaspoon minced fresh cilantro
1 teaspoon paprika
½ teaspoon plus ⅛ teaspoon salt
¾ teaspoon cayenne pepper
¼ teaspoon ground black pepper
2 ounces (¼ cup) cream cheese
1 cup cheddar–Monterey Jack
    shredded cheese blend

10 small (7-inch) flour tortillas
1 egg, beaten
6 to 10 cups vegetable oil or
    shortening

3 to 4 cups roughly chopped
    romaine lettuce
Prairie Dust Seasoning (clone
    recipe on page 220)
1 medium roma tomato, chopped

1. Make the avocado-lime dipping sauce by combining all the ingredients in a small bowl. Cover and chill until needed. Stir the sauce a couple times as it chills.
2. Preheat the grill to high heat. Rub a chicken breast with vegetable oil, then grill it for 4 minutes per side, or until cooked through. When cool, finely chop the chicken until the pieces are no bigger than a kernel of corn.
3. Heat 1 tablespoon of vegetable oil in a sauté pan over medium/low heat. Add the onion, diced peppers, and garlic. Cook

slowly for 4 to 5 minutes, or until the edges of the onion begin to turn translucent. Stir in the chicken and cilantro. Add the paprika, salt, cayenne pepper, and black pepper. Remove the mixture from the heat and pour it into a large bowl. Stir in the cream cheese and shredded cheese blend until it is a pasty consistency.

4. Warm the tortillas in a tortilla warmer. You can also wrap the tortillas in a moist towel and microwave for 1 minute on high.

5. Spoon 2 tablespoons of filling into a tortilla near one edge. Fold the tortilla over the filling and roll it up tightly like a cigar. Brush some beaten egg on the edge of the tortilla before you finish rolling it up so that it sticks. Arrange each folded tortilla on a platter and let them sit in the refrigerator for at least 30 minutes (or as long as overnight) so that the beaten egg "glue" sets up.

6. Preheat the oil in your fryer or in a large pot to 350 degrees F.

7. When the oil is hot, fry 3 to 4 of the wraps at a time for 3 to 4 minutes, or until golden brown. Drain on a rack or on a paper towel–lined plate.

8. While the wraps are frying, line a serving platter with the chopped romaine lettuce. Pour most of the dipping sauce into a small bowl and set it in the middle of the platter. Save some of the sauce to drizzle over the wraps.

9. Slice each of the fried wraps at a slight angle through the middle. Arrange the wraps in a spoke-like fashion on the lettuce around the bowl of dipping sauce. Sprinkle the wraps with a little of the Prairie Dust clone from page 220. Use a spoon to drizzle the reserved sauce over the wraps in a circular motion, then sprinkle the chopped tomato over the whole dish, and serve.

• SERVES 6 TO 8 AS AN APPETIZER.

•　•　•　•

LONGHORN STEAKHOUSE PRAIRIE DUST

Peruse a menu at one of the 270-unit LongHorn Steakhouses located throughout the eastern half of the U.S. and you'll find this seasoning blend on battered onion petals, spicy fried shrimp, pork chops, and steaks. Just combine these eight common ingredients in the comfort of your home, and you will have quickly cloned a versatile seasoned salt that can be added to everything that needs flavor, from steaks to chicken to seafood. It's also good sprinkled over eggs, burgers, and even popcorn.

1 tablespoon salt
1 ¼ teaspoons paprika
1 ¼ teaspoons ground black pepper
½ teaspoon onion powder
½ teaspoon garlic powder

¼ teaspoon ground cayenne pepper
¼ teaspoon ground turmeric
¼ teaspoon ground coriander

Combine all ingredients in a small bowl. Pour into an empty spice shaker.

• MAKES 7 TEASPOONS.

• • • •

MARGARITAVILLE HAVANAS AND BANANAS COCKTAIL

MENU DESCRIPTION: *"This one brings you back down there. Made with Cruzan dark rum, Bailey's Irish Cream, Creme de Banana, and piña colada mix."*

Bring the islands to you with this clone of the trademarked signature cocktail from Jimmy Buffett's successful theme chain. This is a blender drink similar to a piña colada, but with the addition of Bailey's Irish Cream and crème de banana I think it's way better than a piña colada. I've listed the brand names for the booze as specified on the restaurant menu, but the recipe works just as well with any brands you prefer.

¾ ounce Cruzan dark rum
¾ ounce Bols Crème de
    Bananes
1 ½ ounces Bailey's Irish Cream
4 ounces (½ cup) piña colada
    mix
2 cups ice

GARNISH
orange wedge

Combine all of the ingredients in a blender and blend on high speed until the ice is crushed and the drink is slushy. Pour into a 16-ounce glass and garnish with an orange wedge on a cocktail toothpick.

MAKES 1 DRINK.

• • • •

MARGARITAVILLE INCOMMUNICADO COCKTAIL

MENU DESCRIPTION: *"Close your eyes and imagine you're there. Margaritaville Gold Tequila, Bols Triple Sec, vodka, rum and gin mixed with cranberry juice, pineapple juice, sour mix and grenadine."*

You know how a Long Island Iced Tea has 5 different liquors in it? Well, this is like that, but better, with 2 kinds of juice, plus grenadine and sweet-and-sour mix. Watch yourself with this one folks, or you could become the name of this drink.

¾ ounce light rum

¾ ounce Bols triple sec

¾ ounce vodka

¾ ounce gin

¾ ounce Margaritaville gold
   tequila

¾ ounce grenadine

1 ½ ounces cranberry juice

1 ½ ounces pineapple juice

1 ½ ounces sweet-and-sour mix

GARNISH
lime wedge

Drop a handful of ice into a shaker and add all the liquid ingredients. Shake well and pour drink into a 16-ounce glass. Garnish with a lime wedge on a cocktail toothpick.

• MAKES 1 DRINK.

• • • •

MARGARITAVILLE
VOLCANO NACHOS

MENU DESCRIPTION: *"Topped with chili, cheese, guacamole, sour cream, jalapeños, tomato, and scallions."*

This giant pile of nachos lives up to its name, and they are by far the best nachos I have ever had at any casual chain. The secret is in the stacking of the ingredients. You start with a layer of yellow corn tortilla chips and then spoon on some creamy, slightly spicy nacho cheese. I found that Tostitos makes the perfect cheese for this: Tostitos Salsa Con Queso. More chips go on top, then more cheese, then more chips, followed by chili and a shredded cheese blend. You can either use a premade chili that can be found in the deli section of many grocery stores where the soups are sold, or use the recipe in this book for the clone of Red Robin Red's Homemade Chili Chili on page 331. After the nachos are baked and the cheese is melted, diced tomato, green onion, sour cream, guacamole, and jalapeño slices are added on top, and the party can now erupt.

GUACAMOLE

1 Hass avocado
2 teaspoons diced yellow onion
1 teaspoon diced jalapeño
    pepper

½ teaspoon lime juice
⅛ teaspoon salt
½ pound yellow corn tortilla chips

1 cup Tostitos Salsa Con Queso

1 cup chili (from clone recipe for
   Red Robin Red's Homemade
   Chili Chili on page 331, or
   from supermarket deli)

1 ¼ cups shredded cheddar and
   Monterey Jack cheese blend

1 small tomato, diced

¼ cup diced green onion

⅓ cup sour cream

12 to 15 canned jalapeño slices
   (nacho slices)

1. Preheat the oven to 400 degrees F.
2. Make the guacamole by mashing the avocado in a medium bowl, then mixing in the other ingredients. Set aside.
3. Build the nachos on an oven-safe ceramic plate. First arrange one layer of tortilla chips on the plate. Spoon ½ cup of cheese sauce over the chips. Arrange another layer of chips, followed by the remaining ½ cup of cheese sauce. Stack the remaining chips on the pile, followed by the chili and shredded cheese blend. Bake for 7 to 8 minutes, or until the cheese is melted and beginning to bubble.
4. Remove the nachos from the oven and pile the diced tomato on top, followed by the green onion.
5. Use an ice cream scoop to position scoops of the guacamole and sour cream side by side on top.
6. Pile the jalapeño slices on top of the guacamole and sour cream and serve pronto.

- SERVES 4 TO 6.

• • • •

MARGARITAVILLE
JERK SALMON

MENU DESCRIPTION: *"From Boston Bay, the birthplace of Jamaican Jerk. Salmon rubbed with our signature Jerk spices and seared in a skillet, finished with Jerk BBQ sauce and a side of mango chutney."*

Perk up your next salmon feast with the sweet and spicy flavors of Margaritaville's jerk seasoning. After duplicating the secret jerk rub, add just a little bit of it to either Cattlemen's Golden Honey barbecue sauce or KC Masterpiece Honey barbecue sauce for the perfect after-baking baste. The chain's delicious mango chutney is also cloned here so you get the true Margaritaville Jerk Salmon experience. If you can, make the chutney a couple hours ahead— it seems to get tastier over time. Serve this salmon with some rice and your favorite steamed vegetables.

MANGO CHUTNEY

1 ripe mango, diced
2 tablespoons diced white onion
2 tablespoons diced red bell
 pepper
2 tablespoons diced Anaheim chile

1 ½ teaspoons granulated sugar
1 teaspoon lime juice
¼ teaspoon curry powder
⅛ teaspoon salt

JERK SEASONING

2 teaspoons dark brown sugar
¾ teaspoon salt

½ teaspoon dried thyme
½ teaspoon ground black pepper

½ teaspoon paprika

½ teaspoon crushed red pepper flakes

¼ teaspoon ground allspice

¼ teaspoon cayenne pepper

½ cup Cattlemen's Golden Honey barbecue sauce or KC Masterpiece Honey barbecue sauce

four 6-ounce salmon fillets (without skin)

vegetable oil

1. Make the mango chutney by combining all of the chutney ingredients in a medium bowl. Cover and chill for a couple hours if possible.
2. Make the jerk seasoning by combining all of the seasoning ingredients in a small bowl.
3. Make the jerk barbecue sauce by mixing the barbecue sauce with 1 teaspoon of the jerk seasoning and set it aside.
4. When you are ready to make the fish, preheat the oven to 425 degrees F.
5. Place an oven-safe skillet that is large enough to hold all four fillets over medium/high heat. Add about a tablespoon of vegetable oil to the pan.
6. Sprinkle both side sides of each fillet with the jerk seasoning.
7. When the pan is hot, sear the top (not the flat side) of each fillet in the pan for 2 to 3 minutes, or until browned. Flip each fillet over and place the pan into your preheated oven for 6 to 7 minutes, or until the salmon is cooked through.
8. Plate each salmon fillet and brush with the jerk barbecue sauce. Serve the mango chutney on the side along with extra barbecue sauce, if desired.

- SERVES 4.

• • • •

MASTRO'S STEAKHOUSE GORGONZOLA MAC & CHEESE

This 8-unit Scottsdale, Arizona–based chain founded in 1999 was named one of the top ten steakhouses in the country by the Gayot restaurant and travel guide, and is planning to build forty additional restaurants over the next ten years. Mastro's restaurants are known for their elegant settings and delicious prime beef served on 400-degree plates, but this side dish ranks high among the most popular menu choices. As if the creamy gorgonzola cheese sauce isn't incredible enough, this dish is topped with a bubbling cheese layer that includes mozzarella, fontina, and Pecorino, plus a little Grana Padano, which is similar to Parmigiano-Reggiano. You can track down all of these cheeses separately and make your own cloned blend, or you can use a preshredded Italian cheese blend found in most markets that will include four to six Italian cheeses in one bag. Even though the bagged blend is not exactly what is used at the restaurant, I found these cheese blends to be an easy and inexpensive substitute that taste very close to the original. When using the preblended cheese, spread 1½ cups over the top of the pasta and get on with the broiling.

2 tablespoons butter
2 tablespoons all-purpose flour
1 cup whole milk
¼ cup gorgonzola cheese
   (1 ounce)
¼ teaspoon salt
1 cup uncooked elbow macaroni
   (4½ ounces)

⅔ cup shredded mozzarella
   cheese
⅔ cup shredded fontina cheese
2 tablespoons shredded Pecorino
   cheese
2 tablespoons shredded Grana
   Padano cheese (or
   Parmigiano-Reggiano)
½ teaspoon minced fresh parsley

1. Preheat the broiler.
2. Melt the butter in a medium saucepan over medium heat, then whisk in the flour. Cook for 30 seconds, then whisk in the milk and add the gorgonzola and salt. Cook until bubbling, stirring often, then reduce the heat and simmer for 2 to 3 minutes, until the cheese is melted and the sauce is thick. Cover and remove from the heat.
3. While making the cheese sauce, bring 2 quarts of water to a boil and cook the macaroni until tender, about 10 minutes. Strain the pasta and mix with the cheese sauce in the saucepan.
4. Pour the pasta and sauce into an oven-safe casserole dish. Combine the shredded cheeses and spread the blend over the top of the pasta. Broil the pasta for 3 to 4 minutes, or until the cheese is melted and browned in spots.
5. Sprinkle the minced parsley over the top and serve.

• SERVES 4.

• • • •

MASTRO'S STEAKHOUSE STEAK SEASONING

One of the best tools I have for analyzing seasoning blends—besides the old taste buds—is a video microscope. I've saved a directory of potential ingredients to a flash disk, which I can resort to when zooming in tight on a small sample of seasoning. Using this microscope makes it easy to determine, for example, if the little white specks in the mix are onion or garlic (one is translucent, one isn't), and whether there are ground herbs in there (bits of leaves and stems). With this microscope I was able to clearly see that the salt used in an acquired sample of Mastro's secret steak seasoning was fine salt like the stuff used on popcorn, and that there was some flour in there, probably to help the seasoning stick to the meat. Identifying those ingredients plus a few more made it very easy to assemble a clone of the blend that you can now use on your favorite cuts at home.

2½ teaspoons popcorn salt (fine salt)
2 teaspoons paprika
1½ teaspoons all-purpose flour
¼ teaspoon onion powder
¼ teaspoon garlic powder
¼ teaspoon ground black pepper

Combine all the ingredients in a small bowl. Sprinkle over steaks before cooking.

- MAKES 7 TEASPOONS.

• • • •

MASTRO'S
STEAKHOUSE
WARM BUTTER CAKE

Mastro's signature dessert is sinfully good. How can it not be? It's buttery pound cake with a sweetened cream cheese layer that melts into the cake when reheated just before being crowned with vanilla ice cream and a drizzle of homemade raspberry sauce. This formula makes four cakes when you bake them in five-inch ramekins, which gives you cakes that are the same size as those served in the restaurant. And each one will easily serve two people. You can make this dessert the day before you plan to serve it just as the chefs at the restaurant do. When each butter cake order comes into the Mastro's kitchen, a cake is microwaved until hot, the sugar topping is melted with a chef's torch (the kind often used for crème brûlée), then the cake is topped with ice cream and raspberry sauce. If you don't have a torch to melt the sugar crystals, you can just skip that step and serve the cake with the raw sugar untorched. It still tastes great.

CAKE

1 cup (2 sticks) butter, softened
1 1/3 cups granulated sugar
2 eggs
2 egg yolks
1 tablespoon vanilla extract
1/4 teaspoon minced orange zest

1 1/2 cups all-purpose flour
1 teaspoon salt
1/2 teaspoon baking powder
1 cup Sugar in the Raw for
    dipping the bottoms

CREAM CHEESE LAYER

8 ounces cream cheese, softened
1/3 cup granulated sugar
1 egg

1 tablespoon all-purpose flour
1 tablespoon sour cream
1/2 teaspoon vanilla extract

RASPBERRY SAUCE

2 cups frozen raspberries (about
    8 ounces)
1 cup water

2/3 cup granulated sugar
2 teaspoons cornstarch

WHIPPED CREAM

1 cup heavy cream
1/4 cup granulated sugar
1/4 teaspoon vanilla extract

ON TOP

3 scoops vanilla ice cream

GARNISH

8 strawberries, quartered
12 orange slices
4 sprigs of mint

1. Preheat the oven to 325 degrees F.
2. Make the butter cakes by blending the softened butter and granulated sugar together in a large bowl with an electric mixer on high speed for about 1 minute. Add the whole eggs, egg yolks, vanilla, and orange zest and mix for another minute.
3. In a separate medium bowl, combine the flour, salt, and baking powder. Pour this dry mixture into the wet mixture and beat with an electric mixer for 1 minute.
4. Mix together cream cheese, sugar, egg, flour, sour cream, and vanilla in another medium bowl until smooth.
5. Butter the inside of four 5-inch ramekins. Cut 4 disks out of parchment paper to fit into the bottom of each ramekin. This will help the cakes come out. Spoon a little more than 1 cup of batter into each ramekin. Spread 1/3 cup of the cream cheese mixture over the top of the batter in each ramekin (you will have some leftover cream cheese filling).

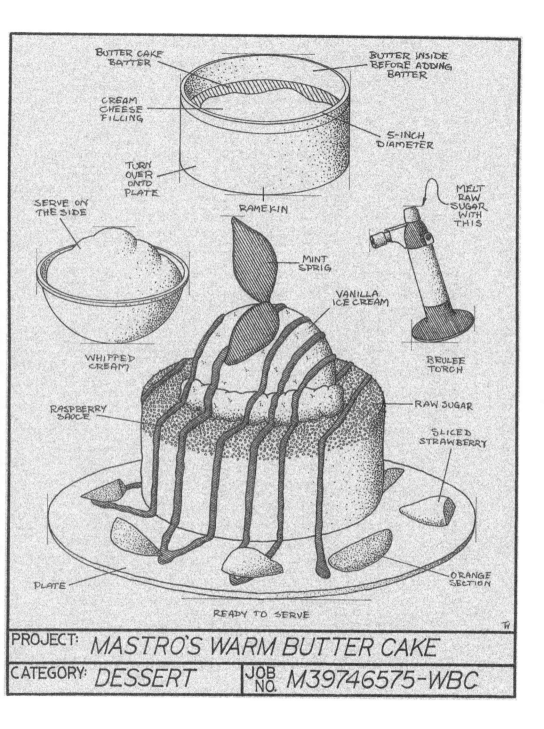

BUTTER CAKE BATTER

BUTTER INSIDE BEFORE ADDING BATTER

CREAM CHEESE FILLING

5-INCH DIAMETER

TURN OVER ONTO PLATE

RAMEKIN

MELT RAW SUGAR WITH THIS

SERVE ON THE SIDE

MINT SPRIG

VANILLA ICE CREAM

WHIPPED CREAM

BRULEE TORCH

RASPBERRY SAUCE

RAW SUGAR

SLICED STRAWBERRY

PLATE

ORANGE SECTION

READY TO SERVE

PROJECT:	*MASTRO'S WARM BUTTER CAKE*
CATEGORY: *DESSERT*	JOB NO. *M39746575-WBC*

6. Bake for 45 to 50 minutes, or until the tops are browned. Cool for 60 minutes so that when the cakes are removed from the ramekins they won't fall apart.

7. Make the raspberry sauce by combining the raspberries, water, and sugar in a medium saucepan over medium heat. When the berries begin to boil, reduce the heat and simmer for 5 minutes. Strain to remove the seeds, then pour the strained sauce back into the pan, whisk in the cornstarch until it's completely dissolved, and bring the sauce up to a boil again. Reduce the heat and simmer for 6 to 8 minutes, or until the sauce is thick and syrupy, then pour into a container, cover, and chill until needed.

8. Make the whipped cream by beating all the ingredients on high speed with an electric mixer until the cream forms stiff peaks. Cover and chill until needed.

9. Run a butter knife around the inside edge of each ramekin, then invert the dish to remove each cake. Dip the bottom of each cake into the raw sugar. The cake is served upside down, so invert the cakes onto a platter, then cover and chill them if planning to serve later. If you want to serve the cakes now, zap them one at a time in the microwave on high, sugared-side up, for 30 to 45 seconds, or until hot. Use a chef's torch (a crème brûlée torch) to melt the raw sugar on top, then go to step 11.

10. To serve a cake that has been refrigerated, place it onto the center of a plate, with the sugar-coated-side up. Microwave each cake on high for 60 to 90 seconds, or until it's hot. Use a chef's torch (a crème brûlée torch) to caramelize the raw sugar on top.

11. Place a scoop of vanilla ice cream on the cake, drizzle raspberry sauce over the top, then arrange 8 strawberry slices and 3 orange slices around the plate. Stick a sprig of fresh mint into the scoop of ice cream and serve fresh whipped cream on the side.

• MAKES 4 CAKES (SERVES 8).

•   •   •   •

MAX & ERMA'S
TORTILLA SOUP

After years of fielding requests to clone the delicious signature soup from this growing 100-unit chain, I was finally able to secure a couple carry-out samples from Max & Erma's at the Cleveland airport while I was there on a media tour for my last book. Wrapped in a bundle of napkins and tucked into a carry-on bag, my samples arrived home in Vegas still warm, believe it or not, and ready for analysis. For this one you'll need to snag some white and dark fillets of chicken and get shredding on a half-pound hunk of cheese. It's all that cheddar cheese that makes this tortilla soup unique. And you'll definitely want to shred your own, since I've found that the preshredded stuff—while also more expensive—just doesn't melt as well in the chicken broth as cheese that's been shredded just before it goes into the pot.

1 skinless chicken breast fillet
1 skinless chicken thigh fillet
2 tablespoons vegetable oil
¼ cup minced white onion
¼ cup minced Anaheim pepper
1 teaspoon minced garlic
4 cups chicken broth
2 tablespoons cornstarch
8 ounces mild cheddar cheese, shredded

three 6-inch corn tortillas, minced
2 tablespoons lime juice (2 limes)
¼ cup canned diced tomatoes
½ teaspoon ground cumin
½ teaspoon ground cayenne pepper
¼ teaspoon ground Mexican oregano
¼ teaspoon salt

CRISPY TORTILLA GARNISH

2 to 3 cups vegetable oil
two 6-inch flour tortillas, thinly
    sliced

1. Cook the chicken in a sauté pan with a little oil on medium heat for 4 or 5 minutes per side. You won't need to cook the chicken all the way through, since it will finish cooking in the soup. When the chicken is cool, chop it into bite-size pieces.
2. In a large saucepan, heat up the vegetable oil over medium/low heat. Add onion, minced pepper, and garlic and sweat (cook slowly) for 15 minutes or until the minced onion begins to turn translucent.
3. Dissolve the cornstarch in the chicken broth, then add the mixture to the pan, along with the remaining ingredients. Bring heat to medium while stirring constantly to help the cheese melt. When the soup begins to bubble, reduce heat and simmer for 20 minutes.
4. While the soup simmers, heat 2 to 3 cups of vegetable oil to 325 degrees F in a medium saucepan or deep fryer. Drop the thinly sliced flour tortillas in the oil and fry for 1 to 1½ minutes, until golden brown. Drain on paper towels.
5. Serve 1¼ cups of soup in a bowl with some crispy tortillas on top.

• MAKES 4 SERVINGS.

• • • •

MIMI'S CAFE BUTTERMILK SPICE MUFFINS

The Web site for Mimi's Cafe features a recipe that claims to duplicate the buttermilk spice muffins that are so popular at the restaurant chain, but I found the recipe there to be slightly lacking. While the recipe produced very good muffins, I discovered the Web site formula required more sugar, more nutmeg, and the addition of salt to produce muffins that could be considered clones of the popular version baked fresh every day in Mimi's kitchens. To make this recipe work best, use a large (Texas-size) muffin pan and line each cup with large paper muffin cups. You could also make the muffins in a smaller, standard-size muffin pan by reducing the baking time by 5 to 10 minutes, and adding only 1 teaspoon of topping on the batter in each cup rather than the 2 teaspoons described here. But for the absolute best clone, I say go big.

1 ¼ cups granulated sugar
½ cup (1 stick) butter, softened
2 tablespoons vegetable oil
3 eggs
2½ cups all-purpose flour

2 teaspoons baking soda
1 ¼ teaspoons ground nutmeg
½ teaspoon ground cinnamon
½ teaspoon salt
¾ cup buttermilk

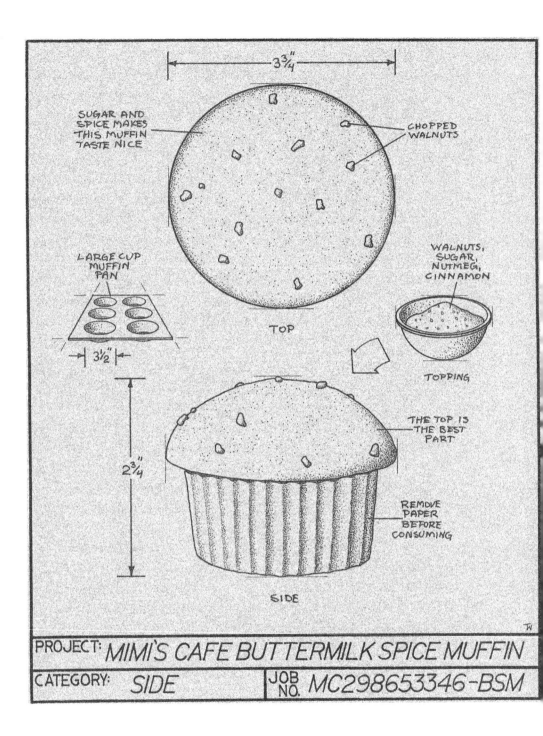

3¾"

SUGAR AND
SPICE MAKES
THIS MUFFIN
TASTE NICE

CHOPPED
WALNUTS

LARGE CUP
MUFFIN
PAN

3½"

WALNUTS,
SUGAR,
NUTMEG,
CINNAMON

TOP

TOPPING

2¾"

THE TOP IS
THE BEST
PART

REMOVE
PAPER
BEFORE
CONSUMING

SIDE

PROJECT: *MIMI'S CAFE BUTTERMILK SPICE MUFFIN*

CATEGORY: *SIDE*

JOB
NO. *MC298653346-BSM*

240

TOPPING

¼ cup chopped walnuts

2 tablespoons granulated sugar

⅛ teaspoon ground nutmeg

⅛ teaspoon ground cinnamon

1. Preheat the oven to 350 degrees F.
2. Use an electric mixer on high speed to combine the sugar and butter in a large bowl. Mix for 30 seconds, then add the oil and eggs and mix until smooth and creamy.
3. Mix the flour with the baking soda, nutmeg, cinnamon, and salt in a medium bowl. Pour the dry ingredients into the wet ingredients, add the buttermilk, and mix until smooth, about 1 minute.
4. Pour the batter into a large muffin pan lined with large paper muffin cups.
5. Combine the topping ingredients in a small bowl. Sprinkle 2 teaspoons over the top of the batter in each muffin cup.
6. Bake for 30 to 35 minutes, or until the muffins are dark brown on top.

- Makes 6 large muffins.

• • • •

MIMI'S CAFE CARROT RAISIN NUT MUFFINS

These muffins and the buttermilk spice muffins are the two top sellers among the several muffins baked every day at the Irvine, California–based chain. If you like the combo of carrots, raisins, and walnuts in a super-moist cake, this is the muffin for you. The real thing is made dark with the addition of caramel coloring, which you can find in many supermarkets or in stores that sell cake-decorating supplies. You can choose to skip this ingredient and your muffins will still come out great. They'll just be a little lighter in color. This recipe is designed for a large muffin pan with 6 large muffins cups, but you can also use a standard-size 12-cup pan. Just reduce the baking time by 5 to 10 minutes.

1 cup granulated sugar
¼ cup (½ stick) butter, softened
¼ cup molasses
½ cup plus 1 tablespoon
     vegetable oil
3 eggs
2 tablespoons buttermilk
1 teaspoon caramel food coloring
     (optional)

½ teaspoon vanilla extract
2½ cups all-purpose flour
2 teaspoons baking soda
½ teaspoon salt
1 cup shredded carrots
1 cup raisins
½ cup chopped walnuts

3¾"

RAISIN

CHOPPED
WALNUTS

SHREDDED
CARROT

LARGE SIZE
MUFFIN PAN

3½"

TOP

RAISINS

SHRED
THESE

CARROTS

CHOPPED
WALNUTS

2¾"

MUFFIN IS
FILLED WITH
FLAVOR

PAPER CUP,
NOT SO MUCH

SIDE

TW

PROJECT: *MIMI'S CAFE CARROT RAISIN NUT MUFFIN*

CATEGORY: *SIDE*   **JOB NO.** *MCI69465492-CRNM*

1. Preheat the oven to 350 degrees F.
2. Use an electric mixer to combine the sugar with the butter and molasses in a large bowl. Add the vegetable oil, eggs, buttermilk, coloring (if using), and vanilla and mix well for 1 minute, or until smooth and creamy.
3. In a separate bowl, stir together the flour, baking soda, and salt.
4. Combine the dry mixture with the wet ingredients and mix well by hand.
5. Add the carrots, raisins, and walnuts and distribute the batter evenly into in a large muffin pan lined with 6 large paper muffin cups. Bake for 35 to 40 minutes, or until a toothpick stuck in the center of a muffin comes out clean.

• MAKES 6 LARGE MUFFINS.

• • • •

MIMI'S CAFE
FIVE-WAY
GRILLED CHEESE

When I think back on all the grilled cheese sandwiches I was served as a kid, I don't get very nostalgic. Around my neighborhood the recipe was plain and simple: Slap some American cheese between a couple slices of white Wonder Bread and grill in a hot skillet until browned on both sides. Good enough grub for a kid I guess, but what if moms back in the day had a grilled cheese recipe like the one served at Mimi's Cafe? Would my young palate have been able to appreciate the five different cheeses? Would the sourdough bread brushed with soft garlic butter and sprinkled with Parmesan cheese have won over a littler version of me? I don't know the answers to these questions, but I do know that as an adult this is the best grilled cheese I've ever had. It's been on Mimi's menu since the first day the restaurant opened back in 1978 in Anaheim, California, and the chain now serves around 18,000 of these sandwiches every year—surely to both adults and kids alike. Grab yourself some sliced Swiss, cheddar, Jack, mozzarella, shredded Parmesan, and sourdough bread. This is a super-easy recipe, so you'll have no trouble quickly cranking out four amazing grilled cheese sandwiches that I'm sure absolutely anyone will totally dig.

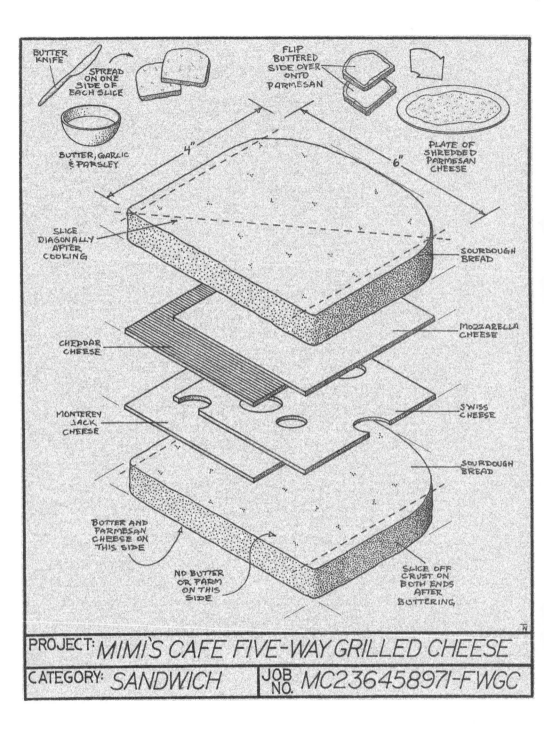

BUTTER KNIFE

SPREAD ON ONE SIDE OF EACH SLICE

FLIP BUTTERED SIDE OVER ONTO PARMESAN

BUTTER, GARLIC & PARSLEY

PLATE OF SHREDDED PARMESAN CHEESE

4"

6"

SLICE DIAGONALLY AFTER COOKING

SOURDOUGH BREAD

MOZZARELLA CHEESE

CHEDDAR CHEESE

SWISS CHEESE

MONTEREY JACK CHEESE

SOURDOUGH BREAD

BUTTER AND PARMESAN CHEESE ON THIS SIDE

NO BUTTER OR PARM ON THIS SIDE

SLICE OFF CRUST ON BOTH ENDS AFTER BUTTERING.

| PROJECT: | MIMI'S CAFE FIVE-WAY GRILLED CHEESE |
| CATEGORY: SANDWICH | JOB NO. MC236458971-FWGC |

246

½ cup (1 stick) salted butter, softened

1 teaspoon finely minced garlic (about 1 clove)

¼ teaspoon minced fresh parsley

8 slices sourdough bread

¾ cup shredded Parmesan cheese

4 slices Swiss cheese

4 slices cheddar cheese

4 slices Monterey Jack cheese

4 slices mozzarella cheese

1. Combine the butter, garlic, and parsley in a small bowl.
2. Preheat a large sauté pan or griddle pan over medium heat. The pan should be big enough to fit two slices of sourdough bread.
3. To make each sandwich, spread garlic butter on one side of each slice of sourdough bread. Cut the crust off of the left and right ends of each slice of bread—leave the crust on the top and bottom. Sprinkle Parmesan cheese onto a plate, and then turn each slice of bread over onto the cheese so that it sticks to the garlic butter. Allow the excess cheese to fall off the bread, then gently place each slice of bread, cheese-side down, onto the hot pan.
4. Immediately place a slice of Swiss and a slice of cheddar on one slice of bread, and then place a slice of Jack and a slice of mozzarella on the other slice of bread.
5. In 2½ to 3½ minutes, when the Parmesan cheese has browned, use a spatula to flip one slice of bread over onto the other, and then remove the sandwich from the pan. Let the sandwich sit for 1 minute, then slice it diagonally through the middle and serve hot.

• MAKES 4 SANDWICHES.

•   •   •   •

OLIVE GARDEN POMEGRANATE MARGARITA MARTINI

If you're into tequila, try this. It's made with Patrón silver tequila and Patrón's 80-proof Citrónge orange liqueur. You'll also need to track down some real grenadine syrup—that's the kind made with pomegranate juice, not flavoring. Stirrings is the brand I found. You can alternately use pure pomegranate juice here, such as the stuff made by Pom Wonderful, but you'll also have to add a little simple syrup to sweeten the drink since pomegranate juice is fairly tart. This drink is served straight up in a large martini glass, but it works just as well over ice in a poolside tumbler with a bendy straw.

1 ounce Patrón silver tequila
¾ ounce Patrón Citrónge orange
    liqueur
1 ½ ounces real grenadine syrup
    (or ¾ ounce pomegranate
    juice, plus ¾ ounce simple
    syrup)

1 teaspoon lemon juice
1 teaspoon lime juice
2 teaspoons orange juice
2 ounces sweet-and-sour mix

GARNISH
thin lemon slice
thin lime slice

1. Drop a handful of ice into a cocktail shaker.
2. Pour everything the shaker and shake thoroughly.
3. Strain entire contents of the shaker into a chilled 10-ounce martini glass.
4. Float a thin slice of lemon and a thin slice of lime on the surface of the drink.

• MAKES 1 DRINK.

•   •   •   •

OLIVE GARDEN
MANGO MARTINI

Today I find myself at the Olive Garden bar tasting several new martinis displayed in full color on the front of the drink menu. And this is a good one. It features Malibu's great mango-flavored Caribbean rum, triple sec, sweet-and-sour mix, and a little Kern's mango nectar (which you'll find in 12-ounce cans) for a clone that's identical to the original. Shake everything up with ice and strain into a chilled martini glass and find out for yourself how hard it is to drink just one.

2 ounces Malibu mango-flavored
    Caribbean rum
¾ ounce triple sec

2 ounces Kern's mango nectar
2 ounces sweet-and-sour mix

GARNISH
lime slice

1. Drop a handful of ice into a cocktail shaker.
2. Pour everything into the shaker and shake thoroughly.
3. Strain entire contents of the shaker into a chilled 10-ounce martini glass.
4. Add a slice of lime to the rim of the glass.

• MAKES 1 DRINK.

• • • •

OLIVE GARDEN
BREADSTICKS

Anyone who loves Olive Garden is probably also a big fan of the bottomless basket of warm, garlicky breadsticks served before each meal at the huge Italian casual chain. My guess is that the breadsticks are proofed, and then sent to each restaurant, where they are baked until golden brown, brushed with butter, and sprinkled with garlic salt. Getting the bread just right for a good clone was tricky—I tried several different amounts of yeast in all-purpose flour, but then finally settled on bread flour to give these breadsticks the same chewy bite as the originals. I discovered that the two-stage rising process is also a crucial step to making the perfect *Top Secret Recipe* for these very popular soft breadsticks.

2 tablespoons granulated sugar
¾ teaspoon active dry yeast
I cup plus I tablespoon warm
    water (105 to 115 degrees F)

16 ounces bread flour (3 cups)
1½ teaspoons salt
¼ cup (½ stick) butter, softened

ON TOP
2 tablespoons butter, melted
½ teaspoon garlic salt

1.   Dissolve the sugar and yeast in the warm water in a small bowl or measuring cup and let the mixture sit for 5 minutes, or until it becomes foamy on top.

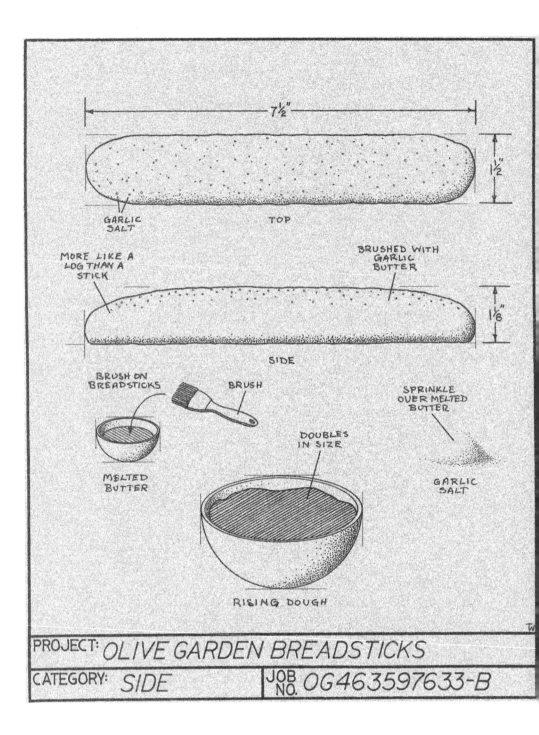

7½"

1½

GARLIC SALT

TOP

MORE LIKE A LOG THAN A STICK

BRUSHED WITH GARLIC BUTTER

1⅛"

SIDE

BRUSH ON BREADSTICKS

BRUSH

SPRINKLE OVER MELTED BUTTER

DOUBLES IN SIZE

MELTED BUTTER

GARLIC SALT

RISING DOUGH

PROJECT: OLIVE GARDEN BREADSTICKS

CATEGORY: SIDE

JOB NO. OG463597633-B

2.	Combine the flour and salt in a large bowl. Use the paddle attachment on a stand mixer to mix the softened butter into the flour. If you don't have a stand mixer, use a mixing spoon to combine the butter with the flour. When the yeast mixture is foamy, pour it into the flour mixture and use a dough hook on your mixture to combine the ingredients and knead the dough for approximately 10 minutes. If you don't have a stand mixer, combine the ingredients and then knead the dough by hand on a countertop for 10 minutes. Place the dough in a covered container and let it sit for 1 to 1½ hours, until it doubles in size.

3.	When the dough has doubled, measure out 2-ounce portions and roll the dough between your hands or on a countertop to form sticks that are 7 inches long. Place the dough on parchment paper–lined baking sheets, cover, and set aside for 1 to 1½ hours, or until the dough doubles in size once again.

4.	Preheat the oven to 400 degrees F.

5.	Bake the breadsticks for 12 minutes, or until golden brown. When the breadsticks come out of the oven, immediately brush each one with melted butter and sprinkle with a little garlic salt.

• MAKES 12 TO 13 BREADSTICKS.

•   •   •   •

OLIVE GARDEN DIPPING SAUCES FOR BREADSTICKS

MENU DESCRIPTION: *"Freshly prepared Alfredo or marinara sauce, served warm."*

The soft breadsticks served at Olive Garden taste awesome by themselves, but dunk 'em in one of these warm sauces and . . . fahgeddaboutit! You can use these clones as dipping sauces or pour them over the pasta of your choice to duplicate a variety of entrée items available at the chain. Use the Alfredo sauce over fettuccine and you duplicate the Fettuccine Alfredo. Pour the marinara sauce on linguine and you've cloned Olive Garden's Linguine alla Marinara. Make up your own dishes, adding sausage, chicken, or whatever you have on hand for an endless variety of Italian grub.

ALFREDO SAUCE

½ cup (1 stick) butter
1 tablespoon minced garlic (about 3 cloves)
2 cups heavy cream

¼ teaspoon salt
¼ teaspoon ground black pepper
¾ cup grated Parmesan cheese

Make the Alfredo sauce by melting the butter in a medium saucepan over medium heat. Add the garlic to the butter and cook for 1 minute, then whisk in the cream, salt, pepper, and cheese. Bring the mixture to a boil, then reduce the heat to medium/low and simmer for 12 to 15 minutes, or until thick, stirring often.

- MAKES 2½ CUPS.

MARINARA SAUCE

3 tablespoons extra virgin olive oil
⅓ cup diced onion
1½ teaspoons minced garlic
  (1½ cloves)
one 28-ounce can crushed
  tomatoes
¾ cup water

1½ teaspoons granulated sugar
¼ teaspoon salt
¼ teaspoon ground black pepper
¼ teaspoon dried basil
¼ teaspoon Italian seasoning
  herb blend

Heat the olive oil in a medium saucepan over medium heat. Add the onion and garlic and sauté for 1 to 2 minutes, or until the garlic begins to turn light brown. Stir in the crushed tomatoes, and then add the remaining ingredients. Bring the mixture to a boil, then reduce the heat and simmer uncovered for 25 minutes, stirring often.

- MAKES 3 CUPS.

• • • •

OLIVE GARDEN CHICKEN & GNOCCHI SOUP

MENU DESCRIPTION: *"A creamy soup made with roasted chicken, traditional Italian dumplings, and spinach."*

It's hard to find premade gnocchi that is as good as the stuff Olive Garden uses in their new hit soup. The gnocchi are perfectly tender and seasoned with a bit of nutmeg. But making gnocchi at home from scratch doesn't have to be hard. In this secret recipe for gnocchi made the Olive Garden way I found it best to use instant mashed potatoes. This way I could not only save time but also be certain that the gnocchi would turn out exactly the same with each batch. Once you make the gnocchi and form each chunk of dough into small disks, you can start on the soup. For the chicken, just grab a roasted chicken in your supermarket. Take off the skin, then remove the meat and chop it up before adding it to the soup. When the soup simmers until thick you will have eight 1-cup servings of a soup that tastes exactly like the new Olive Garden top menu choice.

GNOCCHI

1 cup Potato Buds
¾ teaspoon plus ⅛ teaspoon salt
¼ scant teaspoon ground nutmeg

1 cup boiling water
1 egg yolk
⅔ cup all-purpose flour

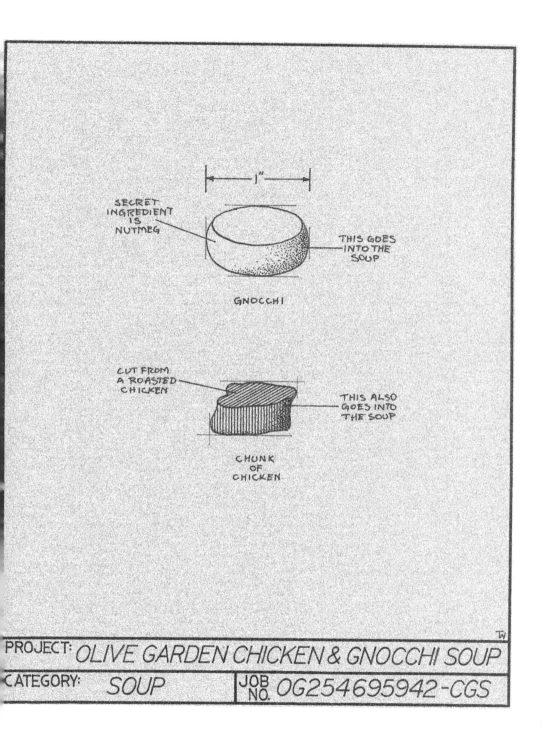

SECRET INGREDIENT IS NUTMEG

1"

THIS GOES INTO THE SOUP

GNOCCHI

CUT FROM A ROASTED CHICKEN

THIS ALSO GOES INTO THE SOUP

CHUNK OF CHICKEN

PROJECT: *OLIVE GARDEN CHICKEN & GNOCCHI SOUP*

CATEGORY: *SOUP*

JOB NO. *OG254695942-CGS*

2 tablespoons vegetable oil
½ cup shredded carrot
¼ cup diced onion
¼ cup chopped celery
1 teaspoon minced garlic
2 tablespoons cornstarch
4 cups chicken broth
4 cups water

1 ½ teaspoons salt
½ teaspoon ground black pepper
⅛ teaspoon ground nutmeg
1 ½ cups half-and-half
1 roasted chicken with meat
   removed and chopped (about
   1 pound meat)
2 cups chopped fresh spinach

1. Make the gnocchi by mixing the Potato Buds with the salt and nutmeg. Stir in the boiling water and continue mixing until no dry flakes remain. Stir in the egg yolk until the mashed potato mixture has an even pale yellow color throughout.

2. Stir in the flour and knead for about a minute with your hands.

3. Use a ½ teaspoon to measure out small portions of the dough. Using floured hands, roll the small dough portion around between the palms of your hands, making a ball, then press each ball down onto floured wax paper, making a small disk. When all the gnocchi is made, you can begin to make the soup.

4. Heat up the oil in a large soup pot or Dutch oven over medium heat. Add the carrot, onion, celery, and garlic and sauté for 3 minutes. Whisk the cornstarch into the chicken broth and add to the vegetables along with the water. When the mixture begins to boil, add the gnocchi. Reduce the heat and simmer for 10 minutes. Add the half-and-half and simmer for another 10 to 15 minutes, or until the soup begins to thicken. Add the chicken and spinach and simmer for another 10 minutes, or until the soup has thickened and the spinach is tender.

• MAKES 8 CUPS.

•   •   •   •

OLIVE GARDEN SMOKED MOZZARELLA FONDUTA

MENU DESCRIPTION: *"Oven-baked smoked mozzarella, provolone, Parmesan, and Romano cheese. Served with Tuscan bread."*

Olive Garden's take on the Italian melted cheese dip includes smoked mozzarella combined with grated Parmesan, Romano, and provolone cheese, and lots of thyme. When making your clone, be sure to slice the waxy rind off the smoked mozzarella before you grate it. That part does not taste good. After slowly melting the mozzarella, Parmesan, and Romano in a small saucepan with half-and-half, pour the creamy mixture into a shallow dish, top it with a slice of provolone, and pop it under the broiler until light brown. Serve your hot fonduta with baguette slices, bagel chips, or crackers.

1 ½ cups shredded smoked
    mozzarella cheese
1 ½ tablespoons grated Parmesan
    cheese
1 ½ tablespoons grated Romano
    cheese

⅓ cup half-and-half
½ teaspoon dried thyme
⅛ teaspoon crushed red pepper
    flakes
1 slice provolone cheese

GARNISH
1 tablespoon diced tomato
pinch or 2 minced parsley

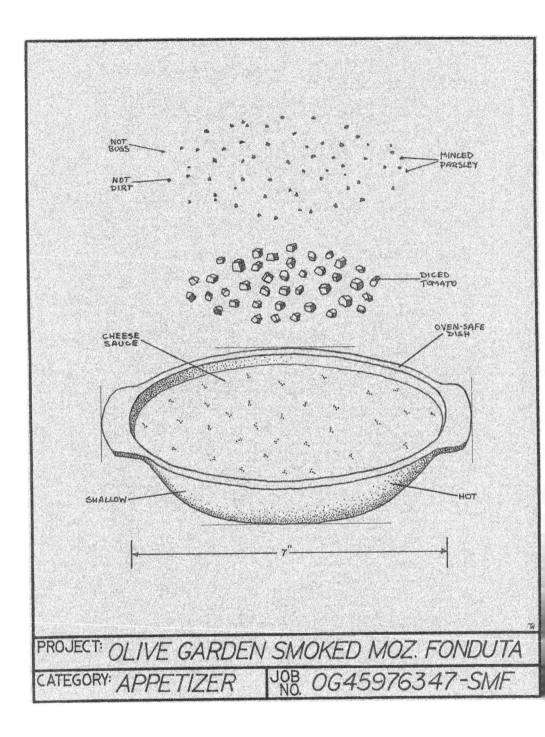

NOT BUGS

NOT DIRT

MINCED PARSLEY

DICED TOMATO

CHEESE SAUCE

OVEN-SAFE DISH

SHALLOW

HOT

7"

PROJECT: *OLIVE GARDEN SMOKED MOZ. FONDUTA*

CATEGORY: *APPETIZER*

JOB NO. *OG45976347-SMF*

ON THE SIDE

12 slices Tuscan bread, baguette,
crackers, or chips

1. Preheat broiler to high.
2. Combine mozzarella, Parmesan, Romano, half-and-half, thyme, and pepper flakes in a small saucepan over low heat. Stir constantly as cheese melts for 8 to 10 minutes, until mixture is smooth. Pour the mixture into a shallow oven-safe bowl, ramekin, or crème brûlée dish, and top it with a slice of provolone cheese.
3. Broil for 2 to 3 minutes, until the provolone is light brown. Spoon diced tomato onto the center of the fonduta, sprinkle with minced parsley, and serve it up with sliced bread, crackers, or chips on the side.

• MAKES 2 APPETIZER SERVINGS.

• • • •

OLIVE GARDEN STEAK GORGONZOLA ALFREDO

MENU DESCRIPTION: *"Grilled beef medallions drizzled with balsamic glaze, served over fettuccine tossed with spinach and gorgonzola-Alfredo sauce."*

This new menu item builds on Olive Garden's great Alfredo sauce recipe with the addition of gorgonzola cheese. The tangy cheese sauce works well with the sweet-and-sour balsamic reduction that is drizzled over the beef medallions. Find three 6-ounce sirloin steaks (or whatever cut you prefer) and slice each of them into four 1½-ounce fillets. Get pounding with a kitchen mallet and make those steaks about ½-inch thick and they will grill up to same size as the medallions on the original dish. Between the pounding and the meat tenderizer in the beef seasoning, you will turn even the cheapest cut of beef into a tender morsel. Build your dish as described below and you will have re-created the taste and presentation of the original rich, tasty, fulfilling dish.

BALSAMIC GLAZE

½ cup balsamic vinegar
½ cup honey
1½ teaspoons Knox unflavored
    gelatin powder

ALFREDO SAUCE

½ cup (1 stick) salted butter
2 cups heavy cream
¼ teaspoon garlic powder
⅛ teaspoon ground black pepper

½ cup crumbled gorgonzola
   cheese
¼ cup grated Parmesan cheese

one 12-ounce box fettuccine pasta

BEEF SEASONING

½ teaspoon meat tenderizer
   (McCormick brand works
   well)
¼ teaspoon ground black pepper

¼ teaspoon garlic powder
⅛ teaspoon dried thyme

three 6-ounce sirloin steaks
   each cut into four 1½-ounce
   medallions

4 cups chopped fresh spinach
3 tablespoons chopped green
   onions (about 2 onions)

GARNISH

3 tablespoons crumbled
   gorgonzola cheese

2 tablespoons chopped sun-dried
   tomatoes

1. Make balsamic glaze by combining balsamic vinegar, honey, and unflavored gelatin in a small saucepan over low heat. Stir often as mixture comes to a simmer. Turn off heat when mixture begins to boil, then remove it from the heat and cool at room temperature. The glaze will thicken even more as it cools.

2. Make the Alfredo sauce by melting the butter in a medium saucepan over medium heat. Add the cream, garlic powder,

pepper, and cheeses, and simmer over medium/low heat for 10 to 12 minutes or until thick.

3. Bring 4 to 6 quarts of water to a boil and add the pasta. Cook until done, then drain.

4. Preheat grill to high. Combine the beef seasoning ingredients. Pound beef medallions to about ½-inch thick and sprinkle both sides with the seasoning blend. When your grill is hot, cook beef medallions for 2 to 3 minutes per side, until cooked to your preference.

5. Just before serving the dish, add the chopped spinach and chopped green onions to the Alfredo sauce. For each serving toss approximately ⅓ of the fettuccine pasta with about ¾ cup of the Alfredo sauce in a medium bowl. Spoon onto a serving plate, and then arrange 4 beef medallions on the pasta. Drizzle balsamic vinegar glaze over each beef medallion. Combine gorgonzola cheese crumbles with chopped sun-dried tomatoes and sprinkle about 1½ tablespoons of this mixture over the beef medallions. Repeat for the remaining servings.

• MAKES 3 SERVINGS.

• • • •

OLIVE GARDEN
BLACK TIE MOUSSE CAKE

MENU DESCRIPTION: *"Rich layers of chocolate cake, dark chocolate cheesecake, and creamy custard mousse."*

There are four delicious layers in this amazing cake that has been a signature dessert at the Italian chain for years, but assembling your own home clone is not difficult. For the two cheesecake layers in the middle I created a custom "no-bake" recipe since the chocolate cake on the bottom is already baked and we don't want to bake it twice. The top layer is made by slowly cooking egg, cream, and sugar until thick, then stirring in chocolate chips. White chocolate drizzle is swirled into this fudgy topping, dark chocolate buttercream frosting is added, then mini chocolate chips are pressed all around the side of the cake. This dessert takes a little time only because each layer needs to set up in your chillin' box before the next one is added. But when it's all done you'll have 12 servings of a really great-looking dessert that will bring you much worship from each and every chocoholic in the room.

CHOCOLATE CAKE LAYER

9 tablespoons granulated sugar
1 egg
½ teaspoon vanilla extract
2 tablespoons vegetable oil
1 tablespoon shortening
¼ cup water

½ cup all-purpose flour
3 tablespoons Hershey's (not dark) cocoa powder
½ teaspoon baking powder
¼ teaspoon baking soda
¼ teaspoon salt

CHOCOLATE CHEESECAKE LAYER

¾ cup heavy cream
½ cup granulated sugar
½ teaspoon vanilla extract

8 ounces cream cheese, softened
1¾ cups semisweet chocolate
  chips

FLUFFY CHEESECAKE LAYER

¾ cup heavy cream
¼ cup granulated sugar

½ teaspoon vanilla extract
8 ounces cream cheese, softened

CHOCOLATE CUSTARD MOUSSE LAYER

1 egg
¾ cup heavy cream
¼ cup granulated sugar

½ teaspoon vanilla extract
1¼ cups semisweet chocolate
  chips

WHITE SWIRL

2 tablespoons white chocolate
  chips (about ¾ ounce)

1 tablespoon heavy cream
1 tablespoon powdered sugar

DARK CHOCOLATE BUTTERCREAM FROSTING

2 cups powdered sugar
3 tablespoons dark cocoa powder
  (Hershey's Special Dark)
¼ cup (½ stick) butter, softened

⅓ cup heavy cream
½ teaspoon black food coloring
  (optional)

6 ounces mini chocolate chips (½ bag)

1. Preheat the oven to 350 degrees F.
2. Make the chocolate cake by combining the sugar, egg, and vanilla in a medium bowl and mixing with an electric mixer on high for 1 minute. Add the oil and shortening and mix well, then add the water and mix until smooth.
3. In another medium bowl, combine the flour, cocoa powder, baking powder, baking soda, and salt. Pour this dry blend into the bowl with the wet ingredients and mix until smooth. Pour into a well-greased 10-inch springform pan and bake in the preheated oven for 25 minutes.
4. While the cake cools, make the chocolate cheesecake layer by mixing the heavy cream, sugar, and vanilla in a medium bowl with an electric mixer on high until the cream forms stiff peaks. Mix in the softened cream cheese until smooth. Melt the chocolate chips in your microwave in a small glass or ceramic bowl on high for 30 seconds. Stir the chips and then heat on high for another 15 to 30 seconds. Stir the chips until smooth, then mix the melted chocolate chips into cream cheese mixture. Spoon the chocolate cream cheese over the chocolate cake in the springform pan, cover, and chill for 1 hour.
5. Make the fluffy cheesecake layer by mixing the heavy cream, sugar, and vanilla in a medium bowl with an electric mixer on high until the cream forms stiff peaks. Mix in the softened cream cheese until smooth. Spread over the chocolate cream cheese layer and chill for 1 hour.
6. Make the chocolate custard layer by whisking together the egg, cream, and sugar in a medium metal bowl. Set the bowl over water that is simmering in a medium saucepan over medium/low heat (you can also use a double boiler pan for this) and whisk for 6 minutes, or until thick. Remove the bowl from the heat, add the chocolate chips, and mix with a spoon until smooth. Spread the chocolate custard over the fluffy cream cheese layer.
7. Make the white swirl by combining the white chocolate chips with the cream and powdered sugar in a small microwave-

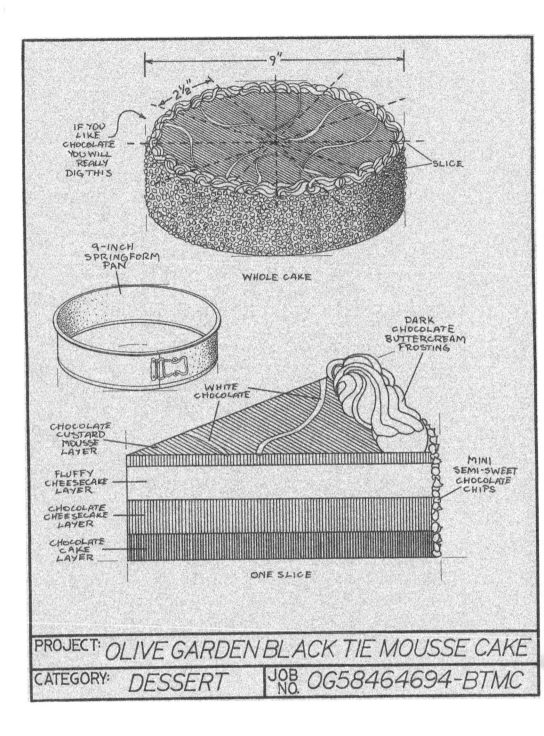

9"

2½"

IF YOU
LIKE
CHOCOLATE
YOU WILL
REALLY
DIG THIS

SLICE

WHOLE CAKE

9-INCH
SPRINGFORM
PAN

DARK
CHOCOLATE
BUTTERCREAM
FROSTING

WHITE
CHOCOLATE

CHOCOLATE
CUSTARD
MOUSSE
LAYER

FLUFFY
CHEESECAKE
LAYER

CHOCOLATE
CHEESECAKE
LAYER

CHOCOLATE
CAKE
LAYER

MINI
SEMI-SWEET
CHOCOLATE
CHIPS

ONE SLICE

PROJECT: *OLIVE GARDEN BLACK TIE MOUSSE CAKE*

CATEGORY: *DESSERT*

JOB NO. *OG58464694-BTMC*

safe glass or ceramic bowl. Heat on high for 30 seconds and stir. Heat for an additional 15 seconds if the chips haven't melted completely. Stir until smooth, then drizzle a little of this over the chocolate custard layer. Use a knife to swirl the white chocolate into the chocolate custard and chill until firm.

8. Make the dark chocolate buttercream frosting by combining the powdered sugar and dark cocoa powder in a small bowl. Add the butter, cream, and black food coloring (if using), and mix with an electric mixer until smooth. Load the frosting into a pastry bag fitted with a large star tip.

9. Remove the cake from the springform pan and pipe the frosting around the top edge of the cake.

10. Press mini chocolate chips around the sides of the cake. Press firmly so that the chips stick. Chill the cake for at least another hour, then use a serrated knife to cut the cake into 12 slices and serve.

• MAKES 12 SERVINGS.

•   •   •   •

ON THE BORDER MEXICAN MOJITO

You don't need rum to make a great mojito—just check out this variation on one of the most popular cocktails of the new millennium. Where white rum is usually found in this drink, America's largest casual Mexican food chain mixes in 1800 silver tequila and Cointreau orange liqueur. Add to that a little sweet-and-sour mix and a squirt of agave syrup and you have a tasty mash-up of margarita and mojito. Agave syrup is used as a sugar substitute, and it can be found in many markets now or in specialty and health food stores. The same brand of agave syrup On the Border uses in this drink (Wholesome) can be found at Whole Foods.

6 to 8 mint leaves
2 lime wedges
¾ ounce 1800 silver tequila
¾ ounce Cointreau liqueur

¼ cup sweet-and-sour mix
½ ounce agave syrup
splash soda

GARNISH
sprig of mint

1. Drop mint leaves and lime wedges into a 16-ounce glass and use a muddler (or a wooden spoon) to smash mint and lime, extracting juices.
2. Fill glass with ice.

⊙ TARGET
EXPECT MORE. PAY LESS.

SAN DIEGO MISSION VALLEY - 619-542-0025
02/04/2011 11:02 AM EXPIRES 05/05/11

CLOTHING
076062989   SS TEE   T $7.99

ENTERTAINMENT-ELECTRONICS
059043285   TOP SECRET   T $12.80

SUBTOTAL	$20.79
T = CA TAX 8.7500% on $20.79	$1.82
TOTAL	$22.61

        *0077 VISA CHARGE $22.61

Target Pharmacy   We're here to help!
        9am - 9pm M-F
        9am - 6pm Sat
        9am - 6pm Sun

REC#2-1035-1410-0086-8300-0 VCD#751-259-140

Thanks! Your purchase
helps give 5% of our
income to communities

Win a $5000 GiftCard

Tell us about your last shopping experience
at Target for a chance to win a
$5000 Target GiftCard!

Locate the Gift Registry
Kiosk and select GUEST SURVEY.
Or at home, log onto:

www.Target.com/survey
User ID: 7896 4859 0991
Password: 317 000

Cuéntanos acerca de tu última experiencia
de compra en Target y tendrás la oportunidad
de ganar una tarjeta de regalo
Target GiftCard de $5000.
En el kiosco del registro de regalos,
selecciona "Guest Survey" o visita
www.target.com desde tu casa e ingresa
la contraseña y N° de usuario de arriba.
Normas disponibles en "Servicio al huésped"

ONE WINNER PER MONTH!
Guest must be 18 or older to enter.
Sweepstakes runs from
2/01/2011 through 04/30/2011
Complete rules at Guest
Service Desk and Target.com/survey.
(Target team and family not eligible.)

3. Add tequila, orange liqueur, sweet-and-sour mix, and agave syrup. Slide a shaker over the top of the glass and invert it a couple times until agave nectar is incorporated. Remove the shaker from the glass, add a splash of soda, a straw, and a sprig of mint.

• MAKES 1 DRINK.

• • • •

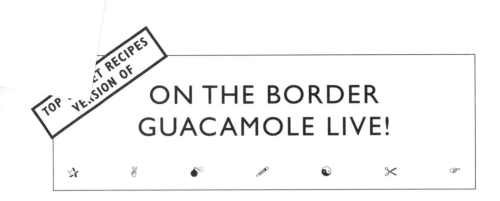

ON THE BORDER
GUACAMOLE LIVE!

MENU DESCRIPTION: *"Made fresh to order, with two whole avocados, plus your choice of tomatoes, jalapeños, cilantro, red onions, and fresh lime juice."*

This 160-unit casual Mexican chain makes a nice tableside guacamole that you can easily duplicate for your amigos. This is the basic formula, so now you can freely adjust it to suit the tastes of your crew. It's also easy to double (or more) this recipe for a bigger fiesta, if that's the plan. Just be sure to toss (gently!) the avocados into the fridge for an hour or two before you open them up. This guac is much better when slightly chilled.

2 ripe medium avocados, chilled
1 lime wedge
1 tablespoon chopped red onion
½ tablespoon minced jalapeño

1 tablespoon chopped cilantro
2 tablespoons diced tomato
⅛ to ¼ teaspoon salt

1. Mash avocados in a medium bowl, then add the juice of 1 lime wedge.
2. Stir in onion, jalapeño, cilantro, tomato and salt to taste. Serve with tortilla chips.

• MAKES 2 TO 4 APPETIZER SERVINGS.

• • • •

PIT
(DO NOT
EAT)

USE
THIS
PART

DON'T
USE
SKIN

AVOCADOS

LIME
WEDGE

MINCED
JALAPENO

DICED
TOMATO

CHOPPED
CILANTRO

CHOPPED
RED ONION

SALT

EVERYTHING
GOES IN
HERE

HARD NOT
TO
"DOUBLE-
DIP"

FINISHED GUACAMOLE

PROJECT:	ON THE BORDER GUACAMOLE LIVE!	
CATEGORY: SIDE	JOB NO.	OTB2459767113-GL

ON THE BORDER SMOKED JALAPEÑO VINAIGRETTE

One of the top dressing choices for your salad at this popular Mexican chain is this delicious, slightly spicy chipotle-flavored vinaigrette A clone for this one is made easily by combining several ingredients in a small pan over medium heat and simmering for 5 minutes. The final step involves creating an emulsion to thicken the dressing and to keep the oil from separating. I suggest measuring the oil into a spouted measuring cup. This will make it easy to drizzle the oil in a thin stream into the dressing while you are rapidly whipping the mixture with a wire whisk. If you break a slight sweat, you're doing it right.

4 teaspoons granulated sugar	¼ teaspoon ground chipotle chile
¼ cup water	½ teaspoon crushed red pepper
½ cup red wine vinegar	flakes
½ teaspoon paprika	¼ teaspoon dried oregano
¼ teaspoon ground black pepper	½ teaspoon salt
½ teaspoon garlic powder	¼ cup vegetable oil
½ teaspoon onion powder	

1. Combine all the ingredients except the oil in a small saucepan and place over medium heat. When the mixture reaches a boil, reduce the heat and simmer for 5 minutes.

2. Pour the dressing into a bowl. Drizzle the oil into the dressing in a thin stream while whisking quickly. Pour into a covered container and chill until cold.

• MAKES ¾ CUP.

• • • •

OUTBACK STEAKHOUSE BLEU CHEESE PECAN CHOPPED SALAD

This cheesy little number is one of the most popular salad choices that come with any entree order at America's favorite steakhouse chain. Cinnamon pecans and fried angel hair pasta are tossed with salad greens and a delicious sweet-and-sour bleu cheese vinaigrette. The crunchy angel hair pasta pieces are made by first boiling 24 strands of pasta for half of the usual cooking time. When the pasta is cool, you simply fry it in a bit of oil until light brown and crispy. The cinnamon pecans are easily candied in a small saucepan with a few basic ingredients. The recipe here makes two large salad servings, which will require only half of the dressing. This way, if you want to serve more salads you can easily double up on the other ingredients, and you'll have just the right amount of dressing to go around.

BLEU CHEESE VINAIGRETTE

⅔ cup extra virgin olive oil

¼ cup crumbled blue cheese

¼ cup honey

2 tablespoons grated Parmesan cheese

1 tablespoon granulated sugar

1 tablespoon minced garlic

1 ¼ teaspoons salt

1 teaspoon Italian herb seasoning blend

¼ teaspoon ground black pepper flakes

¼ teaspoon crushed red pepper

½ cup rice vinegar

2 teaspoons lemon juice

CINNAMON PECANS

3 tablespoons granulated sugar
1 tablespoon water
1 teaspoon salted butter

¼ teaspoon ground cinnamon
pinch salt
½ cup chopped pecans

CRUNCHY ANGEL HAIR PASTA

24 pieces uncooked angel hair
    pasta

1 cup vegetable oil

4 cups chopped iceberg lettuce
2 cups chopped romaine lettuce
⅓ cup chopped green onion

¼ cup chopped red cabbage
¼ cup shredded carrot
¼ cup crumbled bleu cheese

1. Make bleu cheese vinaigrette by combining all ingredients except vinegar and lemon juice in a small saucepan over medium heat. When the mixture begins to bubble, turn off the heat. When the mixture is cool, combine it with the rice vinegar and lemon juice in a blender. Blend on high speed for 1 minute, cover, and chill.
2. Make cinnamon pecans by combining the sugar, water, butter, cinnwamon, and salt in a small pan over medium heat. When the mixture begins to bubble, add pecans. Stir constantly until the liquid evaporates and the sugar begins to crystallize on the nuts. Don't allow the nuts to smoke or burn. Pour the nuts out onto a plate to cool.
3. To make the crunchy angel hair pasta, bring several cups of water to a boil in a large saucepan. Break the pasta into quarters and boil for 2 minutes, then drain and rinse with cold water. Bring 1 cup of oil to 325 degrees F. Fry the pasta in several batches in the oil for 1 minute or until light brown. Drain on paper towels. When the fried pasta is cool, break it into smaller bite-size pieces.

4. Assemble the salad by combining lettuces, green onion, red cabbage, shredded carrot, pecans, and pasta in a large bowl. Toss with ¾ cup of the dressing and serve in two bowls with 2 tablespoons crumbled blue cheese on top of each serving.

- MAKES 2 SERVINGS.

TIDBITS

You can save some time by substituting crispy chow mein noodles for the fried angel hair pasta. Just be sure to break the noodles up a bit before tossing them into the salad. Find chow mein noodles in the supermarket aisle where the Asian foods are stocked.

• • • •

OUTBACK STEAKHOUSE MASHED SWEET POTATOES

TOP SECRET RECIPES VERSION OF

This special side may not always be available at your local Outback Steakhouse, so just in case it gets yanked, here's a clone recipe to satisfy your craving. The butter, sugar, and spices added to the baked and mashed sweet potatoes make this dish great with salmon, chicken, turkey, and pork; and it totally rocks as a holiday feast side. The original version is so sweet and rich that it could double as pie filling. I've actually had to back off a bit on the butter and brown sugar compared to the helping I was served at the restaurant. And just check out the amazing finishing touch: pecans, corn flakes, and oats mixed with butter, brown sugar, and cinnamon for a streusel-like crunchy topping. You'll be tempted to eat this topping by itself with a spoon!

4 medium sweet potatoes
⅔ cup dark brown sugar
6 tablespoons salted butter
½ teaspoon salt

½ teaspoon ground cinnamon
¼ teaspoon ground nutmeg
¼ teaspoon ground allspice

TOPPING

1 tablespoon salted butter
6 tablespoons chopped pecans
¼ cup rolled oats (not instant)

2 tablespoons crumbled corn flakes
2 tablespoons dark brown sugar
½ teaspoon ground cinnamon

1. Bake sweet potatoes on a baking sheet for 60 to 70 minutes in a preheated 400 degrees F oven until soft. When the potatoes are cool enough to handle, slice each one in half and scoop out the good stuff. Toss the skins. Use an electric mixer on high to mash the potatoes in a large bowl until smooth. You should have 4 cups of mashed sweet potatoes. Mix in brown sugar, butter, salt, cinnamon, nutmeg, and allspice.

2. Make the topping by melting 1 tablespoon of butter over medium/low heat. Add the pecans, oats, and corn flakes (coarsely crumble the corn flakes in a bowl or plastic bag before measuring), and stir often over heat for 5 minutes, or until the mixture is hot. Don't let it get brown. Pour this mixture into a medium bowl. Combine brown sugar and cinnamon in a small bowl, and then stir the sugar into the nuts and cereal.

3. When you are ready to serve the mashed sweet potatoes, reheat the potatoes in a saucepan or in a microwave oven until hot. Spoon ¾ cup to 1 cup serving onto a plate and sprinkle with 2 tablespoons of the topping.

• MAKES 4 TO 6 SIDE SERVINGS.

• • • •

OUTBACK STEAKHOUSE THREE CHEESE AU GRATIN POTATOES

When I was there, this amazing side was on the Outback Steakhouse menu for a "limited-time-only." But that's okay, since a *Top Secret Recipe* for the dish is now here to stay. Even better, this cloned version is twice as big as what you get in the restaurant! The preparation is super simple: Peel and slice a couple russets and bake the slices on a sheet pan, then combine the baked slices with the cheese sauce in a casserole dish, sprinkle with cooked bacon, and broil to finish. Most of the work here went into getting the creamy three-cheese sauce to match up to the flavor and consistency of the real thing. With that mission accomplished—after shredding through several pounds of cheese—we've now got a versatile taste-alike dish that works great as a side for a variety of meals, from fancy sit-downs to company cookouts.

2 medium russet potatoes
2 tablespoons salted butter, melted

¼ teaspoon salt
¼ teaspoon ground black pepper

CHEESE SAUCE

1 tablespoon salted butter
1 tablespoon all-purpose flour

½ cup half-and-half
¾ cup shredded gruyère cheese

½ cup shredded Monterey Jack
    cheese
1 tablespoon grated Parmesan
    cheese

3 pieces thick-sliced bacon,
    cooked

GARNISH

½ teaspoon minced parsley

1.   Preheat oven to 450 degrees F.
2.   Peel the potatoes and slice them into ¼-inch-thick slices. Toss
     the potato slices in a bowl with the melted butter, salt, and
     pepper, then spread them out onto a baking sheet and bake
     for 30 minutes or until the edges of the potatoes begin to
     brown.
3.   While the potato slices bake, make the cheese sauce by
     whisking together the butter and flour in a small saucepan
     over medium/low heat. Heat until bubbling, and then stir in
     the half-and-half. When the mixture begins to bubble again,
     add the cheeses. Continue cooking the sauce over medium/
     low heat, stirring often, until smooth.
4.   When the potato slices are done, remove them from the
     oven and set the oven to high broil.
5.   Transfer the potato slices to a shallow casserole dish. Pour the
     cheese sauce over the potato slices. Mince the cooked bacon
     and then sprinkle it over the top of the potatoes.
6.   When the oven is hot, broil the dish for 2 minutes or until
     the top begins to bubble and brown. When it's done, sprinkle
     dish with ½ teaspoon of minced parsley and serve hot.

• MAKES 4 SIDE SERVINGS.

•   •   •   •

OUTBACK STEAKHOUSE OUTBACK RACK

MENU DESCRIPTION: *"A 14-ounce rack of New Zealand lamb served with a Cabernet sauce."*

Since the lamb racks Outback serves are smaller than the racks you'll most likely find at the market, just one New Zealand rack should be enough for two people. The racks I get at Costco weigh in anywhere from 24 to 28 ounces, and I've seen even bigger racks at other markets. Just be sure to trim off most of the extra fat before you sear the lamb. And after the searing, don't wash out that skillet! You want those flavorful little bits (*fond*) in there to make the incredible cabernet sauce that is served alongside the lamb for dipping, dousing, and drenching.

LAMB SEASONING

1 ½ teaspoons salt
1 teaspoon ground black pepper
1 teaspoon paprika
½ teaspoon garlic powder
¼ teaspoon onion powder
¼ teaspoon ground cayenne
    pepper

¼ teaspoon dried thyme
¼ teaspoon dried rosemary
¼ teaspoon dried basil
¼ teaspoon dried marjoram
¼ teaspoon dried oregano

1 tablespoon olive oil

1 rack New Zealand lamb,
    trimmed and cut in half

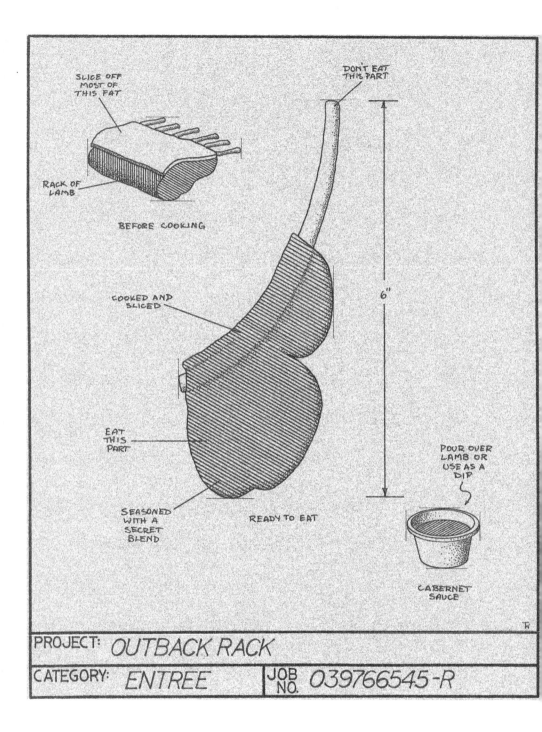

SLICE OFF
MOST OF
THIS FAT

DON'T EAT
THIS PART

RACK OF
LAMB

BEFORE COOKING

COOKED AND
SLICED

6"

EAT
THIS
PART

POUR OVER
LAMB OR
USE AS A
DIP

SEASONED
WITH A
SECRET
BLEND

READY TO EAT

CABERNET
SAUCE

PROJECT: *OUTBACK RACK*

CATEGORY: *ENTREE*   JOB NO. *039766545-R*

CABERNET SAUCE

1 tablespoon salted butter
1 teaspoon all-purpose flour
¼ cup cabernet sauvignon wine
⅓ cup beef broth

2 tablespoons water
1 ½ teaspoons Dijon mustard
1 teaspoon minced parsley
pinch Lamb Seasoning

1. Preheat oven to 425 degrees F.
2. Make the lamb seasoning by combining ingredients in a small bowl.
3. Heat 1 tablespoon of olive oil in a large skillet over medium heat. If the oil begins to smoke, your pan is too hot.
4. Trim the excess fat from the rack of lamb and slice the rack in half so that you have two smaller racks with 4 bones each. Sprinkle each rack with the seasoning blend.
5. Sear the top and bottom of the racks in hot oil for 3 to 4 minutes or until surface is browned. Put racks into an oven-safe roasting pan and bake for 15 minutes or until the internal temperature is 130 degrees F (for medium). When the lamb is done remove it from the oven, cover the pan with foil, and let the lamb rest for 8 to 10 minutes.
6. While the racks are baking, make the cabernet sauce by melting the butter in the searing skillet (make sure you have not washed out this skillet—the browned goodness from the searing should still be in there). When the butter is melted, add the flour and cook for a minute or until the flour begins to turn a tan color. Whisk in the other ingredients in the order listed, then turn off the heat.
7. When the lamb is done resting, cut each rack into chops and serve with cabernet sauce on the side.

• Makes 2 servings.

• • • •

OUTBACK STEAKHOUSE VICTORIA'S "CROWNED" FILET WITH HORSERADISH CRUMB CRUST

Tonight, don't settle for steaks that are served straight off the grill. Instead, blow everyone away when you serve up grilled beef tenderloin fillets that have been "crowned" with buttery horseradish bread crumbs. This presentation looks and tastes great, but the best part is that it's so freakin' easy! The crust is actually prepared ahead of time by combining the ingredients and forming the mixture into crust "wafers" that are chilled until firm. Then, when the steaks come off the grill, you top each one with a crust and broil until bubbling. Now, sit back and watch as your feeders flip when they take one bite. That's right, tonight you rule!

HORSERADISH CRUMB CRUST

¼ cup salted butter, softened

3 tablespoons plain bread crumbs (such as Progresso brand)

1 tablespoon white prepared horseradish

¼ teaspoon coarse grind black pepper

⅛ teaspoon crushed red pepper flakes

pinch salt

pinch dried thyme

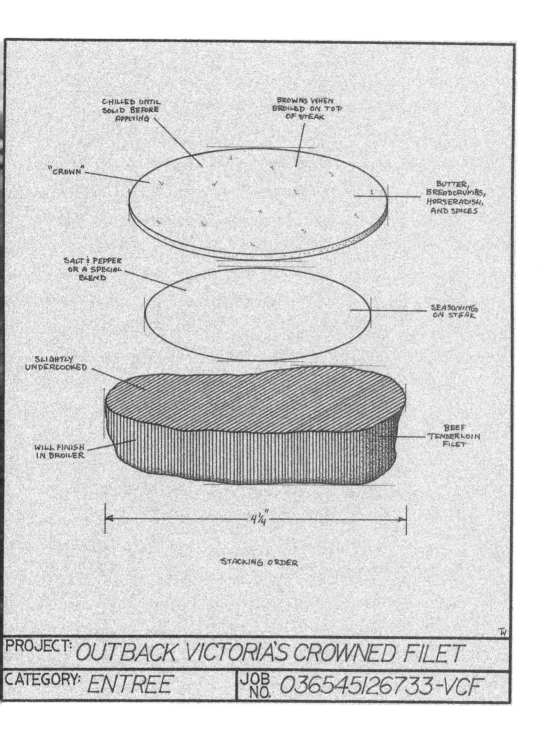

CHILLED UNTIL
SOLID BEFORE
APPLYING

BROWNS WHEN
BROILED ON TOP
OF STEAK

"CROWN"

BUTTER,
BREADCRUMBS,
HORSERADISH,
AND SPICES

SALT & PEPPER
OR A SPECIAL
BLEND

SEASONING
ON STEAK

SLIGHTLY
UNDERCOOKED

BEEF
TENDERLOIN
FILET

WILL FINISH
IN BROILER

4¼"

STACKING ORDER

PROJECT: *OUTBACK VICTORIA'S CROWNED FILET*

CATEGORY: *ENTREE*

JOB NO. *036545126733-VCF*

four 8-ounce beef tenderloin fillets

1. Prepare the crumb crust by combining all the ingredients in a medium bowl. Stir well.
2. Divide the mixture into 4 equal portions and form it into slightly oval-shaped disks that are approximately 2½ × 3 inches across on wax paper. Chill these crumb disks in your refrigerator until firm.
3. When you are ready to prepare the fillets, preheat your grill to high heat. Also preheat your oven broiler.
4. Season the fillets (see Tidbits below) and cook them on the preheated grill until just shy of your desired doneness. Arrange the fillets on a baking sheet, and top each one with a disk of crumb crust. Pop these fillets under the broiler until the crust is bubbling but not brown, and serve.

• MAKES 4 SERVINGS

TIDBITS

To season the fillets you can use salt and pepper or your favorite steak seasoning. If you want a taste that's closer to the steaks served at Outback, use our Top Secret Steak Rub! (www.TopSecret Recipes.com). It's a blend of spices that duplicates the flavor of the stuff used at the chain.

• • • •

OUTBACK STEAKHOUSE CHOCOLATE THUNDER FROM DOWN UNDER®

MENU DESCRIPTION: *"An extra generous pecan brownie is crowned with rich vanilla ice cream, drizzled with our classic warm chocolate sauce, and finished with chocolate shavings and whipped cream. A chocolate lover's dream."*

The gluten-free brownie that is the chocolate thunder under the ice cream and homemade whipped cream is a flourless chocolate pecan cake that is cut into squares. Once the "brownie" is baked, it is chilled and sliced, and then each serving is nuked for about forty-five seconds until gooey hot. The fun really starts when you load a huge scoop of vanilla ice cream on top of the hot brownie and then drizzle on some warm fudge sauce. Outback cooks make the sauce from scratch each day, but it tastes almost exactly like Hershey's Hot Fudge Topping, which you can get in just about any market. Maximum points will be earned when you make the whipped cream from scratch using the ridiculously easy recipe here—and there's nothing like freshly made whipped cream—but you can instead use the less delicious stuff that comes in a can if you're feeling lazy and cumulative point total is not a concern.

PECAN BROWNIE

24 ounces semisweet chocolate
(chips or bars)
¾ cup (1½ sticks) butter
5 eggs

½ cup granulated sugar
1½ teaspoons vanilla extract
¼ teaspoon salt
1 cup chopped pecans

WHIPPED CREAM

2 cups heavy cream
½ cup granulated sugar
½ teaspoon vanilla extract
½ teaspoon cream of tartar

9 large scoops vanilla ice cream
one 16-ounce jar Hershey's Hot
Fudge Topping

GARNISH

shavings from a semisweet chocolate bar

1. Preheat the oven to 325 degrees F.
2. Make the pecan brownie by combining the chocolate with the butter in a medium bowl. Microwave on high for 30 seconds, then stir and repeat 3 more times, or until the chocolate is completely melted and smooth.
3. Beat the eggs, sugar, vanilla, and salt together in a large bowl with an electric mixer on high speed for 1 minute. Mix a little of the warm chocolate into the eggs, then spoon in the rest and mix with the electric mixer until well combined. Mix in the pecans.
4. Pour the batter into a buttered 9 x 9-inch baking pan and bake for 45 to 50 minutes, or until the middle of the brownie rises and begins to firm up. Cool, cover, and chill in the pan for a couple hours. You can also serve the dessert now without chilling the cake—it's just a little more difficult to slice when warm. To serve the cake immediately after baking, just follow the remaining steps but skip the microwave heating in step #7 since the cake will already be warm.

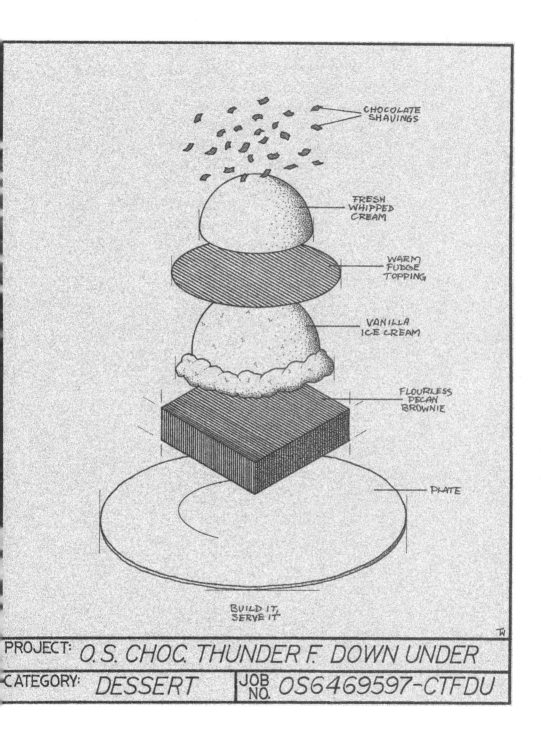

CHOCOLATE
SHAVINGS

FRESH
WHIPPED
CREAM

WARM
FUDGE
TOPPING

VANILLA
ICE CREAM

FLOURLESS
PECAN
BROWNIE

PLATE

BUILD IT,
SERVE IT

PROJECT: *O.S. CHOC. THUNDER F. DOWN UNDER*

CATEGORY: *DESSERT*   JOB NO. *OS6469597-CTFDU*

5. Make the whipped cream by combining the ingredients in a medium bowl and mixing with an electric mixer on high speed until the cream forms stiff peaks. Chill until needed.

6. When the brownie is cold, slice it into 9 even portions. Warm the fudge topping in a small saucepan of simmering water for 3 to 5 minutes or in your microwave for 1 minute on high. Be sure to remove the lid from the jar before heating it up.

7. To serve, arrange one brownie on a plate and microwave it on high for 45 seconds, or until hot. Add a scoop of ice cream on top of the brownie, then spoon some fudge topping over the ice cream. Add a large scoop of whipped cream on top of the ice cream. Use a potato peeler to shave some chocolate off the edge of a semisweet chocolate bar, sprinkle the shavings over the top of the whipped cream, and serve.

• MAKES 9 SERVINGS.

•   •   •   •

P. F. CHANG'S ASIAN PEAR MOJITO

You may be surprised not to find any pear ingredients in this drink. Rather, the flavors of lime juice, sour apple schnapps, citrus rum, and pineapple juice combine to create what P.F. Chang's bartenders claim is a refreshing pear-like flavor. Does it taste like pear to you? Regardless, the drink is excellent, especially if you dig mojitos.

3 lime wedges
5 mint leaves
1 ounce DeKuyper Sour Apple
   Pucker schnapps

1 ½ ounces Bacardi Limón citrus
   rum
splash pineapple juice
club soda

GARNISH
mint sprig
lime wedge

1. Dump 3 lime wedges and 5 mint leaves into a 16-ounce glass. Add the sour apple schnapps and muddle the ingredients until the juice is out of the lime wedges.
2. Fill glass with ice, then add citrus rum, a splash of pineapple juice, and fill the glass the rest of the way up with club soda.
3. Add a sprig of mint and a lime wedge and serve.

• MAKES 1 DRINK

• • • •

P. F. CHANG'S CHANG'S KEY LIME PIE MARTINI

This cocktail clone requires a vanilla-flavored Spanish liqueur called Licor 43. When it's mixed with key lime juice, sugar, and cream in just the right proportions, you get a remarkable liquid version of key lime pie. The restaurant uses bottled key lime juice which can be found at specialty stores such as Trader Joe's, or you can just squeeze your own key limes. And if you can't track down Licor 43, I found that Tuaca liqueur substitutes nicely. Cheers.

lime wedge	1 ounce key lime juice
graham cracker crumbs	¾ ounce half-and-half
1 ½ ounces Licor 43	canned whipped cream
1 teaspoon granulated sugar	

GARNISH
lime slice

1. Rub a wedge of lime on the rim of a chilled 8-ounce martini glass. Turn the glass over onto a small plate of graham cracker crumbs until the rim is thoroughly coated with crumbs.
2. Measure Licor 43 into the martini glass.
3. Measure sugar, key lime juice, and half-and-half into cocktail

shaker. Swirl the canned whipped cream 3 times around the inside of the shaker. Add a handful of ice and shake vigorously.

4. Strain drink into the martini glass and garnish with a thin slice of lime.

• Makes 1 drink.

•   •   •   •

P. F. CHANG'S CHICKEN IN SOOTHING LETTUCE WRAPS (IMPROVED)

MENU DESCRIPTION: *"Quickly cooked spiced chicken served with cool lettuce cups."*

While working on the formula for P. F. Chang's Vegetarian Lettuce Wraps for this book (page 300), I discovered that there were several ways I could improve the clone recipe for the Chicken Wraps that I published in *Top Secret Restaurant Recipes 2.* I've now perfected the flavor of the stir-fry with the addition of mirin (a sweetened sake syrup) and oyster sauce, both of which you can find in your market where the Asian foods are stocked. The "special sauce" that you spoon over your wraps has also been tweaked and perfected. And finally, after reducing the amount of chicken from two breasts fillets to just one, I think this new and improved version of P.F. Chang's most popular dish is the absolute best clone it can be.

SPECIAL SAUCE

2 tablespoons granulated sugar
½ cup water
3 tablespoons soy sauce
1 tablespoon rice vinegar
⅛ teaspoon chili oil

2 tablespoons chopped green onion
½ to 1 teaspoon Chinese hot mustard paste (see Tidbits)
1 to 3 teaspoons chili garlic sauce

STIR-FRY SAUCE

2 tablespoons plus 2 teaspoons
    soy sauce
1 tablespoon water

2 tablespoons mirin
1 tablespoon oyster sauce
2 teaspoons rice vinegar

4 tablespoons vegetable oil
1 large skinless chicken breast
    fillet
one 8-ounce can water chestnuts,
    drained and minced (about
    1 cup)

one 6-ounce can diced straw
    mushrooms, drained and
    minced (about ⅔ cup)
1 teaspoon minced garlic
3 tablespoons chopped green
    onion

1 to 1½ cups fried maifun rice
    sticks (see Tidbits)
4 to 5 iceberg lettuce cups

1. Make the special sauce (for spooning over your lettuce wraps) by dissolving the sugar in the water in a small bowl. Add the soy sauce, rice vinegar, and chili oil. Add the chopped green onion and set the sauce aside until you're ready to serve the lettuce wraps. Eventually you will add Chinese mustard and garlic chili sauce to this special sauce mixture to pour over each of your lettuce wraps. In the restaurant, waiters prepare the sauce at your table the same way based on your desired heat level. We'll get into the specifics of that in step #7.
2. Prepare the stir-fry sauce by mixing all of the ingredients together in a small bowl.
3. To prepare the filling for your lettuce wraps, heat 1 tablespoon of the vegetable oil in a large sauté pan or wok over high heat. Sauté the chicken breast for 4 to 5 minutes per side, or until cooked through. Remove the chicken from the pan to cool. Wipe out the pan.

4. As the chicken cools, chop your water chestnuts and mushrooms into pieces that are about the size of small peas. If you haven't fried the maifun rice sticks, this is a good time to do that.

5. When you can handle the chicken, hack it up with a sharp knife so that no piece is bigger than a dime. With the pan or wok back on high heat, add the 3 remaining tablespoons of oil. When the oil is hot, add the chicken, water chestnuts, mushrooms, and garlic to the pan. Cook the mixture for 2 minutes, stirring often. Add the stir-fry sauce to the pan and sauté the mixture for a couple more minutes, then stir in the green onions and spoon everything out onto a bed of fried maifun rice noodles on a serving dish.

6. Serve the chicken with a side of lettuce cups. Make these lettuce cups by slicing the top off of a head of iceberg lettuce right through the middle of the head. Pull your lettuce cups off of the outside of this slice.

7. Prepare the special sauce at the table by adding your desired measurement of hot mustard and chili sauce to the special sauce blend: 1 teaspoon of chili garlic sauce for mild, ½ teaspoon of mustard paste plus 2 teaspoons chili garlic sauce for medium, and 1 teaspoon of mustard paste and 3 teaspoons of chili garlic sauce for hot. Stir well.

8. Assemble each lettuce wrap by spooning the filling into a lettuce cup, adding special sauce over the top and eating it like a taco.

- SERVES 2 AS AN APPETIZER.

TIDBITS

Follow the directions on the package for frying the maifun rice sticks—usually by pouring 2 inches of vegetable oil into a pan and heating it to around 400 degrees F. Add the maifun, and when it floats to the top remove it to a paper towel.

You can find Chinese hot mustard in bottles sold as a paste or you can use dry Chinese mustard powder and make it into a paste. Follow the direction on the bottle for mixing the dry stuff with water to turn it into a paste, which can then be mixed into the special sauce.

•   •   •   •

P. F. CHANG'S
VEGETARIAN
LETTUCE WRAPS

☆ ✌ ✸ ✏ ☯ ✂ ☞

MENU DESCRIPTION: *"Wok-seared tofu, red onions, water chestnuts with mint and lime. Served with cool lettuce cups."*

After publishing the original version of my clone for this chain's Chicken in Soothing Lettuce Wraps in 2006, the requests for a clone of the vegetarian version began to flow in. I had always been a big fan of the chicken version and was hesitant to even try the vegetarian version, thinking that it could not possibly be as delicious. Man, was I wrong! Chefs at the Chinese bistro chain use finely diced baked tofu where the chicken would be. The red onion, lime juice, and mint add a special flavor combo that many feel makes this dish taste even better than the original. Track down some baked tofu and give this one a try. Baked tofu has a dark exterior and is much firmer than regular tofu. If you can't find it at your supermarket, you can get it at Asian markets or in specialty stores such as Whole Foods. It comes in a variety of flavors, like teriyaki and curry, but you want the unflavored stuff. Slicing it up is as simple as cutting it into thin slices, cutting those slices in half lengthwise, and then cutting across those julienned slices so that you end up with very small diced pieces. Crank your stove up as high as it goes for this one and get ready to not miss the chicken.

SPECIAL SAUCE

2 tablespoons granulated sugar
½ cup water
3 tablespoons soy sauce
1 tablespoon rice vinegar
⅛ teaspoon chili oil

2 tablespoons chopped green
   onion
½ to 1 teaspoon Chinese hot
   mustard paste (see Tidbits)
1 to 3 teaspoons chili garlic sauce

STIR-FRY SAUCE

2 tablespoons plus 2 teaspoons
   soy sauce
1 tablespoon water

2 tablespoons mirin
1 tablespoon oyster sauce
2 teaspoons rice vinegar

3 tablespoons vegetable oil
4 ounces baked tofu (regular
   flavor)
one 8-ounce can water chestnuts,
   drained and minced (about
   1 cup)
¼ cup diced red onion

1 teaspoon minced garlic
juice from a wedge of lime (about
   ½ teaspoon)
1 tablespoon minced mint leaves
2 tablespoons chopped green
   onion

1 to 1½ cups fried maifun rice
   sticks (see Tidbits)
4 to 5 iceberg lettuce cups

GARNISH

2 lime wedges

1. Make the special sauce (for spooning over your lettuce wraps) by dissolving the sugar in the water in a small bowl. Add the soy sauce, rice vinegar, and chili oil. Add the chopped green onion and set the sauce aside until you're ready to serve the lettuce wraps. Eventually you will add Chinese mustard and garlic chili sauce to this special sauce mixture to pour over each of your lettuce wraps. In the restaurant, wait-

ers prepare the sauce at your table the same way based on your desired heat level. I'll tell you more about that later.

2. Prepare the stir-fry sauce by mixing all of the ingredients together in a small bowl.

3. To prepare the filling for your lettuce wraps, heat 3 tablespoons of vegetable oil in a large sauté pan or wok over high heat. Slice the tofu into thin strips, slice the strips in half, and then cut through the strips, making a small dice. Chop the water chestnuts into pieces that are about the size of peas. If you haven't fried the maifun rice sticks, this is a good time to do that.

4. When the oil is hot, add the tofu and sauté for about 20 seconds. Add the water chestnuts, red onion, and garlic, and sauté for 2 minutes. Add the stir-fry sauce and juice from the wedge of a lime and sauté for 2 more minutes. Add the mint and green onion and spoon everything out onto a bed of fried maifun rice noodles on a serving dish. Place 2 wedges of lime on the dish.

5. Serve the dish with a side of lettuce cups. Make these lettuce cups by slicing the top off of a head of iceberg lettuce right through the middle of the head. Pull your lettuce cups off of the outside of this slice.

6. Prepare the special sauce at the table by adding your desired measurement of hot mustard and chili sauce to the special sauce blend: 1 teaspoon of chili garlic sauce for mild, ½ teaspoon of mustard paste plus 2 teaspoons chili garlic sauce for medium, and 1 teaspoon of mustard paste and 3 teaspoons of chili garlic sauce for hot. Stir well.

7. Assemble each lettuce wrap by spooning the filling into a lettuce cup, adding special sauce over the top, and eating it like a taco.

• SERVES 2 AS AN APPETIZER.

Follow the directions on the package for frying the maifun rice sticks—usually by pouring 2 inches of vegetable oil into a pan and heating it to around 400 degrees F. Add the maifun, a little at a time, and when it floats to the top, remove it to a paper towel.

You can find Chinese hot mustard in bottles sold as a paste or you can use dry Chinese mustard powder and make it into a paste. Follow the directions on the bottle for mixing the dry stuff with water to turn it into a paste, which can then be mixed into the special sauce.

•   •   •   •

P. F. CHANG'S
SPICY GREEN BEANS

MENU DESCRIPTION: *"Stir-fried with Sichuan preserves, fiery chili sauce, and garlic."*

Here's an easy side dish that you can start on a day or two before you plan to serve it. Planning ahead like this will allow the spicy Sichuan mixture some quality chill time to pickle in the salt and acids. When you're ready to rock it, a high-heat sauté is put on the beans, preserves are added to the pan, and in less than 5 minutes you've got yourself an impressive, flavorful side that goes great with a slew of entrées—Asian-style or not!

2 tablespoons minced onion
1 tablespoon minced garlic
1 tablespoon canned diced green
   chiles, rinsed and minced
   (see Tidbits)
2½ teaspoons soy sauce
2½ teaspoons chili garlic sauce
   (sambal; see Tidbits)

1½ teaspoons rice vinegar
1 teaspoon lemon juice
¼ teaspoon salt
1½ tablespoons vegetable or
   canola oil
½ pound green beans

1. Combine onion, garlic, chiles, soy sauce, chili garlic sauce, rice vinegar, lemon juice, and salt in a small bowl. Cover and store for several hours or overnight.
2. To prepare the beans, heat 1½ tablespoons of oil in a wok

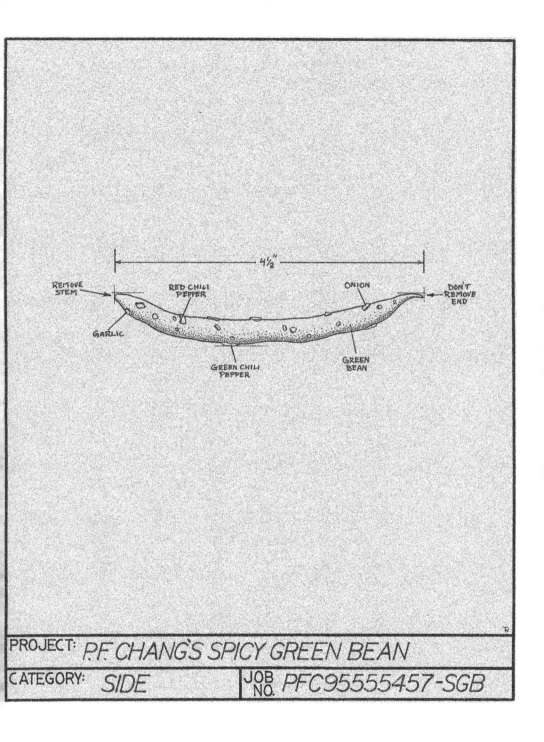

4½"

REMOVE STEM

RED CHILI PEPPER

ONION

DON'T REMOVE END

GARLIC

GREEN CHILI PEPPER

GREEN BEAN

PROJECT: *P.F. CHANG'S SPICY GREEN BEAN*

CATEGORY: *SIDE*   JOB NO. *PFC95555457-SGB*

(or sauté pan) over medium/high heat. Add the beans and cook for 2 minutes or until the beans begin to brown in spots.

3. Add the spicy garlic mixture to the beans and cook for an additional 2 to 3 minutes, until the beans are cooked. Beans should be cooked al dente, or with just a slight snap to them.

• MAKES 2 TO 4 APPETIZER SERVINGS.

TIDBITS

Chili garlic sauce is a deep red sauce that is also called sambal. You can find it in your market where other Asian foods are parked. For the canned green chiles, I used Ortega brand. These "fire-roasted" green chiles can be found in small 4-ounce cans. Drain off the liquid and rinse the chiles, then chop them into finer bits before measuring.

•   •   •   •

P. F. CHANG'S
KUNG PAO CHICKEN

MENU DESCRIPTION: *"Quick-fired with peanuts, chili peppers, and scallions. Our hot favorite."*

My personal favorite chicken dish at P. F. Chang's is also the top spicy chicken entrée at the 89-unit China bistro chain. The secret to creating a great clone is in combining the right ingredients for the perfect marinade that will also become the sauce in the dish. Soy sauce and oyster sauce provide the saltiness. Mirin, which is sweetened sake, contributes the sweet flavor component to offset the saltiness. Chili oil gives the sauce its spicy kick and a little rice vinegar adds the necessary acidity. I worked through several batches of the sauce to find the perfect balance of flavorful ingredients that most closely matches the stuff served at the restaurant. Sliced chicken breasts take a soak in this sauce for about an hour, then the chicken is dusted with a little cornstarch and flash-fried in peanut oil. You can use a wok for the frying stage and then rinse it out for the final sauté, or you can use a medium saucepan to fry the chicken and a sauté pan to finish cooking everything with the reserved sauce. Either way, you'll get a great clone that goes perfectly with a side of white or brown rice. Re-creating a clone of this dish was tough, but it wasn't as hard as picking up peanuts with chopsticks. Still haven't figured out that trick.

MARINADE/SAUCE

3 tablespoons soy sauce

4 teaspoons mirin

1 tablespoon peanut oil

1 tablespoon oyster sauce

1 tablespoon water

1 tablespoon chili oil

2 teaspoons rice vinegar

2 skinless chicken breast fillets

2 tablespoons cornstarch

2 to 3 cups peanut oil or
    vegetable oil

⅓ cup unsalted roasted peanuts

5 to 6 dried arbol chiles

1 teaspoon minced garlic

¼ teaspoon red chile flakes

2 tablespoons chopped green
    onion

ON THE SIDE

cooked white or brown rice

1. Make the marinade by combining all of the ingredients in a small bowl.
2. Cut the chicken into bite-size chunks, then stir it into the marinade, cover, and chill for 1 hour. Stir the chicken a couple times as it marinates.
3. After 1 hour, pour the marinated chicken into a wire mesh strainer over a bowl. When all the liquid has strained off the chicken, dump the chicken into a medium bowl and sprinkle with the cornstarch while tossing to coat each piece evenly. Save the sauce in the bowl.
4. Heat 2 to 3 cups of oil in a large saucepan or wok over medium heat. When the oil begins to shimmer (around 300 degrees F), drop the chicken into the oil and cook for about 2 minutes, or until the chicken begins to brown. Remove the chicken to a plate, then preheat a large sauté pan over medium heat. If using a wok, rinse the wok and preheat it over medium heat.

5. When your pan or wok is hot, add the strained sauce, peanuts, dried chiles, garlic, and chile flakes. When the sauce begins to boil, add the chicken and cook for 1 minute, stirring often. Add the green onion and cook for 1 more minute, or until the sauce has thickened and the chicken has darkened. Pour out onto a serving plate and serve with white or brown rice.

• SERVES 2.

•   •   •   •

PIZZA HUT WINGSTREET TRADITIONAL BUFFALO WINGS (MILD, MEDIUM, BURNIN' HOT)

Pizza Hut added buffalo wings to the chain's menu in 1995, but as the popularity of wings began to grow Yum! Brands (the parent company of Pizza Hut) created WingStreet in 2003, offering eight different sauces on wings cooked three different ways. The Wing-Street stores are almost always co-located in Pizza Hut stores so that you can get 8, 14, 22, or 44 breaded, unbreaded, or boneless wings delivered right to your door along with your pizza. With the variety of flavors and prep options, the chain calculated that there are exactly 162 different ways you can get your wings, although the most popular are always the traditional bone-in unbreaded wings with the spicy buffalo sauce that comes in either burnin' hot, medium, or mild heat flavors. In fact, the medium sauce was named the "Best Medium Traditional Wing Sauce" in 2006, 2008, and 2009 at the National Buffalo Wing Festival held in Buffalo, New York, every fall. After some sleuthing I discovered that margarine is the secret ingredient in this award-winning sauce. It melts perfectly, creating a smooth sauce that coats nicely without the gloopy milk solids that come along for the ride in butter. You can certainly substitute with butter if you like, but if you want the closest copy of the WingStreet originals, margarine is the way to go. Also, be sure the wings you use are small—there should be about 14 wings to 1½ pounds. And fresh chicken is always better than frozen.

MILD

¼ cup water
¼ cup Frank's Red Hot Original
    Cayenne Pepper Sauce
¼ cup margarine

2 teaspoons dark brown sugar
1½ teaspoons paprika
1 teaspoon white vinegar
⅛ teaspoon garlic powder

MEDIUM

½ cup Frank's Red Hot Original
    Cayenne Pepper Sauce
¼ cup margarine
2 tablespoons water

1 teaspoon paprika
2 teaspoons granulated sugar
⅛ teaspoon garlic powder

BURNIN' HOT

½ cup Frank's Red Hot Original
    Cayenne Pepper Sauce
¼ cup margarine
2 tablespoons water

1 teaspoon cayenne pepper
1 teaspoon paprika
2 teaspoons granulated sugar
⅛ teaspoon garlic powder

6 to 10 cups vegetable oil or
    shortening (the amount
    required by your fryer)
14 chicken wings

ON THE SIDE

blue cheese dressing or ranch
    dressing for dipping

1. Make the sauce of your choice by combining the ingredients in a small saucepan over medium heat. When the sauce begins to bubble, reduce the heat and simmer for 3 minutes, then cover and remove from the heat.
2. Heat the oil or shortening in a deep fryer to 350 degrees F.
3. When the oil is hot, drop in the wings and fry for 10 to 12 minutes, or until crispy and light brown.

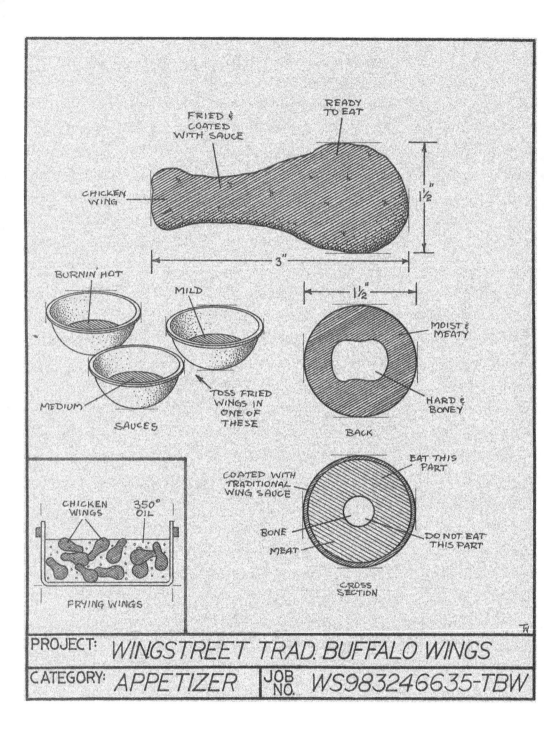

FRIED &
COATED
WITH SAUCE

READY
TO EAT

CHICKEN
WING

1½"

3"

BURNIN' HOT

MILD

1½"

MOIST &
MEATY

MEDIUM

TOSS FRIED
WINGS IN
ONE OF
THESE

HARD &
BONEY

SAUCES

BACK

CHICKEN
WINGS

350°
OIL

EAT THIS
PART

COATED WITH
TRADITIONAL
WING SAUCE

BONE

DO NOT EAT
THIS PART

MEAT

FRYING WINGS

CROSS
SECTION

PROJECT:	*WINGSTREET TRAD. BUFFALO WINGS*
CATEGORY: *APPETIZER*	JOB NO. *WS983246635-TBW*

4. Pour the wings into a large bowl and cover with sauce. Toss until the wings are well coated and serve with blue cheese dressing or ranch dressing on the side for dipping.

• SERVES 2.

• • • •

PIZZA HUT TUSCANI CREAMY CHICKEN ALFREDO PASTA

MENU DESCRIPTION: *"Grilled chicken breast strips and rotini pasta oven baked in a creamy Alfredo sauce with a layer of melted cheese."*

Pizza Hut announced its new pasta dishes in 2008 with an e-mail campaign claiming the company was changing its name to "Pasta Hut." The date was April 1, and the blast was an April Fool's publicity stunt that helped make the chain's new Tuscani pastas one of the company's most popular new product launches. What makes these pastas special is that they are covered with a layer of shredded cheese and then baked in a pizza oven until light brown on top. Of the three varieties available at the chain, the Creamy Chicken Alfredo Pasta garnered the most cloning requests, with everyone pleading to know how to duplicate the delicious Alfredo sauce. I cooked my way through several pounds of pasta and many quarts of cream, but finally discovered the perfect *Top Secret Recipe* that will allow you to make this delicious dish in your own kitchen. And it's remarkably simple.

CHICKEN

2 skinless chicken breast fillets
1 tablespoon salt

2 cups water
1 tablespoon extra light olive oil

ALFREDO SAUCE

½ cup (1 stick) butter
2 teaspoons minced garlic
2 cups heavy cream
½ cup whole milk

½ cup grated Parmesan cheese
1 teaspoon salt
½ teaspoon coarsely ground black
    pepper

1 pound uncooked rotini pasta
2 cups finely shredded mozzarella
    cheese

1. Cover the chicken breasts with plastic wrap and pound them to about ½-inch thick with a kitchen mallet. Dissolve the salt in the water, add the chicken, then cover and chill for exactly 1 hour. When the chicken is done marinating, remove it from the brine, rinse it off, and blot it dry. Heat up 1 teaspoon of oil in a medium sauté pan over medium-high heat and cook the chicken in the pan for 3 to 4 minutes per side, or until cooked through. Cool and chop into bite-size chunks.
2. Make the Alfredo sauce by melting the butter in a medium saucepan over medium/low heat. Add the garlic and cook for 1 minute. Add the remaining ingredients and increase the heat to medium. When the sauce begins to boil, reduce the heat and simmer for 12 minutes, or until thickened.
3. Cook the pasta in 3 to 4 quarts of boiling water for 8 minutes, or until tender. Drain.
4. Preheat the broiler to high.
5. Pour the pasta into a 9 x 13-inch baking pan. Pour the Alfredo sauce over the pasta and toss to coat all of the pasta. Sprinkle the chicken over the top of the pasta, then cover with the shredded cheese.
6. Broil for 2 to 3 minutes, or until the cheese begins to brown. Prepare to modestly accept all kudos.

• SERVES 6.

•   •   •   •

PIZZA HUT
PAN PIZZA

According to my sources, the dough for the pan pizza from Pizza Hut is made fresh in each store every day, and when the day's over any leftovers are tossed out. The secret to perfect pan pizza is pressing the dough into a well-oiled pan (Pizza Hut uses soybean oil), then the pan is covered and the dough rises in a heated cabinet for 45 to 60 minutes. When the dough is topped, the edge is sprayed with a butter-flavored "food release" and the pie is baked at 500 degrees F until perfectly browned on top. You can use a 9-inch, 12-inch, or 15-inch deep dish pizza pan or cake pan for this recipe, and you'll want to preheat your oven with a pizza stone it in to simulate the type of oven used at the chain. The hot ceramic surface of the pizza stone will cause the oil in the pan to cook the bottom of the dough so that it's brown and crispy like an authentic pan pizza crust should be. I tried making the dough with cake flour, all-purpose flour, superfine "00" flour, bread flour, and many combinations of these different flours that all contain varying amounts of gluten. I even tried rising the dough slowly in the refrigerator for various lengths of time as long as up to four days. But after a month of testing and about 30 pan pizzas later, I found the best dough to be straight bread flour, and to let the dough rise at room temperature. I did find that if you let the dough rest for at least 4 hours before the final rise in the pizza pan, the glutens continue to toughen, and you will get the best texture with the perfect chewy bite to it. After about 9 hours, though, the dough is pretty much finished, and it's time to close up shop.

DOUGH

(24 ounces dough—enough for 3 small, 2 medium, or 1 large)

1 tablespoon granulated sugar
1½ teaspoons active dry yeast
1⅓ cups warm water (105 to
    115 degrees F)

3 cups bread flour
1¼ teaspoons salt

SAUCE

one 6-ounce can tomato paste
1⅓ cups water
½ teaspoon dried crushed
    rosemary
½ teaspoon dried minced onion
¼ teaspoon dried oregano
¼ teaspoon salt

¼ teaspoon dried thyme
¼ teaspoon garlic powder
⅛ teaspoon ground black
    pepper
⅛ teaspoon dried basil
⅛ teaspoon citric acid

1 to 2 tablespoons soybean or
    safflower oil
3½ cups shredded mozzarella
    cheese

Pam or Crisco butter-flavored
    nonstick spray

Your choice of toppings: pepperoni, ham, crumbled Italian sausage, bacon pieces, diced cooked chicken, mushrooms, green peppers, sliced onion, black olives, diced tomatoes, jalapeños, pineapple, or roasted red peppers.

1. Make the dough by dissolving the sugar and yeast in the warm water. Allow the solution to sit for about 5 minutes, or until it gets foamy on top.
2. Combine the flour with the salt in a large bowl. It's best to use a stand mixer with a paddle for this, then switch out the paddle for a dough hook.

3. Pour the foamy yeast solution into the flour and combine on low speed until a dough is formed. Turn up the speed a little and knead the dough for 10 minutes. If you don't have a stand mixer, knead by hand for 10 minutes, or until the dough is very smooth and elastic. Cover the dough in the mixing bowl and let the dough rest for 2 hours.

4. Roll out the proper portion of dough to fit in the deep dish pan or cake pan you are using: If you are making a 9-inch pizza (small), divide the dough into three equal portions; for a 12-inch pizza (medium), divide the dough in half; and for a 15-inch pizza (large), use all the dough. Roll out the portion of dough so that it is slightly bigger than the pan you are using. Rub oil around the bottom of the pan: Use 1 tablespoon oil in a 9-inch pan, 1½ tablespoons in a 12-inch pan, and 2 tablespoons in a 15-inch pan. Drop the dough into the bottom of the pan and spread it smooth to the edge of the pan, and then use your fingers to form a raised lip around the edge. Cover the pan with foil and place in a warm spot for 1 hour. If you have two ovens, place the covered dough into one of the ovens with a pan of boiling water, then close the door. If you have only one oven, you can set the pan near that oven, since you will now preheat the oven and it will give off some heat. Place a pizza stone in the oven and set it to 500 degrees F.

5. Make the sauce by combining all the ingredients in a small saucepan and placing it over medium heat. When the mixture begins to boil, reduce the heat and simmer for 10 minutes. Cover the sauce, and let it cool while the dough rises.

6. When the dough has doubled in size, spoon approximately ¼ cup of sauce on a 9-inch pizza, ⅓ cup sauce on a 12-inch pizza, or ½ cup sauce on a 15-inch pizza. Spray the edges of the crust with butter-flavored nonstick spray, then top the pizza with enough shredded mozzarella cheese to cover the sauce. Add your choice of toppings and bake for 10 to 12 minutes, or until the crust and cheese begins to brown. Re-

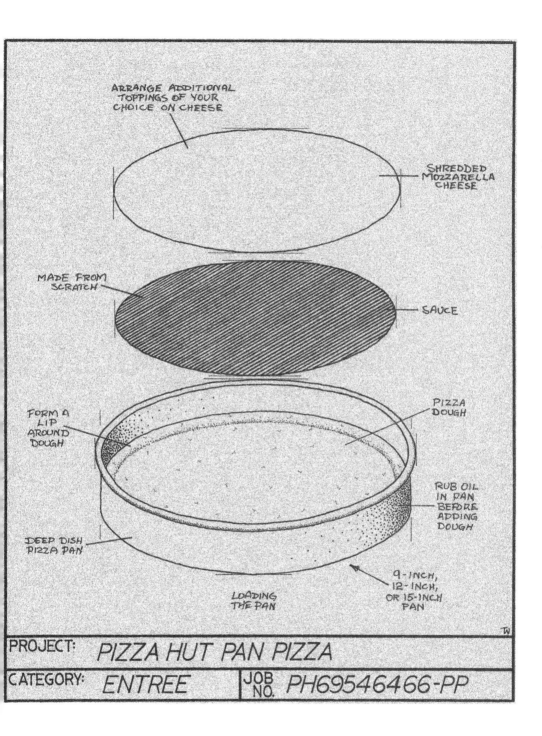

ARRANGE ADDITIONAL
TOPPINGS OF YOUR
CHOICE ON CHEESE

SHREDDED
MOZZARELLA
CHEESE

MADE FROM
SCRATCH

SAUCE

PIZZA
DOUGH

FORM A
LIP
AROUND
DOUGH

RUB OIL
IN PAN
BEFORE
ADDING
DOUGH

DEEP DISH
PIZZA PAN

9-INCH,
12-INCH,
OR 15-INCH
PAN

LOADING
THE PAN

TW

PROJECT: *PIZZA HUT PAN PIZZA*

CATEGORY: *ENTREE*   **JOB NO.** *PH69546466-PP*

move the pizza from the oven, allow it to cool for a few minutes, then slide it out of the pan, slice, and serve. Repeat the process with remaining ingredients if you made the small- or medium-size pizzas.

• MAKES THREE 9-INCH PIZZAS (SMALL), TWO 12-INCH PIZZAS (MEDIUM), OR ONE 15-INCH PIZZA (LARGE).

• • • •

RED LOBSTER
PEACH-BOURBON
BBQ SCALLOPS

MENU DESCRIPTION: *"Wood-grilled, bacon-wrapped sea scallops with a sweet peach-bourbon BBQ sauce, over crispy onion rings with pico de gallo."*

You want a great way to serve scallops? Here you go. This carbon copy of the popular appetizer features scallops that are wrapped with bacon, skewered, grilled, then smothered in a super-secret sweet sauce and topped with fresh pico de gallo. As a bonus, the dish is served with a side of crispy thin onion rings. When you get everything piled on your fork and into your mouth, the flavor and texture combination will make your taste buds forever grateful. I recommend using medium-size sea scallops for this recipe, and wrapping them with center-cut bacon, which is a shorter bacon strip. If you can't find center-cut bacon, use the standard length of bacon and just cut off the ends. What's nice about this dish is that you can make it a couple hours ahead of time by preparing the pico de gallo and sauce, and then baking the scallops, wrapping them with the partially cooked bacon, and storing them covered in the refrigerator until grind time. When you're ready to present the dish to perk up the party, make the crispy onion rings, grill the scallops until hot, dress 'em up with sauce and pico, and serve.

PICO DE GALLO

2 medium tomatoes
¼ cup diced red onion
2 tablespoons minced jalapeño
    pepper (remove seeds)

1 tablespoon minced fresh
    cilantro
½ teaspoon lime juice
⅛ teaspoon salt

PEACH-BOURBON
BBQ SAUCE

1 teaspoon vegetable oil
¼ cup diced onion
1 ¼ cups peach preserves
¼ cup dark brown sugar
⅓ cup apple cider vinegar
¼ cup ketchup
1 tablespoon bourbon whiskey

¼ teaspoon plus ⅛ teaspoon salt
¼ teaspoon coarsely ground black
    pepper
¼ teaspoon ground chipotle chile
    powder
⅛ teaspoon garlic powder

SCALLOPS

12 small to medium sea scallops
12 slices center-cut bacon

4 to 6 metal or wood skewers
vegetable oil

CRISPY ONION RINGS

6 to 10 cups vegetable oil
1 egg, beaten
1 cup milk
¾ cup all-purpose flour
¼ cup cornstarch

½ teaspoon baking soda
¾ teaspoon salt
¼ teaspoon ground black pepper
½ onion, sliced into ¼-inch-thick
    rings

1. Make the pico de gallo by combining all the ingredients in a
    medium bowl. Cover and set aside until needed.
2. Make the peach-bourbon BBQ sauce by heating 1 teaspoon
    of oil in a small saucepan over medium/low heat. Add the

onion and sauté for 2 to 3 minutes, or until the onion begins to brown. Whisk in the remaining ingredients and heat until bubbling, then reduce the heat and simmer uncovered for 10 minutes, or until thick.

3.   Preheat the oven to 350 degrees F and preheat a barbecue grill or indoor grill to high heat.

4.   Cook the bacon in a skillet until about halfway done—it should not be crispy.

5.   Arrange the scallops on a parchment paper–lined or nonstick baking sheet and bake for 15 minutes in the preheated oven, or until they are no longer soft in the middle. Cool for 5 minutes.

6.   Prepare the scallops on skewers by wrapping 1 piece of partially cooked bacon around a scallop. You can slice a little bit of the fat off the bacon and make it thinner so that it is closer to the same height as the scallop when wrapped around it. Pierce the scallop with one skewer slightly offset from the middle of the scallop. Turn the scallop so that you are piercing it through at least one end of the bacon, pinning the end of the bacon to the scallop. Run another skewer through the scallop on the other side parallel to the first skewer. Repeat with 4 scallops per skewer (or more if your skewers are long enough). When all of the scallops are prepped on the skewers, brush them with a little oil. You can now set the scallops aside for up to 30 minutes until you are ready to grill them, or you can chill them, covered, for several hours.

7.   While the scallops bake, make the crispy onion rings by heating oil to 350 degrees F in a fryer or large saucepan. Combine the beaten egg and milk in a shallow bowl or pie pan. Combine the flour, cornstarch, baking soda, salt, and pepper in another shallow bowl or pie pan. Dip each ring into the breading, then into the egg-milk mixture, and then back into the breading until well-coated. Arrange the breaded rings on a plate until all of them are coated. When the oil is hot, fry a handful of the onion rings at a time until golden brown, 2 to 3 minutes.

8. Grill the skewered scallops for 3 to 4 minutes per side on the hot grill until grill marks form. Immediately after removing the scallops from the grill, brush all of them with the peach-bourbon BBQ sauce, then spoon the pico de gallo over the top. Arrange a pile of fried onions around the scallops before serving.

• SERVES 4 AS AN APPETIZER.

• • • •

RED LOBSTER MAPLE-GLAZED SALMON & SHRIMP

MENU DESCRIPTION: *"A Pacific Northwest–inspired combination of fresh salmon and skewered jumbo shrimp, fire-grilled and topped with a maple and cherry glaze. Served over wild rice pilaf with fresh asparagus."*

Whenever a recipe calls for maple syrup, make sure you use the real deal and not the maple-flavored corn syrups that come in plastic squirt bottles with brand names like Aunt Jemima and Log Cabin. Sure, authentic maple syrup is more expensive than the imitation stuff, and it must be refrigerated after opening, but true maple taste is worth the extra *ka-ching*. You will find the real maple flavor dominates in this sweet glaze, but you'll also notice a nice lemony tang and a perfect soy saltiness that work very well with salmon and shrimp—even chicken if you feel like it. Since Red Lobster's executive chef Michael LaDuke added this dish to the menu in July 2007, it's been a big winner for the seafood chain. And now you can add this winning taste to your own repertoire. The clone here is a super simple one, with only 6 ingredients for the glaze including dried cherries that you should find near the raisins and dried cranberries in your market. You can make the sauce several days ahead of time if you like and store it, covered, in the fridge until you bring home the perfect salmon fillets.

MAPLE-CHERRY GLAZE

⅔ cup real maple syrup
½ cup water
2 tablespoons minced dried
   cherries

1 tablespoon granulated sugar
2 teaspoons soy sauce
1½ teaspoons lemon juice

24 peeled medium shrimp
melted butter
four 6-ounce salmon fillets

1. Make the maple-cherry glaze by combining all the ingredients in a small saucepan over medium heat. When the mixture begins to boil, reduce the heat and simmer for 8 to 10 minutes, until thick.
2. Preheat your barbecue grill to high.
3. Skewer 6 shrimps on each of 4 skewers. Brush the shrimp with a little melted butter, and sprinkle with a bit of salt and pepper. Sprinkle the salmon fillets with a little salt and pepper as well.
4. Grill the salmon for 2 to 3 minutes per side until done and grill the shrimp for 1 to 2 minutes per side.
5. Brush the shrimp and salmon with maple-cherry glaze and serve with rice and asparagus or your choice of sides.

• MAKES 4 SERVINGS.

• • • •

RED ROBIN CAMPFIRE SAUCE

Red Robin is known for great gourmet hamburgers and tasty cocktail concoctions, but the 400-plus-unit chain also serves a huge tower of onion rings that comes with a side of this creamy, slightly sweet-and-smoky dipping sauce. An Internet search offered up a few clues about what might be mixed into this mystery sauce, but the complete culinary conundrum was yet to be solved. A mixture of mayonnaise and barbecue sauce was a good starting point, but with so many varieties of barbecue sauce on the market, I had to figure out which came closest to the flavor of the original Campfire Sauce. So, I went back to Red Robin, obtained a sample of the barbecue sauce they use, and conducted a side-by-side taste test of all the major brands on the market. After more spoonfuls of straight barbecue sauce than any human should consume at one sitting, I finally concluded that Bull's-Eye Brown Sugar & Hickory comes the closest to the sauce used at the restaurant. A little more experimentation with this sauce, some mayonnaise, and a couple of other ingredients, and I eventually had in front of me an awesome re-creation of the delicious dipping sauce that can be served with home-baked onion rings, poppers, French fries, or as a really great hamburger spread. Mission accomplished.

½ cup mayonnaise
3 tablespoons Bull's-Eye Brown
    Sugar & Hickory Barbecue
    Sauce

1 tablespoon ketchup
⅛ teaspoon salt

Combine all the ingredients in a small bowl. Cover and chill for about an hour, and then stir once before serving.

- MAKES ½ CUP.

• • • •

RED ROBIN CREAMY ARTICHOKE & SPINACH DIP

MENU DESCRIPTION: *"A creamy, cheesy blend of artichoke hearts, spinach, onions, Parmesan and a hint of bacon."*

Practically every casual restaurant chain has its own version of artichoke and spinach dip, and it's usually one of the top two or three picks from the appetizer menu. Red Robin is no exception, and actually offers a version of the popular dip that is one of the best of the bunch. The basics of the recipe are similar to other formulas, but Red Robin mixes it up with just a little bacon for a hint of smokiness. I like that. I also like that you can easily steam the artichoke hearts, spinach, and onion used here in your microwave oven. Combine the tender veggies with the cheese and other ingredients in a saucepan until thick and creamy, then serve it up with your choice of tortilla chips, sliced pita bread, pita chips, bagel chips, or crackers.

one 10-ounce box frozen chopped spinach, thawed

1 cup artichoke hearts (frozen or canned), diced

¼ cup diced white onion

8 ounces cream cheese, softened

½ cup shredded Parmesan cheese

¾ cup half-and-half

¼ teaspoon garlic powder

½ teaspoon salt

1 piece cooked bacon, minced (about 1 tablespoon)

GARNISH

2 teaspoons shredded Parmesan
 cheese
1 heaping tablespoon diced red
 onion

1. Combine the spinach, artichoke hearts, and onion in a medium microwave-safe bowl, cover with plastic wrap, and cut a slit in the plastic so that the steam can escape. Microwave the bowl on high for 4 minutes, then let the vegetables sit, covered, while you make the cheese sauce.

2. Combine the cream cheese, Parmesan, half-and-half, garlic powder, and salt in a medium saucepan over medium/low heat and cook, stirring often. When the sauce is smooth, stir in the steamed vegetables and add the bacon. Reduce the heat to low and continue to cook for 10 minutes, stirring occasionally. Spoon the hot dip into a serving bowl and top with 2 teaspoons of Parmesan cheese, and a tablespoon of diced red onion. Serve with chips, bread, or crackers on the side.

- SERVES 6 TO 8.

TIDBITS

If you don't have a microwave oven, you can steam the spinach, artichoke hearts, and onion in a saucepan with a steamer basket over medium heat for 10 minutes or until tender.

•   •   •   •

RED ROBIN
RED'S HOMEMADE
CHILI CHILI

MENU DESCRIPTION: *"Lots of fresh ground beef and red kidney beans with a perfect blend of fresh poblano and chipotle peppers and plenty of seasoning. Topped with Cheddar cheese, diced red onions, and tortilla strips. Not too hot, but enough flavor to know you ate it."*

Ah, yes, nothing like a hot bowl of homemade chili on a cool day. Red Robin serves up a great bowl of hot chunky chili topped with cheddar cheese, onions, and crunchy tortilla strips that'll warm your soul. The super-secret clone here can be served up in the same fashion, or you can use this chili as they do in the restaurant to top homemade nachos or an open-faced chili cheeseburger. If you're one of those who prefer a higher-octane, spicier chili, just use more canned chipotles, or add in some of the delicious adobo sauce that's usually included in the can with those chiles.

2 pounds ground beef (at least 15 percent fat)
1 ½ cups diced white onion (about 1 medium onion)
¾ cup diced poblano chile (about 1 medium chile)
2 tablespoons diced canned chipotle chiles
4 teaspoons minced garlic (about 4 cloves)
⅓ cup vegetable oil
⅓ cup all-purpose flour
two 15-ounce cans red kidney beans (with liquid)
one 15-ounce can diced tomatoes
3 tablespoons chili powder
2 ¾ teaspoons salt
1 tablespoon coarsely ground black pepper
1 ½ teaspoons dried oregano

2 cups chicken broth
1 ¾ cups water

GARNISH
2 cups shredded cheddar cheese
1 cup diced red onion
2 cups crumbled tortilla chips

1. Brown the ground beef in a large skillet over medium heat. When there is just a bit of pink visible in the beef, add the onion, poblano chile, chipotle chiles, and garlic. Continue cooking until the diced onion is just beginning to turn translucent on the edges.
2. While the meat is browning, heat up the oil over medium heat in a large saucepan or Dutch oven, and then whisk in the flour to make a roux. Cook for 2 to 3 minutes, or until the roux begins to turn tan in color. Add the browned ground beef mixture and remaining chili ingredients, and bring to a boil. Reduce the heat and simmer for 3 hours, or until the meat is tender and the chili is thick, stirring occasionally.
3. Serve 1 cup of chili in a bowl, topped with shredded cheddar cheese, diced red onion, and crumbled tortilla chips.

• MAKES EIGHT 1-CUP SERVINGS.

•   •   •   •

RED ROBIN
ROYAL RED ROBIN
BURGER

MENU DESCRIPTION: *"This is the aristocrat of all burgers because we crown it with a fresh fried egg. In addition, topped with three strips of hickory-smoked bacon, American cheese, crisp lettuce, tomatoes, and mayo."*

This delicious burger has been on Red Robin's menu since the restaurant first opened in 1969 and it's still a popular pick today. The recipe is a classic bacon cheeseburger, except for one huge difference: There's a jumbo fried egg stacked in the middle! If you've never had an egg on a burger before, I encourage you to give this recipe a try—it's a really great burger. Red Robin serves more than 36 million burgers a year and each of them is sprinkled with the secret seasoning blend called Red Robin Seasoning. You can buy a bottle of the seasoning in the restaurant, or you can just make your own with the *Top Secret Recipe* I've included here. This formula for the seasoning is an improved version of the formula found in *Top Secret Restaurant Recipes 2*, as the tomato soup mix that I required in the recipe in that book is hard to find these days. I discovered that a little bit of the dry mix in a box of Hamburger Helper Italian Lasagna is the perfect way to get dehydrated tomato and a few other tasty ingredients into the seasoning blend— I think this version is a better clone. The restaurant makes each burger with 6 ounces of 80/20 ground beef, which is 20 percent fat. But you can also use 15 percent beef here and your burger will still taste just like the original forty-year-old favorite.

RED ROBIN SEASONING

2 teaspoons salt

2 teaspoons dry mix powder from
    Hamburger Helper Italian
    Lasagna

½ teaspoon chili powder

⅛ teaspoon ground black pepper

6 ounces ground beef (15 percent
    or 20 percent fat)

2 slices American cheese

1 tablespoon butter-flavored
    Crisco shortening (or butter)

1 jumbo egg

one 4½-inch sesame seed
    hamburger bun

3 to 4 teaspoons mayonnaise

2 tomato slices

3 pieces cooked hickory-smoked
    bacon

⅓ cup shredded lettuce

1. Make the seasoning by combining all of the seasoning mix ingredients in a small bowl.

2. Preheat a skillet over medium heat.

3. Form the ground beef into a patty that is about 5 inches in diameter (slightly larger than your bun). Sprinkle with a little of the seasoning blend.

4. Cook the patty in the hot pan for 2 to 3 minutes, flip it over, and place two slices of American cheese on top of the patty. Continue cooking the patty for 2 to 3 minutes, or until it's your desired doneness.

5. Cook the egg by melting the butter-flavored shortening (or butter) in a small pan over medium heat. Crack the egg into the pan and break the yolk. Cook the egg for 2 to 3 minutes per side, or until done.

6. While the burger patty and egg are cooking, brown the face of the top and bottom of the sesame bun in another hot skillet. When the buns are browned, spread the mayonnaise on both the top and bottom bun.

7. When the burger is done, place it on the bottom bun.

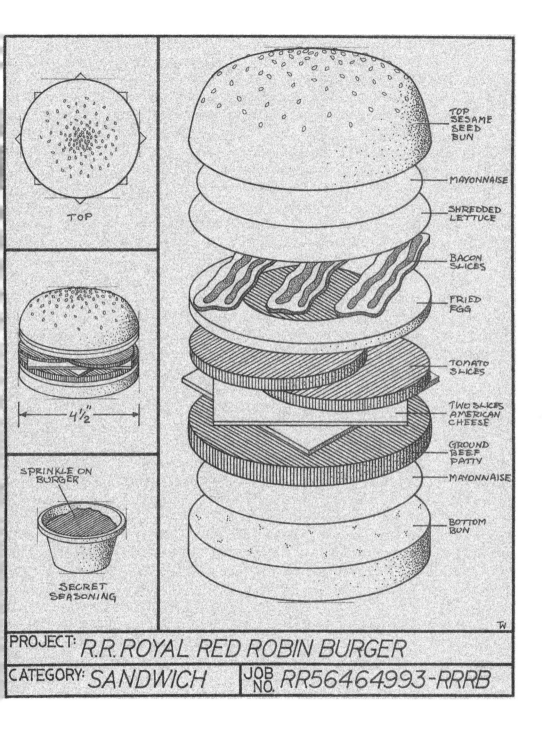

TOP

TOP
SESAME
SEED
BUN

MAYONNAISE

SHREDDED
LETTUCE

BACON
SLICES

FRIED
EGG

TOMATO
SLICES

TWO SLICES
AMERICAN
CHEESE

GROUND
BEEF
PATTY

MAYONNAISE

BOTTOM
BUN

4½"

SPRINKLE ON
BURGER

SECRET
SEASONING

PROJECT: *R.R. ROYAL RED ROBIN BURGER*

CATEGORY: *SANDWICH*   JOB NO. *RR56464993-RRRB*

8. Position two tomato slices on the melted cheese, followed by the cooked egg.
9. Place the 3 bacon slices on the egg.
10. Pile the lettuce on the mayonnaise on the top bun and turn the bun over onto the bottom of the hamburger. Serve with a napkin and cold drink. And fries, if you've got 'em.

• MAKES 1 HAMBURGER.

•   •   •   •

ROMANO'S MACARONI GRILL LEMON PASSION

MENU DESCRIPTION: *"Citrus cake soaked in a sweet cream, topped with lemon mousse and finished off with our fresh Italian whipped cream and caramel."*

When creating this delicious dessert, chefs at Romano's must have been thinking about the tres leches cake that is popular throughout Latin America. The traditional Mexican recipe describes a dense vanilla cake soaked with three types of milk: whole milk, sweetened condensed milk, and evaporated milk. This creates a very moist and rich dessert that is an excellent finish to pretty much any meal. Romano's twist on the traditional favorite is the addition of citrus juices to the cake, a creamier soaking liquid, and a tangy lemon topping. I first tried re-creating the cake with boxed mixes, but they all produce cakes that are much too light and moist and inevitably turn to mush when soaked in the sweet liquid. The final solution is a scratch cake recipe that yields a denser yet still moist citrus cake that holds up to the eventual drenching. Nevertheless, you will want to eat this dessert within a day or two of the soaking or it may start to get all gooey on you. And be sure to store any leftovers in the fridge.

CAKE

1 ¾ cups all-purpose flour
2 teaspoons baking powder

½ cup salted butter, softened
1 cup granulated sugar

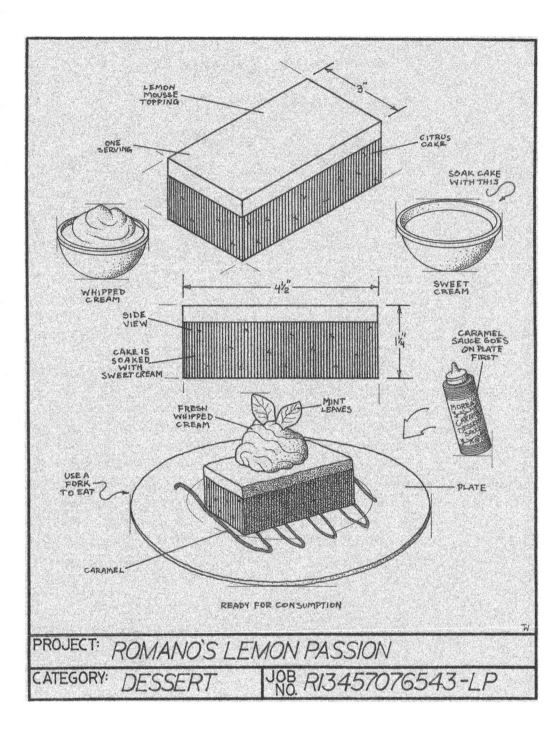

LEMON MOUSSE TOPPING

ONE SERVING

3"

CITRUS CAKE

SOAK CAKE WITH THIS

WHIPPED CREAM

SWEET CREAM

SIDE VIEW

4½"

1¼"

CAKE IS SOAKED WITH SWEET CREAM

CARAMEL SAUCE GOES ON PLATE FIRST

FRESH WHIPPED CREAM

MINT LEAVES

USE A FORK TO EAT

PLATE

CARAMEL

MORE CARAMEL DESERT SAUCE

READY FOR CONSUMPTION

PROJECT: *ROMANO'S LEMON PASSION*

CATEGORY: *DESSERT*

JOB NO. *R13457076543-LP*

4 eggs

½ teaspoon vanilla extract

¼ cup lemon juice

¼ cup orange juice

LEMON MOUSSE TOPPING

8 ounces cream cheese, softened

1¾ cups powdered sugar

3 tablespoons lemon juice

1 drop yellow food coloring

⅓ cup heavy cream

SWEET CREAM

1½ cups half-and-half

one 14-ounce can sweetened
    condensed milk

WHIPPED CREAM

1¼ cups heavy cream

2 tablespoons granulated sugar

¼ teaspoon vanilla extract

GARNISH

caramel topping
    (Preferably in a squirt bottle)
mint leaves

1.   Preheat oven to 350 degrees F.
2.   Sift together the flour and baking powder into a medium bowl. In a separate larger bowl, beat together the softened butter and sugar for 1 minute. Add eggs and beat until the mixture is a light yellow color. Mix in vanilla and juices.
3.   Combine the flour with the wet mixture a little at a time while beating until the batter is smooth. Be sure to scrape the sides of the bowl while mixing. Pour this batter into a greased 9 x 9- inch baking pan and bake for 35 to 40 minutes, until the top begins to brown and a toothpick stuck in the center comes out clean. Let the cake cool in the pan.
4.   As your cake is baking make the lemon mousse topping by beating the softened cream cheese with an electric mixer in

a medium bowl until smooth. Add the powdered sugar a little at a time while blending with the electric mixer on low speed. When all of the sugar is incorporated, add the lemon juice and a drop of food coloring. In a separate bowl, beat ⅓ cup heavy cream until it forms stiff peaks. Gently fold this whipped cream into the cream cheese mixture until completely combined, then cover and chill.

5. Make the sweet cream by combining half-and-half with sweetened condensed milk in a 4-cup measuring cup with a spout or in a small pitcher. Cover and chill this as well.

6. Make the whipped cream by combining 1¼ cups heavy cream, 2 tablespoons granulated sugar, and ¼ teaspoon vanilla in a large bowl. Beat with an electric mixer on high speed until it forms stiff peaks. Cover and park this in the chiller, too.

7. When the cake is completely cool, slice it down the middle once, then across twice, creating 6 rectangular slices. Run a knife along the edges of the cake as well. Poke holes in the top of each slice of cake with a fork—one poke in the center of each piece should do the trick.

8. Pour the sweet cream mixture over the cake while it's still in the baking pan. Allow the liquid to soak into the cake for a few minutes, and then frost the cake with the lemon mousse. Serve each slice on a plate that has been drizzled with caramel. Top each slice with whipped cream and a garnish of a couple mint leaves stuck into the whipped cream.

• MAKES 6 SERVINGS.

• • • •

ROY'S
HAWAIIAN MARTINI

Roy Yamaguchi's national chain of Hawaiian fusion restaurants serves a martini that will have you singing "Tiny Bubbles" with your imaginary monkey friend Cecil. Whole bottles of Skyy vodka, Stoli Vanil, and Malibu rum are dumped into a giant decanter along with some sugar and pineapple chunks. After three days, when all the hunks of pineapple are floating, the cocktail is ready to be served—shaken, not stirred—in a chilled martini glass. This is a perfect clone to prepare in advance of your next swinging pool party, since the recipe makes around 36 drinks.

two 750-ml bottles Skyy vodka   *one 6-ounce can pineapple juice*
one 750-ml bottle Stoli Vanil vodka   *1 cup sugar*
one 750-ml bottle Malibu rum   *1 fresh pineapple, sliced*

1. Combine the vodkas, rum, and pineapple juice in a large decanter or 5-quart jug. Add the sugar and stir until dissolved.
2. Slice the top and bottom off of a fresh pineapple. Slice the pineapple in half, then slice the halves in half to make quarters. Cut the rind from each of the quarters, then slice the quarters into ½-inch-thick slices. This will make several bite-size wedges. Add the pineapple slices to the decanter, and let the mixture sit for 3 days at room temperature.
3. To make the drink, shake 3 ounces of the martini blend

with ice and strain into a chilled martini glass. Garnish with one piece of pineapple from the decanter, speared on a toothpick.

• MAKES ABOUT 36 SERVINGS.

• • • •

ROY'S CLASSIC ROASTED MACADAMIA NUT CRUSTED MAHI MAHI

☆ ✌ 💣 ✏ ☯ ✂ ☞

MENU DESCRIPTION: *"Lobster cognac butter sauce."*

Next time you make lobster, save the shells, because that's what you'll need to whip up the delicious lobster cognac sauce that makes this signature entrée from Roy's so special. This recipe is great for entertaining, not only for the nice presentation, but also because the two sauces can be made in advance and chilled, then reheated in small saucepans—or even in the microwave—just before preparing the fish.

LOBSTER COGNAC SAUCE

lobster shell(s) from ½ pound
    lobster (1 big tail or 2 small
    tails)
2 tablespoons olive oil
¼ cup chopped carrot
¼ cup chopped celery
¼ cup chopped onion
1 clove garlic, quartered
1 small tomato, quartered

3 to 4 basil leaves
1 bay leaf
2 tablespoons white wine
1 tablespoon cognac
1 cup water
½ cup chicken broth
1 cup heavy cream
⅛ teaspoon salt
pinch white pepper

BEURRE BLANC SAUCE

⅔ cup white wine
1 teaspoon lemon juice
4 teaspoons minced shallot

½ cup (1 stick) salted butter, cut
   into pieces
⅓ cup heavy cream
⅛ teaspoon white pepper

MAHI MAHI

½ cup chopped macadamia nuts
½ cup panko (Japanese bread
   crumbs)
¼ teaspoon salt

⅛ teaspoon freshly ground black
   pepper
½ cup all-purpose flour
1 egg, beaten

four 6-ounce mahi mahi fillets
extra virgin olive oil

1. Make the lobster cognac sauce by preheating the oven to 375 degrees F. Bake the lobster shells for 20 minutes, or until the shells begin to turn brown around the edges.
2. Heat the olive oil in a medium saucepan over medium heat. Add the carrot, celery, onion, and garlic to the pan and sauté for 3 to 4 minutes, or until the vegetables begin to brown. Stir in the tomato, basil, bay leaf, and lobster shells and cook for 1 minute. Add the white wine and cognac and cook for an additional 2 minutes. Add the water and chicken broth. When the mixture begins to boil, reduce the heat and simmer for 15 minutes, or until the liquid reduces by half. Pour the mixture into a fine-mesh strainer over another saucepan to strain out the liquid. Add the cream, salt, and pepper, reduce the heat to medium/low, and simmer for 15 to 20 minutes, stirring often, until thick. Remove from the heat, cover, and set aside.
3. Make the beurre blanc sauce by combining the white wine, lemon juice, and shallots in a small saucepan and place it over

medium heat. Simmer for 4 minutes, or until the liquid reduces by about one-half, then add the butter and cream and cook until the butter melts. Strain out the liquid using a fine-mesh strainer over another small saucepan. Add the white pepper to the sauce, place over medium heat, and heat until the sauce begins to simmer, stirring often, then reduce the heat to medium/low and simmer for 10 to 15 minutes, or until the sauce thickens. Remove from the heat, cover, and set aside.

4. To prepare the mahi mahi, preheat the oven to 425 degrees F.

5. Combine macadamia nuts, panko, salt, and ground black pepper in a food processor and pulse until the mixture is the texture of coarse sand. Pour the breading into a pie pan.

6. Pour the flour into another pie pan and the beaten egg into a third pie pan or a shallow bowl.

7. Bread one side of each mahi mahi fillet by first pressing it into the flour. Dip the floured side into the egg and then into the macadamia-panko mixture, completely coating one side of each fillet. Arrange all of the fillets on a plate until your sauté pan is hot.

8. Drizzle a couple tablespoons of extra virgin olive oil into a large oven-safe sauté pan and place it over medium heat. When the pan is hot, place each fillet with the breading-side down into the pan and cook for 1 minute, or until the macadamia-panko breading has browned. Flip each fillet over in the pan, place the pan in the preheated oven, and bake for 5 to 6 minutes, until the mahi mahi is cooked through.

9. To prepare each serving, spoon a little lobster cognac sauce onto a plate, followed by a little of the beurre blanc sauce. Carefully place a mahi mahi fillet onto the center of the plate and serve.

- SERVES 4.

TIDBITS

If you don't have lobster shells, you can substitute shells from 6 large shrimp. The taste is not exactly the same as lobster, but it stills work well for this dish.

•   •   •   •

ROY'S MELTING HOT CHOCOLATE SOUFFLÉ

Roy's chefs bake this signature "lava cake" dessert in parchment paper–lined metal cylindrical molds that are slipped off the soufflé when plating the dish. Fortunately we don't have to locate a restaurant supply outlet to obtain similar molds when the tool we need is easily found in every supermarket. Just save the 4-ounce cans that hold diced peppers or whatever you may find that comes in these small cans with a 2½-inch diameter. Cut off the top and bottom, remove the label, wash the cans, and you have the exact same size mold as those used at Roy's. The recipe for the batter is simple, with only 6 ingredients, but plan ahead for this dessert because the batter needs to chill in the molds before baking so that the centers stay gooey and uncooked like the original.

4 ounces bittersweet chocolate
½ cup (1 stick) unsalted butter
½ cup granulated sugar

2 eggs
¼ teaspoon vanilla extract
pinch salt

GARNISH
raspberry sauce (premade, or use
    the recipe from Mastro's
    Steakhouse Warm Butter
    Cake clone on page 233)
powdered sugar

ON THE SIDE
4 scoops vanilla ice cream

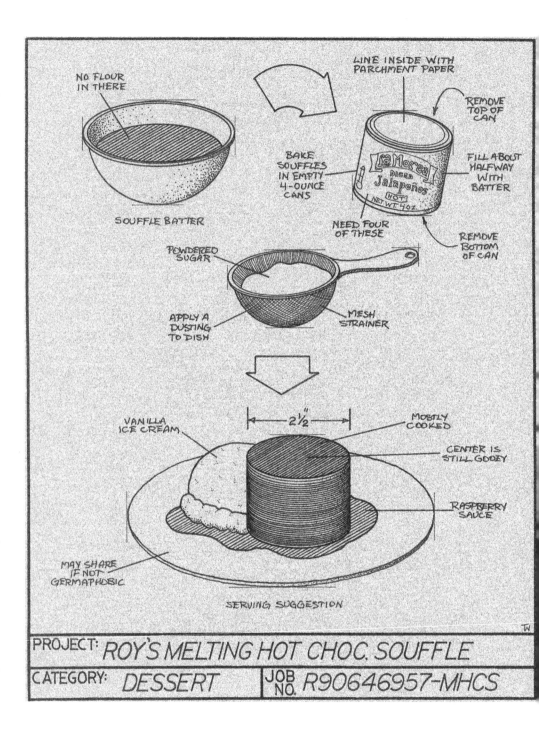

NO FLOUR
IN THERE

SOUFFLE BATTER

LINE INSIDE WITH
PARCHMENT PAPER

REMOVE
TOP OF
CAN

BAKE
SOUFFLES
IN EMPTY
4-OUNCE
CANS

La Morena
DICED
Jalapeños
HOT
NET WT. 4 oz.

FILL ABOUT
HALFWAY
WITH
BATTER

NEED FOUR
OF THESE

REMOVE
BOTTOM
OF CAN

POWDERED
SUGAR

APPLY A
DUSTING
TO DISH

MESH
STRAINER

2½"

VANILLA
ICE CREAM

MOSTLY
COOKED

CENTER IS
STILL GOOEY

RASPBERRY
SAUCE

MAY SHARE
IF NOT
GERMAPHOBIC

SERVING SUGGESTION

PROJECT: ROY'S MELTING HOT CHOC. SOUFFLE

CATEGORY: DESSERT

JOB NO. R90646957-MHCS

1. Melt the chocolate and butter together in a medium glass or ceramic microwave-safe bowl in the microwave on high for 30 seconds. Stir, then nuke it again for another 30 seconds.
2. Add the sugar and mix with electric mixer on high speed for 1 minute. Add the eggs, vanilla, and salt and mix for another minute.
3. Open the top and bottom of four 4-ounce cans (such as the kind that hold diced peppers), remove the labels, and clean out the cans. Line the inside of each can with parchment paper. Make sure the paper is pushed all the way down to the bottom of the can so that the soufflé will slip out easily when cooked. Position each lined can on an additional piece of parchment paper on a baking sheet.
4. Fill each can with an equal amount of cake batter, cover all of them with plastic wrap, and chill for at least 2 hours or overnight.
5. When you are ready to bake the desserts, preheat the oven to 425 degrees F.
6. Place the soufflés in the oven, bake for 20 minutes or until they nearly double in size, then remove them from the oven and cool for 2 minutes.
7. Place each molded soufflé onto the center of a serving plate, carefully remove the can, and peel away the parchment paper. Drizzle the raspberry sauce onto the plate and dust the soufflé with a little powdered sugar. Add a scoop of vanilla ice cream to each plate and serve.

- SERVES 4.

• • • •

RUBY TUESDAY
APPLE SALAD

Mosey on over to the salad bar at Ruby Tuesday and you'll find this sweet, creamy apple salad somewhere down near the end. It's a simple recipe to clone with just 9 ingredients, and it makes a great side for any casual cookout, picnic, reunion, or mandatory boring office party. Dried cranberries rehydrate to add notes of concentrated sweetness, and the celery and chopped pecans contribute extra crunch. You'll need two kinds of apples—one green and one red—just be sure to dice them into pieces that are about the size of almonds. Plan ahead on this one so that you can let the salad sit for several hours before you serve it. It tastes much better after a good fridge nap. This recipe yields enough for 6 servings, but it can easily be doubled or quadrupled to fill more mouths.

½ cup sour cream
½ cup mayonnaise
¼ cup granulated sugar
1 ½ teaspoons lemon juice
1 Granny Smith apple, diced

1 Gala or Fuji apple, diced
½ cup dried cranberries
⅓ cup chopped pecans
¼ cup minced celery

1. Combine sour cream, mayonnaise, sugar, and lemon juice in a medium bowl and whisk until sugar has dissolved.
2. Add the remaining ingredients and stir. Store the salad in a sealed container in your refrigerator for 3 to 4 hours before serving.

• MAKES 6 SERVINGS.

• • • •

RUBY TUESDAY
QUESO DIP AND BEEF
QUESO DIP

MENU DESCRIPTION: *"Smooth and spicy cheese dip. Served with un-limited crisp tortilla chips."*

Many who have tried the original say it's the best queso dip they've ever had, so I absolutely had to get on the case! Talking to a store manager, I found out that the dip is made with American cheese and a little Parmesan, but the rest of the ingredients were going to have to be determined in the Top Secret underground lab. When I got down there (using the elevator hidden in a fake outhouse in the corner of a vacant lot), I immediately washed the dip in a strainer and discovered bits of spinach, onion, and two kinds of peppers. The red pepper, which is responsible for the kick, appeared to be rehydrated dry peppers. It looks like they're red jalapeños, but since the red ones can be hard to find, I chopped up some red Fresno peppers and the dip tasted great—full of flavor with a nice spicy kick. Just be sure to remove the inner membranes and seeds from the peppers before you mince them up or your super-cool dip may end up packing way too much heat. I'm also including a clone recipe for the new variation of the queso that is topped with spicy ground beef, just to mix it up a bit.

QUESO DIP

1 tablespoon vegetable oil
¼ cup minced red Fresno or red
    jalapeño pepper
    (approximately 3 peppers),
    seeded and deribbed
2 tablespoons minced white onion
2 tablespoons chopped canned
    mild green chiles
⅔ cup whole milk

½ cup sour cream
12 slices American cheese
¼ cup La Victoria medium taco
    sauce
¼ cup grated Parmesan cheese
½ teaspoon chili powder
¼ teaspoon salt
¼ cup chopped fresh spinach

SERVE WITH

tortilla chips

1. Heat the oil in a medium saucepan over medium heat. Add the red pepper, onion, and canned chiles and sauté for 5 minutes. Be sure to remove the seeds from the red peppers before you mince them.
2. Stir in the milk and sour cream. Add the American cheese and stir until the cheese is melted.
3. Add the remaining ingredients, reduce the heat to medium/low, and cook for 15 minutes, stirring often, until thickened. If the mixture begins to bubble, reduce the heat.
4. Spoon the queso dip into a serving bowl and serve with tortilla chips for dipping.

• MAKES 2½ CUPS.

BEEF QUESO DIP

¼ pound ground sirloin
½ teaspoon chili powder
⅛ teaspoon salt

⅛ teaspoon onion powder
½ cup water

1. Brown the ground beef in a small skillet over medium/low heat using a wooden spoon to break it up into small pieces as it cooks.
2. When there is no pink in the beef, add the remaining ingredients and simmer for 20 to 25 minutes, or until all of the water has cooked off.
3. Sprinkle the spicy ground beef over the top of the queso dip made in the recipe above, and serve with tortilla chips.

• MAKES 3 CUPS.

• • • •

RUBY TUESDAY
THAI PHOON SHRIMP

MENU DESCRIPTION: *"Tender, crispy shrimp with a sweet and spicy chili sauce that's got just the right kick."*

It was another job for the microscreen sieve. Rinsing away the mayo from a spoonful of this delicious chili sauce reveals just what I expected: sambal chunks. The minced chile peppers that sat there, naked, in the bottom of the sieve looked just like the type of red pepper used in sambal chili sauce. And since there were bits of garlic in there, too, it was clear that the bright red chili garlic sauce you find near the Asian foods in your market is the perfect secret ingredient for the fiery mixture that's used on this popular dish on Ruby Tuesday's new appetizer menu. Once you make the sauce, whip up some of the secret breading for the shrimp and get on with the frying. You can use shortening or oil here, but I think shortening works best, and it doesn't stink up the house. The no–trans fat stuff is da bomb. Once all of your shrimp are fried to a nice golden brown, carefully coat the little suckers with about half of the sauce, and then serve the rest of the sauce on the side for dipping, just like they do at the restaurant.

CHILI SAUCE

½ cup mayonnaise
4 teaspoons chili garlic sauce
    (sambal)
2 teaspoons granulated sugar

¼ teaspoon ground cayenne
    pepper
⅛ teaspoon paprika

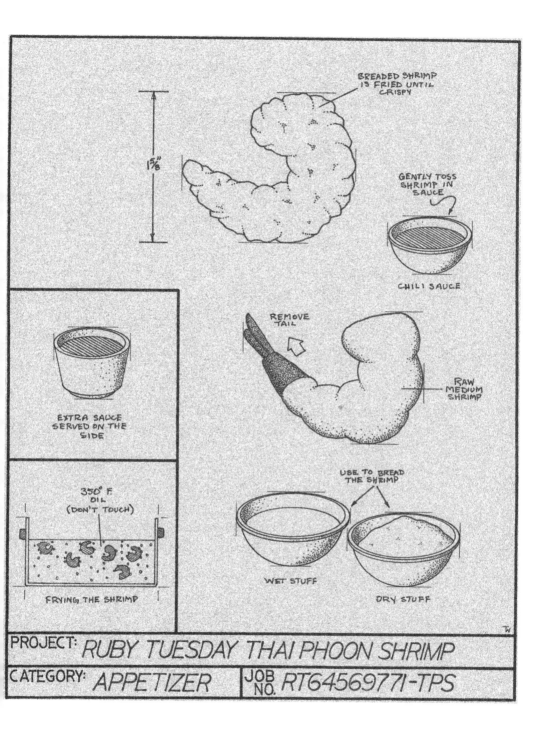

BREADED SHRIMP
IS FRIED UNTIL
CRISPY

$1\frac{5}{8}$"

GENTLY TOSS
SHRIMP IN
SAUCE

CHILI SAUCE

EXTRA SAUCE
SERVED ON THE
SIDE

REMOVE
TAIL

RAW
MEDIUM
SHRIMP

350° F.
OIL
(DON'T TOUCH)

FRYING THE SHRIMP

USE TO BREAD
THE SHRIMP

WET STUFF

DRY STUFF

PROJECT: *RUBY TUESDAY THAI PHOON SHRIMP*

CATEGORY: *APPETIZER*

JOB NO. *RT64569771-TPS*

COATING

1 egg, beaten
1 cup milk
1 cup all-purpose flour
1 teaspoon salt
¾ teaspoon baking soda

½ teaspoon ground black pepper
¼ teaspoon onion powder
¼ teaspoon garlic powder
¼ teaspoon ground cayenne
   pepper

6 to 10 cups vegetable shortening
   or oil

30 medium shrimp, peeled and
   deveined, tails removed

OPTIONAL GARNISH

thinly sliced green leaf lettuce

1. Combine all the ingredients for chili sauce in a small bowl. Cover the sauce and set it aside for now.
2. Combine the beaten egg with the milk in a shallow bowl. Measure 1 cup of flour into another shallow bowl. Mix in salt, baking soda, black pepper, onion powder, garlic powder, and cayenne pepper.
3. Bread the shrimp by first coating each one with flour. Dip the floured shrimp into the egg and milk mixture, and then back into the flour. Arrange the coated shrimp on a plate and pop them into the fridge for at least 10 minutes. This step will help the breading stick on the shrimp when frying.
4. Heat shortening or oil to 350 degrees F. Use the amount of oil required by your fryer, or use a pot or sacuepan filled about halfway.
5. When your oil is hot, fry 8 to 10 shrimp at a time for 3 to 4 minutes, until golden brown. Drain on a rack or paper towels. Drop fried shrimp into a large bowl. Spoon about ¼ cup of the sauce over the shrimp and stir the shrimp gently to coat.

Serve immediately on a bed of sliced green leaf lettuce with the remaining chili sauce on the side.

• MAKES 6 APPETIZER SERVINGS.

TIDBITS

You can also make this dish many days ahead by following the directions up to the frying stage. Instead of frying for 3 to 4 minutes, flash fry the shrimp for just 45 seconds, and then let them cool. Pop the shrimp into a zip-top bag and into the freezer. When you want to make the dish, simply fry the shrimp for 3 minutes, or until brown, and then coat with the sauce as instructed.

• • • •

SERENDIPITY 3 FRRROZEN HOT CHOCOLATE

Oprah named this blended concoction from the New York City–based Serendipity 3 one of her "Favorite Things" in 2006, saying that it made her want to "dance on the chandeliers." Started in a basement on East 58th Street in 1954, Serendipity 3 has been a top stop for many celebrities though the years. Tennessee Williams and Jackie Kennedy were regulars, and Andy Warhol used to pay for his meals with original drawings. With locations now open in Boca Raton and Las Vegas, Serendipity 3 is more than just a sweet shop, it also serves omelets, salads, pizza, and ribs. But the joint is best known for its Frrrozen Hot Chocolate, which is ordered by about 10,000 customers each month. In the restaurant, each frosty creation is made by combining a secret dry mix with milk and ice in a blender on high speed until smooth. The dessert is poured into a huge goblet, topped with whipped cream and chocolate shavings, and served with spoons and straws. The chain claims the secret mix is a blend of many different chocolates, and released a recipe to the *Oprah Winfrey Show* a while back (posted on the show's Web site) that supposedly revealed the secret formula. But, as often seen with secret recipes volunteered by restaurant chains, this one is an inaccurate clone. The recipe given to Oprah says to use 6 half-ounce pieces "of your favorite chocolate," but the chocolate in the restaurant's secret dry mix comes only from cocoa powders. Also, the recipe doesn't mention anything about nonfat dry milk, which is a big part of the dry mix. All you have to do is look at the ingredient list on the 5-dollar package of mix to see "sugar, nonfat dry milk, dextrose, and cocoas." That's it. Perhaps the chain doesn't want to surrender a recipe that will compete with the packaged product it sells online and in stores. That's my job. So here is an original *Top Secret Recipe* I've worked up that uses three popular brands of cocoa, plus dry milk and sugar. Blend this mix with whole milk and ice and you'll have a delicious (and cheap!) clone of Oprah's favorite drink that tastes better than any other recipe out there.

⅓ cup granulated sugar
⅓ cup nonfat dry milk powder
2 tablespoons Ghirardelli cocoa
    powder
1 tablespoon Hershey's cocoa
    powder

1 tablespoon Scharffen Berger
    cocoa powder (see *Tidbits*)
pinch salt
1 cup milk
3 cups ice

ON TOP
whipped cream
shavings from a semisweet chocolate bar

1. Combine the sugar, dry milk powder, cocoas, and salt in a small bowl.
2. Pour the milk into a blender. Add the dry mix and ice.
3. Blend until all the ice is crushed and the drink is smooth. Pour into a large goblet or two 16-ounce glasses. Top the drink with whipped cream and shavings from a semisweet chocolate bar (use a carrot peeler), then add a spoon and straw and serve.

• MAKES ONE 30-OUNCE SERVING OR TWO 15-OUNCE DRINKS.

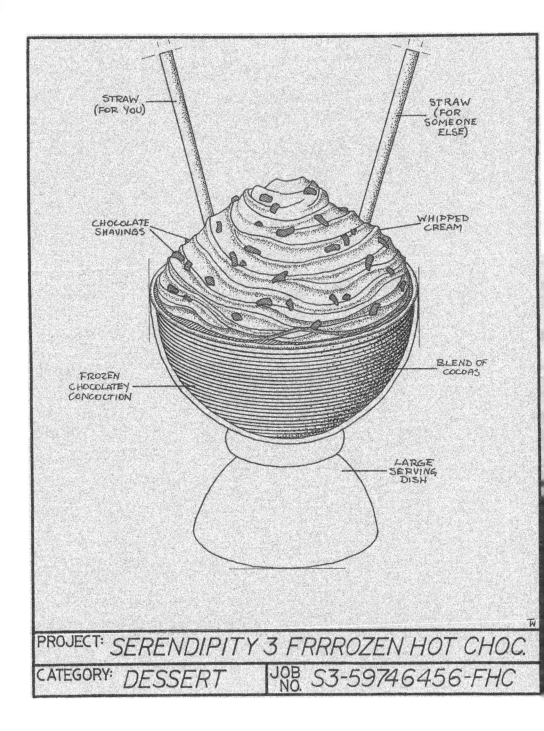

STRAW
(FOR YOU)

STRAW
(FOR
SOMEONE
ELSE)

CHOCOLATE
SHAVINGS

WHIPPED
CREAM

FROZEN
CHOCOLATEY
CONCOCTION

BLEND OF
COCOAS

LARGE
SERVING
DISH

PROJECT: *SERENDIPITY 3 FRRROZEN HOT CHOC.*

CATEGORY: *DESSERT*   **JOB NO.** *S3-59746456-FHC*

TIDBITS

If you can't locate this brand of cocoa, use 3 tablespoons Ghirardelli cocoa powder and 1 tablespoon Hershey's cocoa powder.

• • • •

SIMON
KITCHEN & BAR
WOK-SEARED EDAMAME

In 2008 Chef Kerry Simon packed up his knives at the Hard Rock Casino and Hotel and moved across the Las Vegas Strip into the Palms Place tower at the Palms. The new restaurant features some of the same comfort food favorites as the old joint, such as truffled macaroni and cheese and cotton candy for dessert, but Kerry has now added a sushi bar and a broader menu, which includes breakfast, lunch, and a must-try Sunday brunch where you may be eating alongside the likes of Avril Lavigne or Hugh Hefner and his girlfriends. While you're noodling over which appetizers to try, you must check out this delicious addicting edamame starter: a pile of soybeans are cooked over high heat in a wok until their pods are blackened, then they're tossed in fresh lime juice and a Japanese 7-spice seasoning called shichimi togarashi. Togarashi is a spicy blend of orange peel, sesame seeds, seaweed, and chili that you can purchase in most Asian markets or online. The blend usually doesn't include salt, so you'll have to add some of that as well before you dig in. Or, you can use Szechwan seasoning such as one made by Sun-Bird that's found in most grocery stores where the Asian foods hang out. These blends will usually have salt in them, so you probably don't need to add additional salt if you use the Szechwan seasoning. You'll want to cook these in a wok that's been preheated over high heat, or you can use a cast-iron skillet that's been preheated for at least 10 minutes—you should see a lot of smoke when you drop those beans in the pan! Turn on the vent

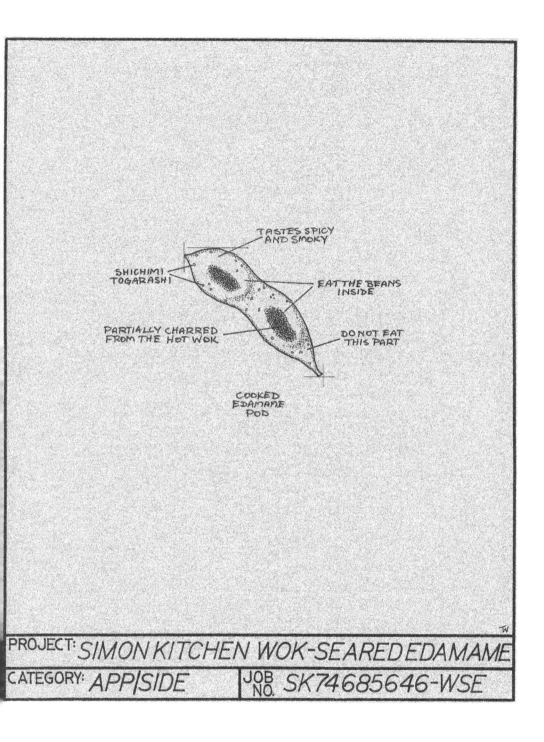

TASTES SPICY
AND SMOKY

SHICHIMI
TOGARASHI

EAT THE BEANS
INSIDE

PARTIALLY CHARRED
FROM THE HOT WOK

DO NOT EAT
THIS PART

COOKED
EDAMAME
POD

TW

PROJECT: *SIMON KITCHEN WOK-SEARED EDAMAME*

CATEGORY: *APP/SIDE*   JOB NO. *SK74685646-WSE*

over your stove before you start cooking unless you feel the need to test your smoke detectors.

½ pound frozen edamame, thawed

1 tablespoon light olive oil

juice of 1 lime

1 teaspoon shichimi togarashi (Japanese 7-spice) or Szechwan seasoning salt

1. Preheat a wok or cast-iron skillet over medium/high heat for several minutes until hot.
2. Toss the edamame in the olive oil in a small bowl until all of the beans are coated with oil, and then use your hands to remove the edamame from the bowl and drop them into the pan (don't dump the bowl into the pan or you will add the excess oil). Cook the edamame for 4 to 5 minutes or until the pods of the beans are blackened in spots. Stir the beans every minute or so.
3. Use tongs to remove the beans from the pan and drop them into a clean bowl. Pour lime juice over the edamame, and toss. Add the seasoning, salt to taste (if using togarashi— about ⅛ teaspoon), toss again, and serve.

• Serves 2 to 4 as an appetizer.

TIDBITS

To eat edamame, squeeze the beans from a pod directly into your mouth and then toss out the pod. The charred pods may look tasty, but you really don't want to eat them.

•   •   •   •

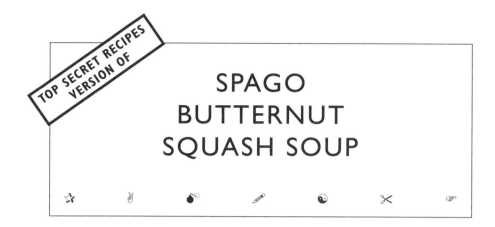

SPAGO BUTTERNUT SQUASH SOUP

I found several delicious variations of Wolfgang Puck's butternut squash soup recipe floating around the Internet, but no version comes close to duplicating the amazing taste of the stuff served at his flagship restaurant. At the Las Vegas Spago in Caesar's Palace, I slurped up the slightly sweetened, pale amber masterpiece with the perfect combination of spices, and then finagled two bowls to go. Since the soup is completely smooth, running it through a strainer revealed no solid evidence of ingredients used therein; only black specks of various spices were visible. This one was not going to be easy. After many attempts, I finally re-created the subtle background flavors with chopped leek slowly sautéed (sweated) in butter, and one Gala apple. I discovered that the apple contributes the sweetness and slight tang I was searching for after failing with sugars and various acids. The rest was easy: Poach the leek, squash, and apple in broth until soft; blend everything until smooth; then reheat with the cream and just a little brown sugar. This is now my new favorite soup.

2 tablespoons butter
½ cup chopped leek (about 1 leek)
1 ½ pounds cubed butternut squash

(about 5 cups or 1 squash)
1 Gala apple, peeled and chopped
3 cups chicken broth
½ teaspoon ground allspice

½ teaspoon ground nutmeg
¼ teaspoon salt
¼ teaspoon ground white pepper
⅛ teaspoon ground ginger

⅛ teaspoon ground cardamom
1¼ cups heavy cream
1 tablespoon light brown sugar

1. Melt the butter in a large saucepan over medium/low heat, then add the leek. Sweat the leaks for 6 minutes, or until soft, and then add butternut squash, apple, chicken broth, and all the spices. Don't add the heavy cream or brown sugar yet. Crank up the heat to medium and bring this mixture to a low boil and cook for 30 minutes, or until the squash softens. Turn off the heat and let the soup cool for 5 to 10 minutes.
2. Pour the soup into a blender and blend on high speed until completely smooth. Add an additional ¼ cup of water to the soup if it's too thick to blend. (To avoid a very messy and very hot situation, press down on the top of the blender with a folded dish towel to keep the lid from popping off.)
3. Pour the soup back into the saucepan and add the cream and sugar. Bring the soup to a simmer over medium/low heat, about 10 minutes. Spoon approximately 1 cup of soup into bowls to serve.

• SERVES 6.

• • • •

SPAGO
PUMPKIN CHEESECAKE

MENU DESCRIPTION: *"Gingerbread crispy crust, cranberry compote, spiced anglaise."*

Every fall we see the same dessert on home dinner tables: A triangular portion of pumpkin pie with a giant dollop of Cool Whip piled up on top. Sure, it's tasty and traditional, but maybe this time around you want to step it up a bit. I've got just the thing. Spago makes a semi-deconstructed pumpkin cheesecake that is the perfect upscale clone for your homemade holiday dessert, and it's totally worth the little extra effort. All four components of the cheesecake are made separately, then when it's dessert time, you pipe the filling onto the crispy gingerbread crusts with a pastry bag (or you can just spoon it on), pile on the garnish, and serve it up with a smile. You can make everything the day before, or on the morning of your celebration, and then build each plate just before serving. If you want an extra garnish for your plates (as in the restaurant), grab some vanilla sauce at the store, or follow the quickie recipe found below in Tidbits.

PUMPKIN CHEESECAKE FILLING

two 8-ounce packages cream
    cheese, softened
one 15-ounce can pumpkin
1 cup granulated sugar
2 eggs

1 teaspoon ground cinnamon
¾ teaspoon salt
½ teaspoon ground ginger
¼ teaspoon ground cloves

CRANBERRY COMPOTE

12 ounces fresh cranberries
1 ¼ cups water
¼ cup orange juice

1 cup granulated sugar
2 tablespoons Grand Marnier
½ teaspoon vanilla extract

SPICED ANGLAISE

2 egg yolks
3 tablespoons sugar
1 ½ cups heavy cream
⅛ teaspoon salt

⅛ teaspoon ground nutmeg
⅛ teaspoon ground allspice
⅛ teaspoon ground cardamom

GINGERBREAD CRISPY CRUST

⅔ cup butter, melted
½ cup dark brown sugar
¼ cup molasses
2 teaspoons ground ginger
2 teaspoons ground cinnamon

½ teaspoon ground allspice
pinch salt
2 cups graham cracker crumbs
½ cup whole wheat flour

1. Make the pumpkin cheesecake filling by combining all the ingredients in a large bowl and mixing with an electric mixer until smooth. Spoon the contents into a large saucepan and set over medium/low heat, stirring often. When mixture begins to bubble—in about 10 minutes—turn off the heat and let it cool down. When the filling cools completely, cover and refrigerate.

2. Make the cranberry compote by combining all the ingredients in a medium saucepan and set over medium heat. Bring the mixture to a boil, then reduce the heat and simmer for 20 to 25 minutes, or until the compote begins to thicken. Turn off the heat and allow the compote to cool off before covering it up and popping it in the refrigerator.

3. For the spiced anglaise, first beat the egg yolks and sugar

together in a bowl for a minute, or until the mixture becomes a lighter shade of yellow. Combine the sweetened yolks with cream, salt, and spices in a medium saucepan and set over medium/low heat. Stir often as the mixture heats up until you see steam coming off it—this should take about 10 minutes. You don't need it to come to a boil. Remove the mixture from the heat, then cover it up and put it in the refrigerator with the other stuff.

4. Now you are ready to make the last component of the cheesecake: The gingerbread crust. First, preheat your oven to 325 degrees F. Next, combine the melted butter with brown sugar, molasses, spices, and salt in a large bowl. In a separate medium bowl, combine the graham cracker crumbs with the flour. Mix the dry ingredients into the wet ingredients with an electric mixer, and press the crust into a 17 x 12-inch baking sheet. Use your fingers to press down on the surface of the crust so that it is an even thickness, from edge to edge. Bake the crust for 20 to 22 minutes, or until it just begins to turn darker brown around the edges. Remove the crust from the oven and cool for a couple minutes, then use a large knife, the flat edge of a metal scraper, or a pizza wheel to cut away ½ inch from around the edges. This edge scrap gets tossed. Now cut lengthwise down the middle, and then cut each of those large portions into 1½-inch-wide slices. You will have approximately 20 crusts (5¼ x 1½ inches). Set these aside to cool until you are ready to assemble your cheesecakes.

5. Build each serving by placing a crust onto a serving plate. Use a pastry bag to pipe two rows of 5 dollops of pumpkin cheesecake filling onto the bottom crust. Place another crust on top of the filling, slightly offset. Spoon a heaping tablespoon of cranberry compote onto one end of the top crust. Use an electric mixer to whip the anglaise until it forms stiff peaks. Spoon a heaping tablespoon of whipped anglaise onto the other end of the top crust.

• MAKES 10 SERVINGS.

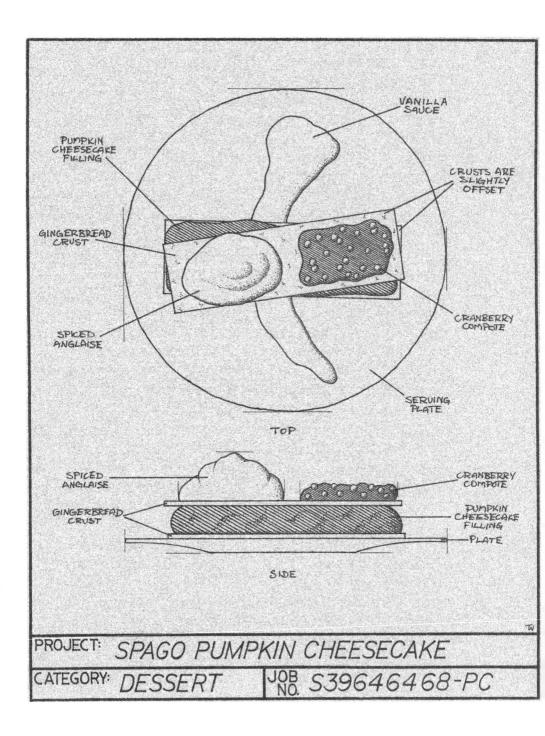

VANILLA
SAUCE

PUMPKIN
CHEESECAKE
FILLING

CRUSTS ARE
SLIGHTLY
OFFSET

GINGERBREAD
CRUST

CRANBERRY
COMPOTE

SPICED
ANGLAISE

SERVING
PLATE

TOP

SPICED
ANGLAISE

CRANBERRY
COMPOTE

GINGERBREAD
CRUST

PUMPKIN
CHEESECAKE
FILLING

PLATE

SIDE

PROJECT: *SPAGO PUMPKIN CHEESECAKE*

CATEGORY: *DESSERT*   JOB NO. *S39646468-PC*

TIDBITS

Before serving you can apply an additional garnish of a strip of vanilla sauce onto the plate before preparing this dessert. Premade vanilla sauces packaged in squirt bottles can be found in most markets. You can also make your own by bringing a mixture of 2 cups of heavy cream, 4 beaten egg yolks, ½ cup of sugar and half of a split vanilla bean to a simmer over medium/low heat and cooking, stirring often, for 10 to 15 minutes. Strain and chill, then use a squirt bottle or spoon to apply a strip of the cooled sauce to the plate before assembling your cheesecake.

• • • •

T.G.I. FRIDAY'S POMEGRANATE MARTINI

Now it seems like every casual restaurant chain has at least one pomegranate cocktail on the drink menu. Friday's hops on with this simple concoction that features PAMA, the first pomegranate liqueur on the market. It's served up in a chilled martini glass, and it's awful. I'm just kidding, it's actually one of the best pomegranate martinis I've had so far.

1 ounce Skyy vodka
1 ½ ounces PAMA pomegranate
  liqueur

½ ounce Cointreau orange liqueur
1 ½ ounces Ocean Spray
  cranberry juice cocktail

GARNISH
orange wedge

1. Fill an 8-ounce martini glass with ice to chill it.
2. Drop a handful of ice into a cocktail shaker. Add vodka, liqueurs, and cranberry juice to the shaker, close it up, and give it a real good shake.
3. Pour the ice out of the martini glass, and then strain the drink into the glass.
4. Make a cut into the orange wedge and place it onto the rim of the glass. Serve it up or take it for yourself.

• MAKES 1 DRINK.

• • • •

T.G.I. FRIDAY'S
CANDY APPLE MARTINI

Celebrate life with this cocktail clone that tastes like you're drinking a caramel apple. And look at that, there's caramel dripping down the apple slice garnish into the bottom of the glass. This one is just way too cool.

1 ounce Stoli Vanil vodka
2 ounces DeKuyper Sour Apple
   Pucker schnapps

1½ ounces Hiram Walker
   butterscotch schnapps

GARNISH
thin apple slice
caramel sauce

1. Fill an 8-ounce martini glass with ice to chill it.
2. Drop a handful of ice into a cocktail shaker. Add vodka and schnapps to the shaker, close it up, and shake thoroughly. Really shake it good, so that you get some tiny ice chips in your drink.
3. Pour the ice out of the martini glass, and then strain drink into the glass.
4. Make a cut halfway through an apple slice, and then slide the slice onto the rim of the glass. Drizzle some caramel over the apple slice so that it drips down into the glass.

• MAKES 1 DRINK.

• • • •

VODKA AND
TWO KINDS
OF SCHNAPPS

CARAMEL
SAUCE

APPLE
SLICE

DRINK THIS
PART

EAT THIS
PART

8-OUNCE
MARTINI
GLASS

READY FOR
CONSUMPTION

PROJECT: *T.G.I. FRIDAY'S CANDY APPLE MARTINI*

CATEGORY: *COCKTAIL* **JOB NO.** *TGIF 35794566-CAM*

T.G.I. FRIDAY'S
CRISPY GREEN BEAN FRIES

MENU DESCRIPTION: *"Crunchy and crisp battered green beans with a cool creamy cucumber-wasabi ranch dip."*

Are you ready for this? T.G.I. Friday's new finger food offering might just make you forget about French fries. At least for a little while. Flavorful green beans are coated with tasty bread crumbs, then fried to a golden brown and served with a side of creamy wasabi dipping sauce. This item has quickly become the top seller off the chain's new appetizer menu as Friday's becomes the first major casual restaurant to introduce a dish that has been popular for several years at upscale chains. But creating a home version isn't just a matter of breading and frying fresh green beans. My first attempts using a breading technique employed for perfect onion rings produced beautiful looking fried beans, but they were undercooked and had an overwhelming green bean flavor that was absent from the Friday's version. So I had to figure out a good way to get the undesirable green bean-ness out of there. After a few tests that included steaming, baking, and boiling, I finally settled on blanching the beans in a flavorful broth. The secret technique, which you'll find here, tenderizes the beans while injecting a pleasant flavor that closely resembles the Friday's favorite.

CUCUMBER-WASABI
RANCH DIP

½ cup Hidden Valley Ranch
   salad dressing

¼ cup minced peeled and seeded
   cucumber

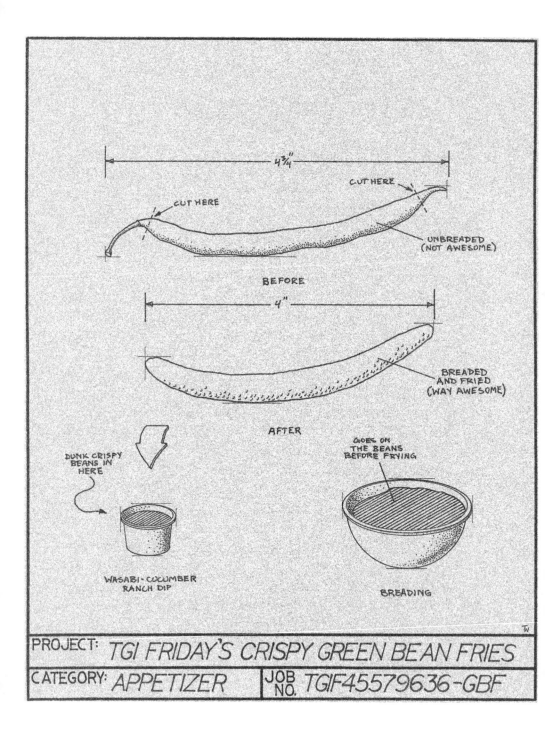

BEFORE

4¾"

CUT HERE

CUT HERE

UNBREADED
(NOT AWESOME)

AFTER

4"

BREADED
AND FRIED
(WAY AWESOME)

DUNK CRISPY
BEANS IN
HERE

WASABI-CUCUMBER
RANCH DIP

GOES ON
THE BEANS
BEFORE FRYING

BREADING

PROJECT:	*TGI FRIDAY'S CRISPY GREEN BEAN FRIES*	
CATEGORY: *APPETIZER*	JOB NO.	*TGIF45579636-GBF*

1 tablespoon whole milk
1 ½ teaspoons white prepared
  horseradish
1 teaspoon white vinegar

1 teaspoon powdered wasabi
⅛ teaspoon salt
pinch ground cayenne pepper

4 cups chicken broth
6 to 8 ounces fresh green beans
1 egg, beaten
1 cup milk
1 cup all-purpose flour
1 cup plain bread crumbs
  (I like Progresso brand)

¾ teaspoon salt
¼ teaspoon onion powder
⅛ teaspoon garlic powder
⅛ teaspoon ground black pepper

6 to 10 cups vegetable shortening
  or oil

1. Make the dip by combining all of the ingredients in a blender on high speed until smooth. Cover and chill. The dip will thicken as it chills.
2. Prepare beans by bringing 4 cups of chicken broth to a boil. Boil the beans in the broth for 15 minutes and then plunge them into ice water to keep them from getting too soft.
3. Combine beaten egg with milk in a shallow bowl. Measure 1 cup of flour into another shallow bowl. Combine bread crumbs, ¾ teaspoon salt, black pepper, onion powder, and garlic powder in a third shallow bowl.
4. Take a small handful of beans out of the water and shake off any excess liquid. Coat the beans with flour. Shake off any excess flour. Dip the beans one at a time into the egg and milk mixture and then coat each one with the bread crumb mixture. Lay the coated beans on a plate in a single layer until all of them have been breaded.

5. Heat the shortening or oil to 350 degrees F in a deep fryer or large saucepan.
6. Fry the beans in bunches for 1½ minutes or until golden brown. Drain on a rack or paper towels, then serve them up with the cucumber-wasabi ranch dip.

• MAKES 2 TO 4 APPETIZER SERVINGS.

•   •   •   •

T.G.I. FRIDAY'S
FRIED MAC & CHEESE

MENU DESCRIPTION: *"Irresistible, creamy cheeses and elbow noodles golden fried to perfection."*

When T.G.I. Friday's vice president of research and development Phil Costner was in Las Vegas at Fix restaurant in the Bellagio in 2006, he tried a version of this fantastic finger food and immediately went to work locating a supplier to develop the dish for his chain of more than 1000 restaurants. Now Fried Mac & Cheese is one of 7 "radically new" finger foods on Friday's appetizer menu that includes Crispy Green Bean Fries, Potato Skinny Dippers, and Triple Meat Fundido. After several hours in the underground lab I decided on a couple ways to approach this particular clone. Since Friday's Fried Mac & Cheese is made with a blend of cheeses, I'll first show you how to re-create the mac and cheese from scratch using cheddar and Monterey Jack cheeses. And for those of you who love shortcuts, head on down to the Tidbits at the end of the recipe and I'll show you how to clone the appetizer much faster using frozen Stouffer's Macaroni & Cheese.

MAC & CHEESE

5 teaspoons all-purpose flour
1 cup skim milk
1 cup (3 ounces) shredded
   medium cheddar cheese

1 cup (3 ounces) shredded
   Monterey Jack cheese
2 teaspoons margarine
¼ teaspoon plus ⅛ teaspoon salt

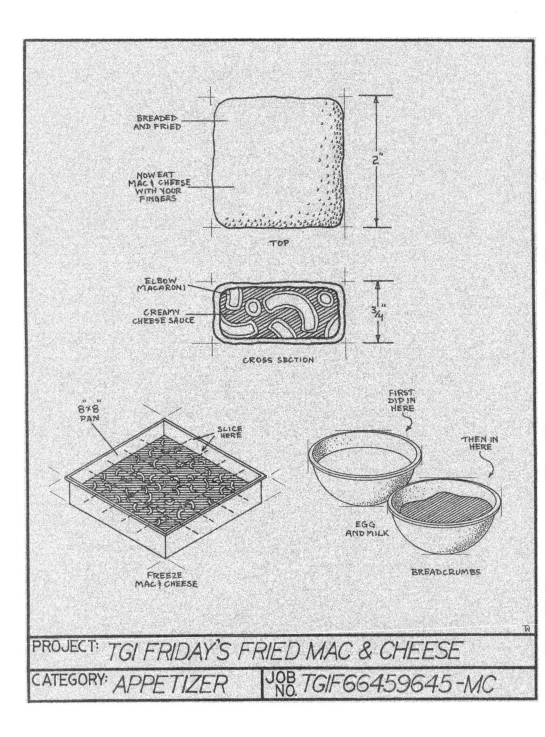

BREADED AND FRIED

NOW EAT MAC & CHEESE WITH YOUR FINGERS

2"

TOP

ELBOW MACARONI

CREAMY CHEESE SAUCE

3/4"

CROSS SECTION

8"×8" PAN

SLICE HERE

FREEZE MAC & CHEESE

FIRST DIP IN HERE

THEN IN HERE

EGG AND MILK

BREADCRUMBS

PROJECT: TGI FRIDAY'S FRIED MAC & CHEESE

CATEGORY: APPETIZER

JOB NO. TGIF66459645-MC

¾ cups uncooked elbow macaroni   margarine
    (about 1¾ cups cooked)

1 egg, beaten   ¾ teaspoon salt
1 cup whole milk   6 to 10 cups vegetable shortening
1 cup all-purpose flour   or oil
1½ cups plain bread crumbs
    (Progresso works well)

GARNISH

½ teaspoon minced fresh
    parsley

1. Whisk flour into skim milk in a small saucepan, then place it
    over medium/low heat.
2. Add the shredded cheeses, margarine, and salt and stir often
    with a spoon until the cheese begins to melt. Reduce heat to
    low and simmer for 30 minutes. Use a whisk to stir the sauce
    every couple of minutes so that it becomes smooth and
    thick.
3. While the sauce thickens, prepare macaroni by dumping ¾
    cup uncooked elbow macaroni into rapidly boiling water. Boil
    for 8 minutes or until tender, and then drain. You should have
    at least 1¾ cups of cooked macaroni.
4. When the cheese sauce has simmered for 30 minutes, re-
    serve 2 tablespoons of the sauce and then pour pasta into a
    medium bowl. Gently stir in remaining cheese sauce and then
    pour the mixture into an 8 x 8-inch pan that has been greased
    with margarine. Cover and chill.
5. When the macaroni and cheese is cold, use a knife to cut
    down 4 times and across 4 times for a total of 25 macaroni
    & cheese chunks. Carefully remove the squares, arrange them

on wax paper, and put them into a covered container in the freezer for a couple hours.

6. When the macaroni and cheese is frozen solid, combine beaten egg and milk in one shallow bowl, pour flour into another shallow bowl, and combine bread crumbs and ¾ teaspoon salt in another bowl.

7. Bread the macaroni and cheese chunks one at time by coating a piece with flour, then dunking it into the egg and milk mixture and coating it with bread crumbs. Dunk the chunk of macaroni & cheese back into the egg and milk and give it another coating of bread crumbs. Repeat this process with all of the macaroni and cheese and arrange the pieces on a plate. Let them sit for 10 minutes so that they can thaw a little bit—this will ensure that the mac & cheese isn't cold inside after the frying.

8. When all of the macaroni & cheese is breaded, heat shortening or oil to 350 degrees F. Fry 4 to 6 pieces at a time in the hot oil for 2 to 3 minutes, until golden brown (you may want to do a test with just one at first so that you can be sure it's warm all the way through). Drain the fried mac and cheese on a rack or paper towels for a minute or two after you pull it out of the oil, then arrange all of the finished fried mac and cheese pieces on a plate. Microwave the remaining 2 tablespoons of cheese sauce for 15 to 20 seconds, until hot. Drizzle this cheese sauce over the top of the fried mac and cheese, sprinkle the dish with parsley, and serve.

• MAKES 6 TO 8 APPETIZER SERVINGS.

TIDBITS

If you'd like a shortcut for this clone, get yourself two 12-ounce boxes of frozen Stouffer's Macaroni & Cheese and let them thaw in the refrigerator. When the mac and cheese is soft, slice lengthwise through the middle of each tray, then slice across three times so that you have 8 rectangles in each tray. Carefully take those slices out, arrange them on wax paper and store them in the freezer until solid, then pick up the recipe at step #6. Using this technique will not give you any extra cheese sauce to drizzle over the top, so you'll have to skip that step at the end. But I doubt anyone will miss it.

•   •   •   •

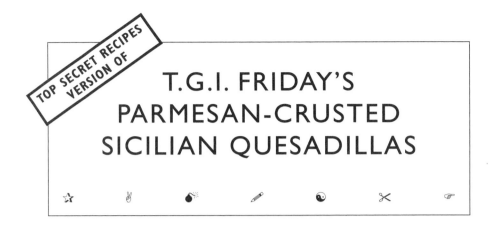

T.G.I. FRIDAY'S PARMESAN-CRUSTED SICILIAN QUESADILLAS

MENU DESCRIPTION: *"Our flour tortilla is packed with sautéed chicken, sausage, bruschetta marinara, bacon, and oozing Monterey Jack cheese. We coat it with Parmesan, and pan-fry it to a crispy, golden brown, then drizzle it with balsamic glaze."*

Italy meets Mexico in this new hit appetizer that combines a cheese-filled tortilla with ingredients you wouldn't usually find in-side a quesadilla, including Friday's bruschetta marinara. You'll love the Parmesan cheese that's crusted on the outside of the tortilla, and the easy balsamic glaze drizzle is the perfect finishing touch. This is an awesome party-dish appetizer since the whole recipe makes 4 quesadillas that can be sliced into as many as 8 pieces each.

BALSAMIC GLAZE
½ cup balsamic vinegar

⅓ cup dark brown sugar

1 teaspoon molasses

⅛ teaspoon salt

BRUSCHETTA MARINARA
1 medium tomato, diced

1 tablespoon tomato sauce

1 tablespoon sliced basil

1 tablespoon olive oil

¼ teaspoon white wine vinegar

½ teaspoon minced garlic

¼ teaspoon ground black pepper

⅛ teaspoon salt

1 chicken breast
olive oil
salt and pepper
½ cup shredded Parmesan
   cheese
four 10-inch flour tortillas

olive oil spray
2 cups shredded Monterey Jack
   cheese
3 pieces cooked bacon, diced
1 ounce cooked Italian sausage,
   diced

GARNISH
4 teaspoons minced fresh parsley

1. Combine the balsamic vinegar, brown sugar, molasses, and salt in a small saucepan. Place over medium/low heat, heat the mixture until bubbling, then simmer for 5 minutes. Remove from the heat and cool.
2. Make the bruschetta marinara by combining tomato, tomato sauce, basil, olive oil, white vinegar, garlic, pepper, and salt in a small bowl. Cover and set aside.
3. Pound the chicken breast until about ½ inch thick, then rub with olive oil and sprinkle it with a little salt and pepper. Heat a sauté pan over medium heat, add the chicken, and sauté for 4 to 5 minutes per side, until cooked. Cool the chicken, then dice it.
4. Prepare each quesadilla by preheating a large nonstick sauté pan over medium heat. Sprinkle 2 tablespoons of Parmesan cheese into the pan. Spray one side of a tortilla with olive oil spray and press it down onto the Parmesan cheese in the pan. Spread ½ cup of Monterey Jack cheese over half of the tortilla. Sprinkle 3 tablespoons of diced chicken on the cheese followed by 1 tablespoon of bacon and 1 tablespoon of sausage. Spoon 2 tablespoons of bruschetta marinara over the cheese and meats, then fold the other half of the tortilla over the fillings. Cook for 1 minute, or until the Parmesan cheese is browed, then flip the quesadilla over and cook it until the Parmesan is browned on that side as well.

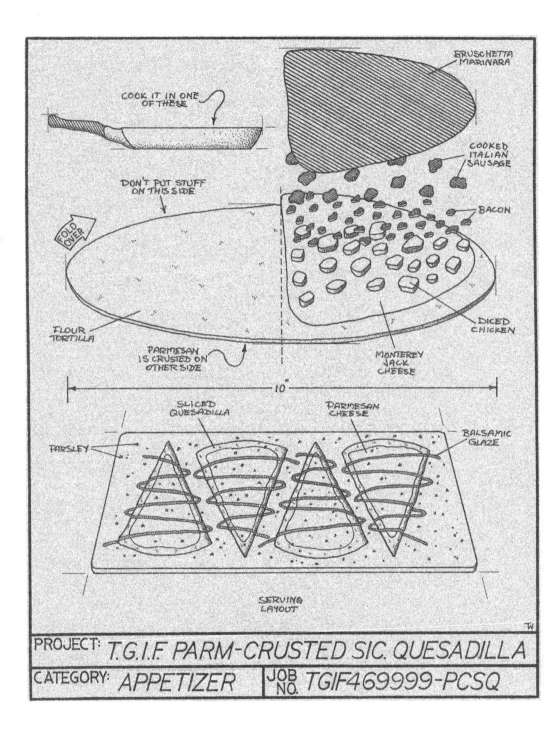

COOK IT IN ONE OF THESE

BRUSCHETTA MARINARA

COOKED ITALIAN SAUSAGE

DON'T PUT STUFF ON THIS SIDE

FOLD OVER

BACON

FLOUR TORTILLA

PARMESAN IS CRUSTED ON OTHER SIDE

MONTEREY JACK CHEESE

DICED CHICKEN

10"

SLICED QUESADILLA

PARMESAN CHEESE

PARSLEY

BALSAMIC GLAZE

SERVING LAYOUT

PROJECT: T.G.I.F PARM-CRUSTED SIC. QUESADILLA

CATEGORY: APPETIZER

JOB NO. TGIF469999-PCSQ

386

5. Slide the quesadilla out onto a cutting board. Use a large chef's knife or a pizza wheel to cut the quesadilla in half, then slice those halves in half, creating 4 slices.

6. Arrange the quesadilla slices on a plate, drizzle with balsamic glaze, and sprinkle with a little parsley. Repeat for the remaining 3 servings.

• MAKES 4 QUESADILLAS.

•   •   •   •

T.G.I. FRIDAY'S
TUSCAN SPINACH DIP

MENU DESCRIPTION: *"Parmesan and Romano cheeses blended with spinach, artichokes, and sauteed onions & peppers. Served with Friday's red and white tortilla chips."*

Many casual chains have their own version of spinach-artichoke dip somewhere on the appetizer menu, but one of the most popular versions is found at this huge national chain. For our clone we'll use marinated artichoke hearts that will contribute the slightly acidic flavor found in the original. The recipe here is a stovetop method, but you can also prepare a version of this dip entirely in your microwave using the technique at the end in the Tidbits.

one 10-ounce box frozen
    chopped spinach, thawed
one 6½-ounce jar marinated
    artichoke hearts, drained,
    rinsed, and chopped (½ cup)
1 teaspoon vegetable oil
1 tablespoon diced onion
1 tablespoon diced red bell
    pepper

4 ounces cream cheese, softened
⅓ cup shredded Parmesan
    cheese
¼ cup shredded Romano cheese
¼ cup heavy cream
1½ teaspoons minced garlic
¼ teaspoon salt
pinch ground black pepper

GARNISH
½ tomato, diced
1 tablespoon shredded Parmesan
    cheese

1 teaspoon minced parsley

1. Steam spinach and artichoke hearts in a steamer basket over boiling water in a covered saucepan for 10 minutes.
2. In another medium saucepan heat 1 teaspoon oil over medium/low heat. Add the diced onion and bell pepper and sauté for 3 to 4 minutes, until onions begin to turn translucent. Add spinach and artichoke hearts plus cheeses, cream, garlic, salt, and pepper to the pan with the sautéed onion and pepper. Cook over medium/low heat, uncovered, for 5 to 6 minutes, or until the cheeses are melted and the dip is hot. Stir occasionally.
3. Spoon the dip into a heat proof serving bowl and garnish with diced tomato, shredded Parmesan cheese, and minced parsley. Serve with chips or crackers on the side.

- MAKES 6 APPETIZER SERVINGS.

TIDBITS

Combine the spinach (don't squeeze any water out of it), artichoke hearts, onion, bell pepper, and garlic in a microwave-safe bowl and cover with plastic wrap. Poke a couple holes in the plastic and microwave everything on high for 6 to 8 minutes, until the spinach is tender. Stir after every 2 minutes. Add cheeses, cream, salt, and pepper and microwave on high for an additional 3 minutes, stirring every minute. Continue the recipe above at step #3.

• • • •

T.G.I. FRIDAY'S JACK DANIEL'S GLAZE

The Jack Daniel's glaze is one of the most scrumptious sauces you will ever taste on just about any meat. Introduced in April of 1997, this glaze has become one of Friday's best-selling items. Its versatile sweet-and-slightly-spicy flavor works well on salmon, baby back ribs, steak, chicken, pork chops ... even on chicken wings. Producers at the *Oprah Winfrey Show* requested that I clone the stuff before I went on the show, and I'm happy to say the clone that resulted from my sleuthing is a dead ringer for the real thing. Try it for yourself. Use it on anything you're grilling, but apply it at the end if your grilling, because the sugar in the sauce will burn over the flames. You'll need this recipe for the Sesame Jack Chicken Strips clone that follows (page 392), and for the clone of Friday's amazing Jack Daniel's Glazed Ribs (page 396).

I head of garlic
I tablespoon olive oil
⅔ cup water
I cup pineapple juice
¼ cup teriyaki sauce
I tablespoon soy sauce
I⅓ cups dark brown sugar

3 tablespoons lemon juice
3 tablespoons minced white onion
I tablespoon Jack Daniel's whiskey
I tablespoon crushed pineapple
¼ teaspoon cayenne pepper

1. Preheat the oven to 325 degrees F.
2. Cut about ½ inch off of the head of garlic. Cut the roots so

that the garlic will sit flat. Remove the excess papery skin from the garlic, but leave enough so that the cloves stay together. Put the garlic into a small casserole dish or baking pan, drizzle the olive oil over it, and cover it with a lid or foil. Bake for 1 hour. Remove the garlic from the oven and let it cool until you can handle it.

3. Combine the water, pineapple juice, teriyaki sauce, soy sauce, and brown sugar in a medium saucepan and place over medium/high heat. Cook, stirring occasionally, until the mixture comes to a boil, then reduce the heat until the mixture is just simmering.

4. Squeeze the sides of the head of garlic until the pasty roasted garlic is squeezed out. Measure 2 teaspoons into the saucepan and whisk to combine. Add the remaining ingredients to the pan and stir.

5. Let the mixture simmer for 30 to 40 minutes, or until the sauce has reduced by about half and is thick and syrupy. Make sure it doesn't boil over.

• Makes 1 cup of glaze.

• • • •

T.G.I. FRIDAY'S
SESAME JACK
CHICKEN STRIPS

MENU DESCRIPTION: *"Golden brown chicken breast strips coated with crispy Japanese panko breadcrumbs with the extra crunch of toasted sesame seeds and tossed in our famous Jack Daniels sauce."*

Although the original recipe is made from sliced chicken breasts, you may consider using the less chewy tenderloin parts in this kitchen copy. Packs of fresh chicken tenderloins are sold in most markets, and you can also find bags of them in the freezer section. I'm a big fan of the more tender meat in the tenderloins, especially when it comes to chicken fingers. The breading here is a simple combination of flour and panko (or Japanese bread crumbs). Look for those where the Asian foods are stocked in your market. When the chicken fingers are done frying, gently toss them in the Jack Daniel's glaze made from the clone recipe on page 390, and you've got a great appetizer than can serve a half dozen finger food fanatics.

1 tablespoon salt
2 cups water

1 pound skinless chicken breast
   fillets (about 3 breasts), or
   tenderloins (9 to 10 pieces)

BREADING

1 cup all-purpose flour
¾ cup panko (Japanese bread
   crumbs)
1 teaspoon paprika

¾ teaspoon salt
½ teaspoon garlic powder
2 eggs
¼ cup milk

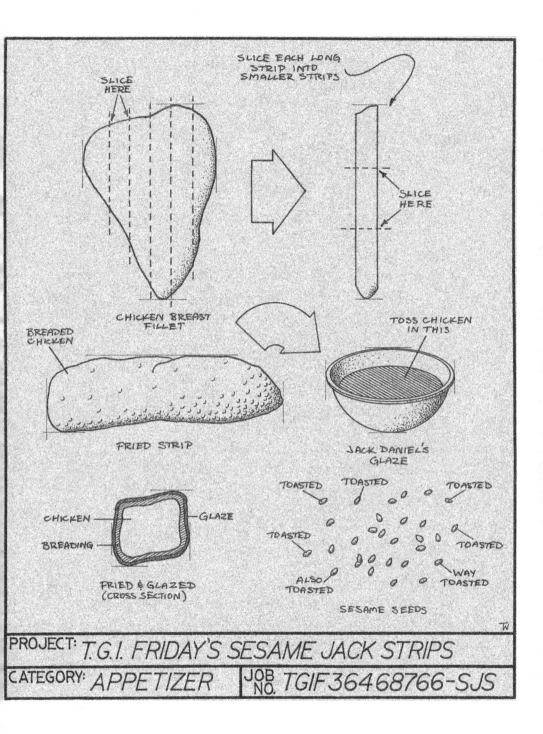

SLICE EACH LONG
STRIP INTO
SMALLER STRIPS

SLICE
HERE

SLICE
HERE

CHICKEN BREAST
FILLET

BREADED
CHICKEN

TOSS CHICKEN
IN THIS

FRIED STRIP

JACK DANIEL'S
GLAZE

CHICKEN — GLAZE

BREADING

FRIED & GLAZED
(CROSS SECTION)

TOASTED   TOASTED   TOASTED

TOASTED   TOASTED

ALSO
TOASTED   WAY
                         TOASTED

SESAME SEEDS

TW

PROJECT: *T.G.I. FRIDAY'S SESAME JACK STRIPS*

CATEGORY: *APPETIZER*   **JOB NO.** *TGIF 36468766-SJS*

393

6 to 12 cups vegetable oil or
shortening for frying

1 cup Jack Daniel's glaze clone
(from page 390)
1 teaspoon sesame seeds

GARNISH (OPTIONAL)
1 cup thinly sliced iceberg lettuce

1. Make the brine by combining the salt and water in a medium bowl. Slice the chicken breasts into strips and cut each of the strips in half or into thirds and drop the pieces into the brine. If using tenderloins, slice each of those in half or into thirds and brine. Cover the chicken and chill in the brine for 1 hour.
2. Heat the oil in a deep fryer, large saucepan, or Dutch oven to 350 degrees F.
3. After the chicken has brined, rinse all the pieces under cold water and blot dry.
4. Combine the flour, panko, paprika, salt, and garlic powder in a shallow bowl or pie pan. Beat the eggs in a separate medium bowl and mix in the milk.
5. First dredge each piece of chicken in the flour mixture, then coat with egg, and toss back into the flour. Do this with about 6 to 8 pieces, allowing them to sit in the flour for a few minutes so that the breading sticks.
6. Fry 6 to 8 pieces at a time for 5 minutes, or until browned and cooked through. Drain on a rack or a plate lined with paper towels.
7. Just before serving, gently toss the wings with the glaze in a large bowl. Arrange the chicken on a bed of thinly sliced lettuce, if using, on a plate, sprinkle with sesame seeds, and serve with extra glaze on the side.

• SERVES 6 AS AN APPETIZER.

TIDBITS

You can find toasted sesame seeds in your market, where Asian foods are stocked. If you can't find toasted sesame seeds, the untoasted kind work fine.

•   •   •   •

T.G.I. FRIDAY'S JACK DANIEL'S GLAZED RIBS

MENU DESCRIPTION: *"This full side of baby back pork ribs is first cooked until it's fall-off-the-bone tender, then seasoned with Cajun spices, fire-grilled and brushed with our famous Jack Daniel's glaze. Served with crispy fries and coleslaw."*

To re-create these great ribs, you first must clone the Cajun seasoning that is sprinkled on them. You'll also need the Jack Daniel's glaze from page 390. Once that's all done you get plenty of time to chill out with your crew while the ribs slowly cook in the oven over the next couple of hours. When the racks come out of the oven, slap 'em on the grill for a few minutes until grill marks form, and chow down.

CAJUN SEASONING

1 teaspoon paprika	¼ teaspoon garlic powder
½ teaspoon salt	¼ teaspoon onion powder
¼ teaspoon dried thyme	¼ teaspoon celery salt
¼ teaspoon ground black pepper	⅛ teaspoon ground cayenne pepper

2 full racks baby back ribs
½ cup Jack Daniel's glaze clone
    (from page 390)

1. Preheat the oven to 300 degrees F.
2. Combine all ingredients for the Cajun seasoning in a small bowl. Sprinkle on both sides of each rack of ribs.
3. Place the ribs on a baking sheet and bake for 2½ hours.
4. Preheat the barbecue grill (or an indoor grill pan) to high heat.
5. Grill the ribs for 3 to 4 minutes per side, or until grill marks form.
6. Immediately after removing the ribs from the grill, brush with Jack Daniel's glaze and serve with extra glaze on the side.

*   SERVES 2.

•   •   •   •

T.G.I. FRIDAY'S BRUSCHETTA CHICKEN PASTA

MENU DESCRIPTION: *"Italian grandmothers everywhere are getting jealous over this recipe. Angel hair pasta tossed with fresh bruschetta marinara, fire-grilled chicken breast in a balsamic glaze, and Parmesan shavings."*

When you combine this balsamic glaze with the angel hair pasta that's been tossed with a slightly tangy bruschetta marinara, you are re-creating the same sweet-and-sour flavor combination that has made this the top pasta choice at T.G.I. Friday's. You'll have to plan ahead a little for this recipe so that the chicken can marinate in the brine. This important step will fill the chicken with the perfect flavor and moistness. You can make the marinara a day ahead if you like and chill it until you need it. Each serving is tossed in a hot skillet so the marinara will be reheated. The glaze can also be made ahead of time and stored in a covered container at room temperature for several days. It's best to use an empty squirt bottle to hold the balsamic glaze so that you can evenly apply it to each serving.

BALSAMIC GLAZE

½ cup balsamic vinegar
⅓ cup dark brown sugar

1 teaspoon molasses
⅛ teaspoon salt

BRUSCHETTA MARINARA

2 cups diced tomatoes (about 4
    medium tomatoes)
¼ cup tomato sauce
¼ cup chopped basil
¼ cup olive oil

1 teaspoon white wine vinegar
2 teaspoons minced garlic
¾ teaspoon ground black pepper
½ teaspoon salt

CHICKEN MARINADE

2 cups water
1 tablespoon salt

½ teaspoon paprika
¼ teaspoon liquid smoke

1 pound skinless chicken breasts
    fillets (about 3 breasts)

olive oil ground black pepper
½ pound uncooked angel hair
    pasta (½ of a box)

FOR FINISHING THE DISH

8 teaspoons olive oil
8 tablespoons Parmesan cheese
4 teaspoons minced parsley

1. Make the balsamic glaze by combining the balsamic vinegar, brown sugar, molasses, and salt in a small saucepan. Place over medium/low heat and heat the mixture until bubbling, then simmer for 5 minutes. Remove from the heat and cool.
2. Make the bruschetta marinara by combining the tomatoes, tomato sauce, basil, olive oil, white vinegar, garlic, pepper, and salt in a small bowl. Cover and set aside.
3. Marinate the chicken by combining the water, salt, paprika, and liquid smoke in a medium bowl. Pound the chicken breasts until about ¾ inch thick, then add to the marinade, cover, and chill for exactly 1 hour.
4. Preheat a grill to high heat.

5. When the chicken has marinated, remove the breasts from the brine, rinse each under cold water, and blot dry. Rub each breast with oil and sprinkle with a little ground black pepper. Grill the chicken for 4 to 5 minutes per side or until chicken is cooked.

6. Break the pasta in half and cook it for 4 minutes in a large saucepan of boiling water. Strain.

7. To prepare each serving, preheat a medium sauté pan over medium heat. Add 2 teaspoons of olive oil to the pan and one quarter of the cooked angel hair pasta. Add ½ cup of the bruschetta marinara and 1 tablespoon grated Parmesan cheese and toss with tongs until hot. Turn out the pasta onto the center of a plate and drizzle with balsamic glaze. Slice the chicken breasts and arrange one quarter of the chicken around the pasta, then sprinkle 1 tablespoon of grated Parmesan cheese over the top, followed by 1 teaspoon of minced parsley. Repeat for the remaining servings.

- SERVES 4.

• • • •

T.G.I. FRIDAY'S DRAGONFIRE CHICKEN

MENU DESCRIPTION: *"Marinated chicken breast topped with fiery kung pao sauce, mandarin oranges and pineapple pico de gallo."*

This Friday's low-fat creation does not skimp on flavor. A marinade, a spicy sauce, and a fresh salsa all pitch in for some big-time taste bud stimulation. Sprinkle mandarin orange sections over the top if you've got 'em, and you will completely re-create the look and taste of this healthy new entree clone.

MARINADE

½ cup olive oil
½ cup honey
3 tablespoons rice vinegar
2 tablespoons lime juice

⅓ cup chopped parsley
1 seeded, chopped jalapeño
2 teaspoons minced garlic
1 tablespoon diced onion
¾ teaspoon salt

2 skinless chicken breast fillets

PINEAPPLE PICO DE GALLO

2 medium tomatoes, diced
½ cup chopped canned sliced
   pineapple
½ cup diced red onion

2 tablespoons minced cilantro
4 teaspoons minced jalapeño
1 tablespoon lime juice
⅛ teaspoon salt

KUNG PAO SAUCE

¼ cup water
2 tablespoons rice vinegar
½ cup dark brown sugar
4 teaspoons soy sauce

1 tablespoon chili sauce
1 tablespoon finely minced garlic
1 teaspoon finely minced ginger

GARNISH

one 11-ounce can mandarin
   orange segments

1. Make the marinade by combining all ingredients in a blender on high speed for 1 minute. Pound the chicken breast fillets flat with a mallet. Combine the chicken with the marinade in a zip-top bag and refrigerate for 2 to 3 hours.
2. Make the pineapple pico de gallo by combining all ingredients. Store in a covered container in your refrigerator until later.
3. Make the kung pao sauce clone by combining all ingredients in a small saucepan over medium heat. When mixture begins to bubble, reduce heat and simmer for 15 minutes. Cover the sauce until it's needed.
4. When the chicken is done marinating, preheat barbecue grill to medium. Wipe the marinade from each chicken breast and grill for 5 to 6 minutes per side, until done. Serve chicken drizzled with cloned kung pao sauce and pico de gallo on the side. Drain the canned mandarin oranges and sprinkle some orange sections over the top of each dish.

• MAKES 2 SERVINGS.

•　•　•　•

T.G.I. FRIDAY'S
TUSCAN PORTOBELLO MELT

MENU DESCRIPTION: *"Sliced portobello mushrooms between layers of provolone and Monterey Jack cheeses, roasted onions, and tomatoes on grilled buttery bread."*

Contestants on the November 1, 2006 episode of *Top Chef* on Bravo were challenged to take a childhood favorite dish and update it with a twist. Friday's senior executive chef Stephen Bulgarelli sat at the judge's table and endured a bizarre wonderland mushroom fantasy plate, a sloppy cheese steak sandwich, and an over salted surf-and-turf tragedy. Finally, it was the delicious variation on a grilled cheese sandwich created by Betty Fraser that took the top spot. As a reward, Betty's sandwich was added to over 500 Friday's menus across the country, and now we have a *Top Secret* clone to easily re-create the tasty winner at home. It's apparent that Friday's modified Betty's recipe to make it easier to prepare in the quick-service environment of the restaurant, and that's the version I've cloned here.

½ cup sliced portobello
   mushroom (about ½ of a
   small portobello)
¼ cup sliced red onion
4 to 5 grape tomatoes, each
   sliced in half
1 teaspoon vegetable oil
¼ teaspoon balsamic vinegar
pinch salt

pinch ground black pepper
pinch dried thyme
2 slices sourdough bread
1 slice provolone cheese
1 teaspoon Grey Poupon Country
   Dijon mustard
1 slice Monterey Jack cheese
butter, softened

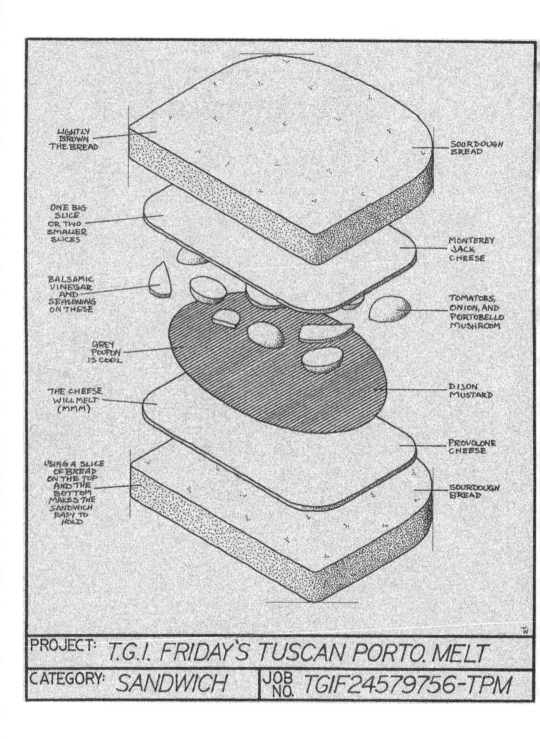

1. Preheat broiler to high.
2. Combine portobello, onion, and tomatoes with oil, vinegar, and pinches of salt, pepper, and thyme in a small roasting pan or oven-safe skillet. Place the mixture under the broiler for 5 to 6 minutes or until the vegetables soften. Stir halfway through cooking time.
3. Heat a griddle or large sauté pan over medium heat. Lightly brown one side of each bread slice and then build this sandwich on the browned side of one slice. Lay a slice of provolone cheese on the bread. Spread mustard on the cheese, and then spoon the roasted vegetables onto the cheese. Place the slice of Jack cheese on the veggies, and then top off the sandwich with the other slice of bread (browned side facing cheese).
4. Spread a little butter on one side of the sandwich, then place the sandwich, buttered-side down, onto the griddle or hot pan. Spread a little butter on top of sandwich. Grill for 1 to 2 minutes, until browned. Flip the sandwich and grill for another 1 to 2 minutes, until brown. Slice diagonally and serve.

• MAKES 1 SANDWICH.

•　•　•　•

TRADER VIC'S
WORLD FAMOUS MAI TAI

Restaurateur Victor Bergeron well-documented the original se-cret formula of the cocktail he created in 1944: a delicious blend of seventeen-year-old rum, lime juice, Orange Curaçao, simple syrup, plus orgeat syrup for a subtle almond flavor. When Vic's Tahitian friends sipped his new creation, they said "Mai Tai Roa Ae," which is Tahitian for "out of this world, the best." Vic named his drink "Mai Tai," and the rest is cocktail history. The recipe has changed through the years with younger rums and various fruit and citrus juice measurements. Many versions of the recipe can be found everywhere. There is even a Trader Vic's Mai Tai mixer avail-able in some stores. But nowhere will you find a formula for the "World Famous" $9.50 caramel-colored cocktail currently served at the 23 Trader Vic's restaurants that dot the globe, since the se-cret ingredient in the current recipe is a concentrated syrup that is produced specifically for use at the restaurant chain. I secured some of this "secret" concentrated mix, and figured out how to clone it by making a super-sweet simple syrup solution, then add-ing orange and almond extracts. Once the syrup is made, you combine it with lime juice, lemon juice, and dark rum in a glass full of crushed ice. Add a few garnishes and you have cloned two re-freshing servings of one of the world's most famous cocktails.

¼ cup granulated sugar
2 tablespoons hot water
1 teaspoon orange extract
½ teaspoon almond extract

1 small lime
2 ounces fresh lemon juice
4 ounces dark rum (such as
  Myers's)

MINT
SPRING

PINEAPPLE
WEDGE

MARASCHINO
CHERRY

CRUSHED
ICE

HALF OF A
LIME

ORGEAT,
CITRUS JUICES,
DARK RUM

12-OUNCE
GLASS

READY FOR
CONSUMPTION

TW

PROJECT: *TRADER VIC'S MAI TAI*

CATEGORY: *COCKTAIL*   JOB NO. *TV87654646-MT*

GARNISH

2 pineapple wedges
2 maraschino cherries
2 sprigs of mint

1. Make the Mai Tai syrup by combining the sugar and hot water. Stir until the sugar dissolves. Add the orange and almond extracts.
2. Make each drink by filling a 12-ounce glass with crushed ice. Add the juice of half of a small lime, 1 ounce of lemon juice, 2 ounces of dark rum, and 1 ounce of the Mai Tai syrup. Pour the drink into a cocktail shaker, shake well, and pour it back into the glass.
3. Garnish each drink with the squeezed lime halves, plus a wedge of fresh pineapple and a maraschino cherry speared on a skewer. Stick a sprig of mint in there, add a straw to each, and serve.

* MAKES 2 DRINKS.

• • • •

TRADER VIC'S
TOM KA GAI SOUP

☆　　✌　　💣　　✎　　☯　　✂　　☞

Packed with the sweet, sour, spicy, and salty flavors that are traditional to Thai cuisine, tom ka gai soup is a party on your palate. It's also a soup that I have been itching to clone for years, but I could not find a famous chain with a popular version. That is until Trader Vic's finally landed in Las Vegas at the new Planet Hollywood Hotel and Casino. This upscale, worldwide Polynesian-themed chain adds eggplant to the soup where you would traditionally find straw mushrooms, and thinly julienned peppers where Thai chiles would usually be swimming. Other than that, the soup has the same traditional flavors of some of the best tom ka gai soups I have eagerly slurped. For this clone you'll need to track down a couple stalks of lemongrass—a whole stalk is about a foot long. Cut each in half and get medieval on it with a kitchen mallet so that the flavors are released into the soup as it cooks. Before serving the soup, be sure to fish out the lemongrass and the chunks of ginger or you may be quickly brushing up on your Heimlich maneuver.

4 cups chicken broth
two 14-ounce cans coconut milk
1 cup diced Japanese eggplant
　　(about ½ eggplant)
2 stalks lemongrass, each cut in
　　half and pounded
¼ cup lime juice
2 tablespoons fish sauce

1 strawberry-size knob of ginger,
　　peeled and halved
1 clove garlic, minced
2 teaspoons red curry paste
1 teaspoon ground coriander
2 skinless chicken breast fillets
2 jalapeño peppers, seeded and
　　julienned

1 red chile, seeded and julienned
⅓ cup chopped green onions (green part only)

GARNISH
6 lime wedges

1. Preheat the barbecue grill to high heat.
2. Combine the chicken broth, coconut milk, eggplant, lemongrass (pound it with a kitchen mallet to release its flavors), lime juice, fish sauce, ginger, garlic, red curry paste, and coriander in a large soup pot and bring to a boil over medium heat. Reduce the heat and simmer for 20 minutes.
3. As the soup simmers, pound the chicken breast fillets flat with a kitchen mallet, rub each with oil, and grill for 4 to 5 minutes per side on the hot grill. The chicken shouldn't be thoroughly cooked, since it will cook more in the soup. When the chicken is done, let it cool, then dice it.
4. When the soup has simmered for 20 minutes, add the chicken and chiles. Be sure the chiles are julienned very thin. Continue to simmer the soup for 10 minutes, and then add the green onions. To prepare the soup for serving, spoon approximately 1½ cups of soup into a bowl, squeeze a lime wedge into the soup, drop the lime into the bowl, and serve it up.

- MAKES 6 SERVINGS.

TIDBITS

Find fish sauce and red curry paste where Asian or Thai foods are stocked in your market.

• • • •

TRADEMARKS

Applebee's is a registered trademark of Applebee's International, Inc.

Bahama Breeze, LongHorn Steakhouse, Olive Garden and Red Lobster are registered trademarks of Darden Concepts, Inc.

BJ's Restaurant & Brewhouse is a registered trademark of BJ's Restaurants.

Bonefish Grill, Carrabba's Cheeseburger in Paradise, Fleming's Prime Steakhouse, Outback Steakhouse, Outback Rack, Victoria "Crowned" Filet, Chocolate Thunder from Down Under, and Roy's are registered trademarks of OSI Restaurant Partners, LLC.

Buca Di Beppo is a registered trademark of Buca, Inc.

Buffalo Wild Wings, Asian Zing, and Parmesan Garlic are registered trademarks of Buffalo Wild Wings, Inc.

California Pizza Kitchen is a registered trademark of California Pizza Kitchen, Inc.

The Cheesecake Factory is a registered trademark of The Cheesecake Factory, Inc.

Chili's, Chicken Crispers, On the Border, and Romano's Macaroni Grill are registered trademarks of Brinker International.

Cracker Barrel and Double Fudge Coca-Cola Cake are registered trademarks of CBOCS Properties, Inc.

Denny's is a registered trademark of DFO, Inc.

Famous Dave's is a registered trademark of Famous Dave's of America, Inc.

Fuddruckers is a registered trademark of Magic Brands, LLC.

Gordon Biersch is a registered trademark of Gordon Biersch Brewery Restaurant Group, Inc.

Hard Rock Café is a registered trademark of Hard Rock Café International, Inc.

Hooter's is a registered trademark of Hooter's of America.

Houston's is a registered trademark of Hillstone Restaurant Group.

IHOP is a registered trademark of IHOP Corp.

INDEX

GET 12 RECIPES FREE WITH THE PURCHASE OF THIS BOOK!

An exclusive special for Target guests*

CAN'T GET ENOUGH OF TODD'S TOP SECRET RECIPES?

WANT TO MAKE MORE OF YOUR RESTAURANT FAVORITES?

Here's the scoop for you cloning sleuths:

1. Go to www.topsecretrecipes.com and click on "Recipes"
2. Add 12 delicious recipes to your shopping cart
3. Enter coupon code: target_recipes
4. Go to your kitchen and start cloning!

*Offer expires 6/1/2011

Plume
Penguin Group (USA) Inc.
www.penguin.com